Graphic STEM Adventures

with Max Axiom™ Super Scientist

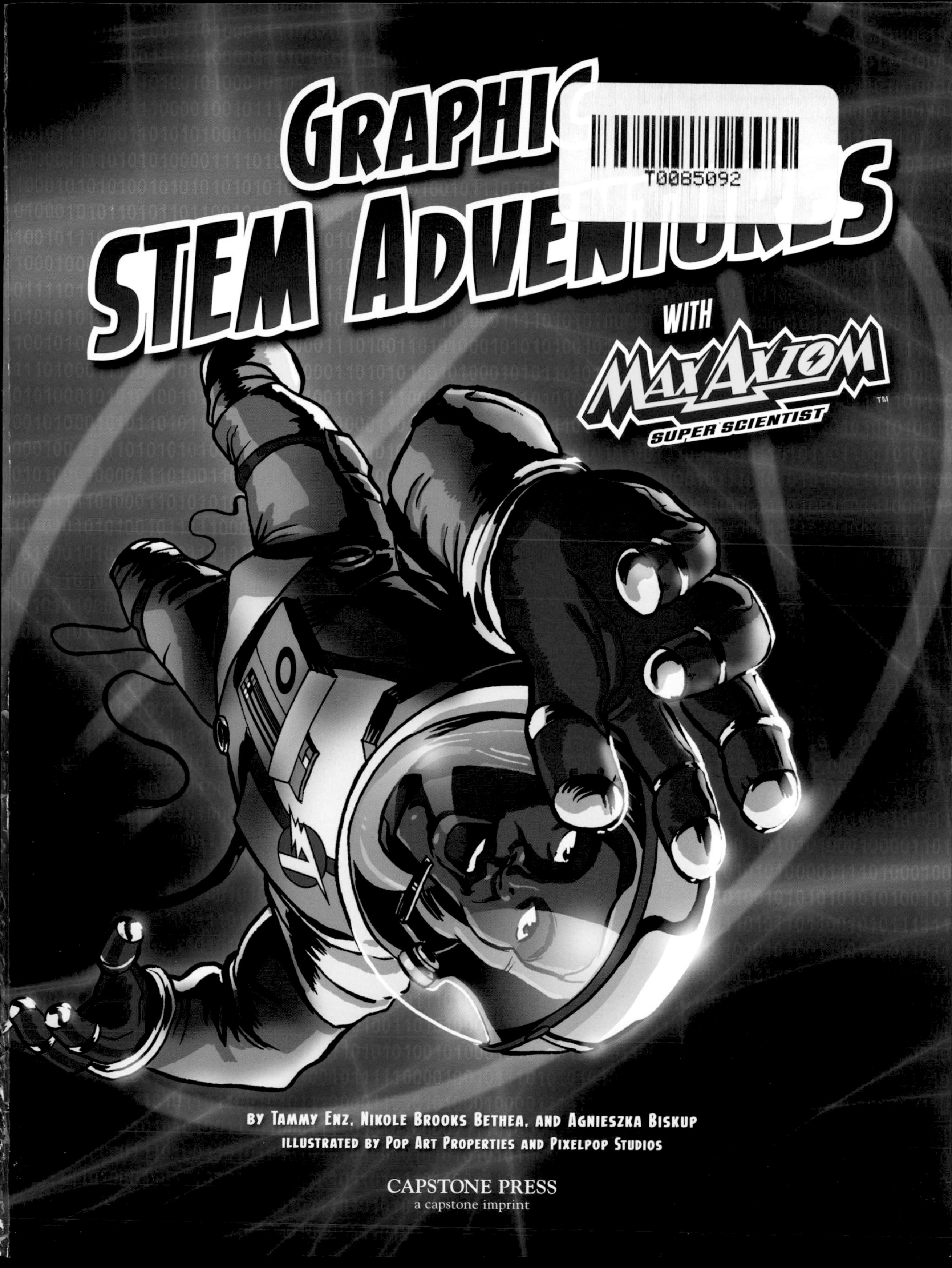

By Tammy Enz, Nikole Brooks Bethea, and Agnieszka Biskup
Illustrated by Pop Art Properties and Pixelpop Studios

Capstone Press
a capstone imprint

Graphic Library is published by Capstone Press, an imprint of Capstone.
1710 Roe Crest Drive, North Mankato, Minnesota 56003
www.capstonepub.com

Library of Congress Cataloging-in-Publication Data is available on the Library of Congress website.

ISBN: 978-1-4966-6662-8 (paperback)

Summary: Follows super scientist Max Axiom as he explores cell phones, drones, robots, and space travel.

Image Credits
NASA: 96,101

Editorial Credits
Christopher Harbo, editor; Charmaine Whitman, designer; Kelly Garvin, media researcher; Tori Abraham, production specialist

Additional Illustrator Credits
Marcelo Baez, cover (top left, middle right), 5, 83; Tommy Ade Hutomo, colorist (Drones, Robots)

Printed in China.
002493

TABLE OF CONTENTS

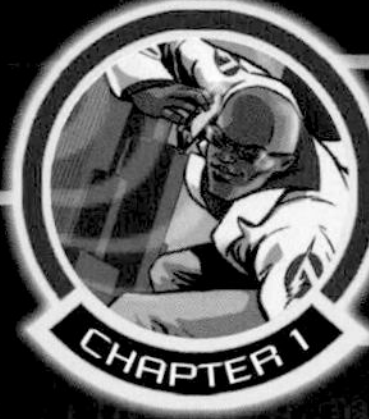
CHAPTER 1

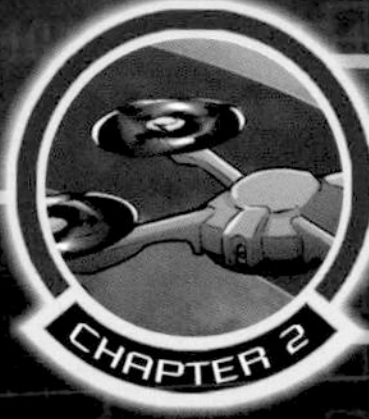
CHAPTER 2

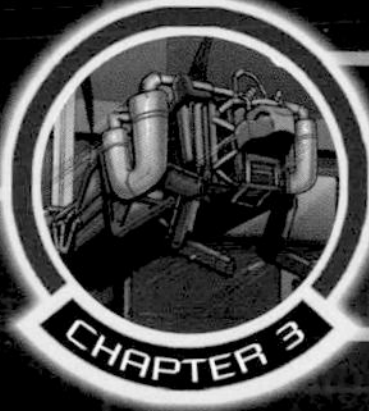
CHAPTER 3

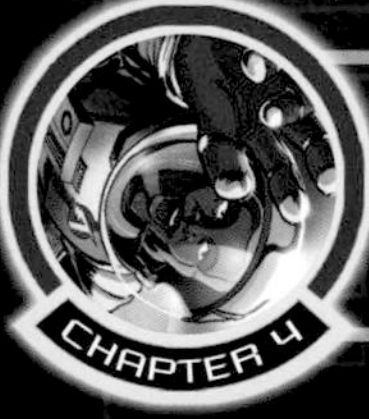
CHAPTER 4

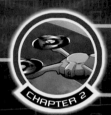

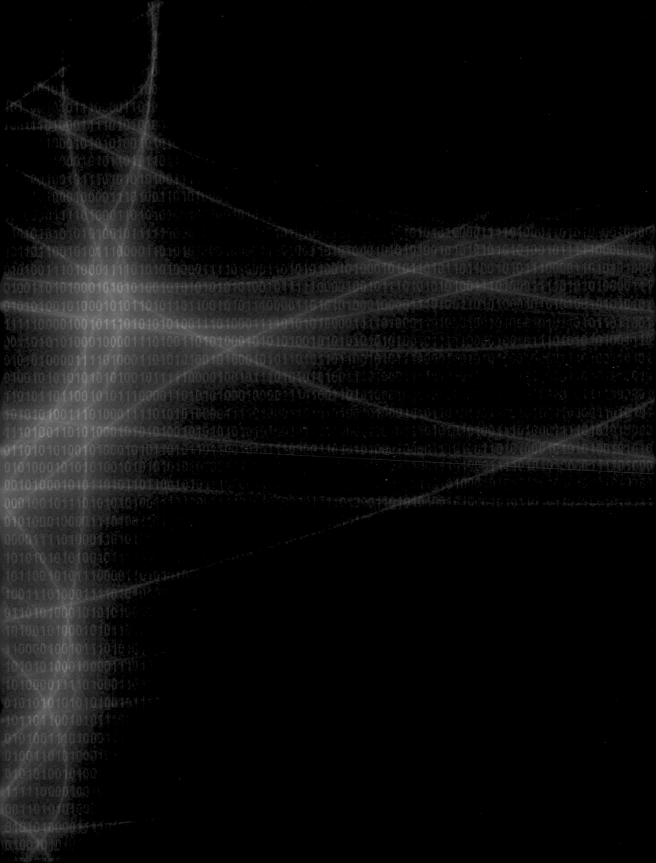

CHAPTER 1

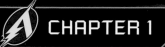

The Amazing Story of Cell Phone Technology

by Tammy Enz

illustrated by Pop Art Properties

Consultant: Akbar M. Sayeed, PhD
Professor
Department of Electrical and Computer Engineering
College of Engineering
University of Wisconsin-Madison

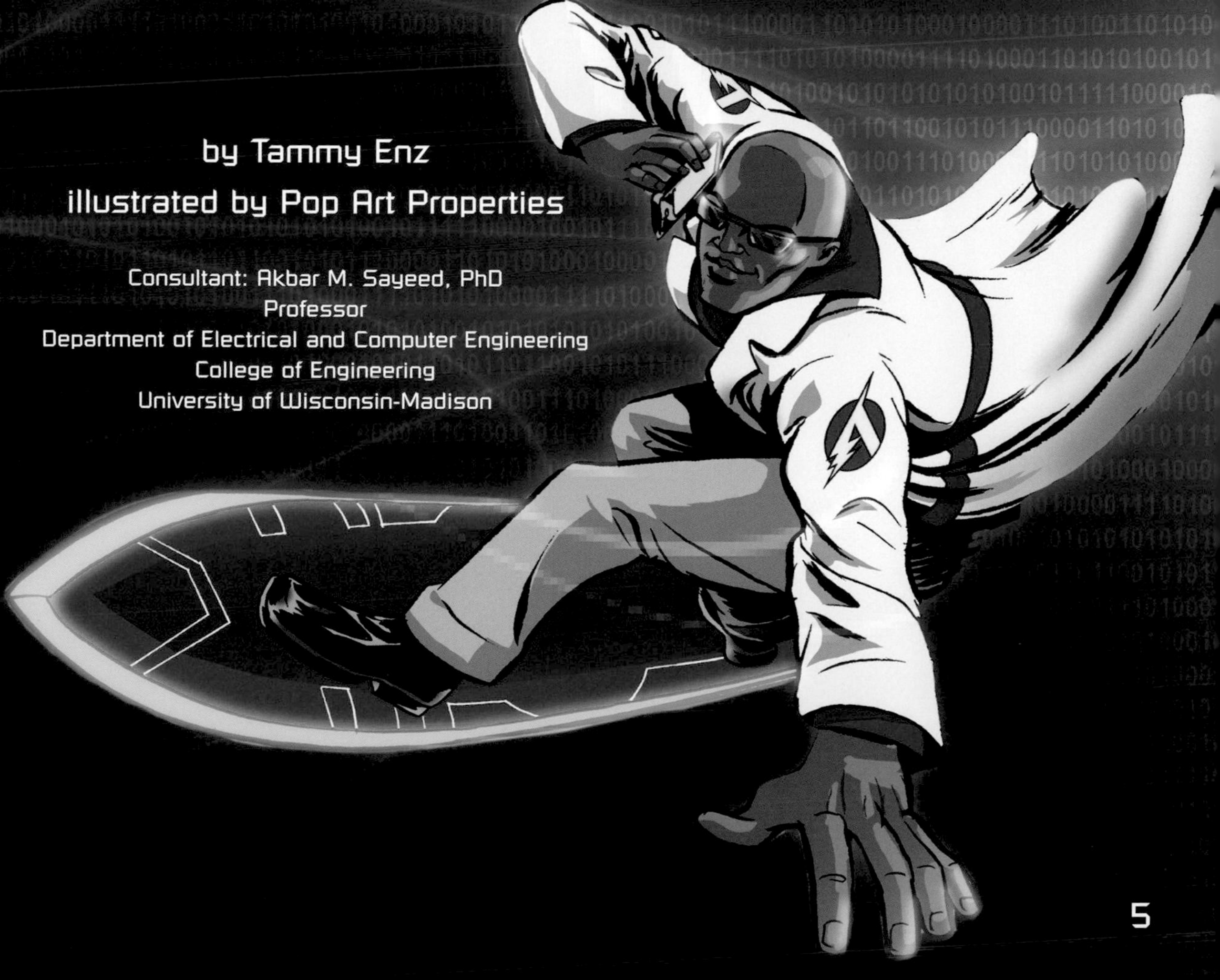

SECTION 1 A DYNAMIC DEVICE

A visit to the Grand Canyon sparks an investigation into cell phone technology for Max Axiom, Super Scientist.

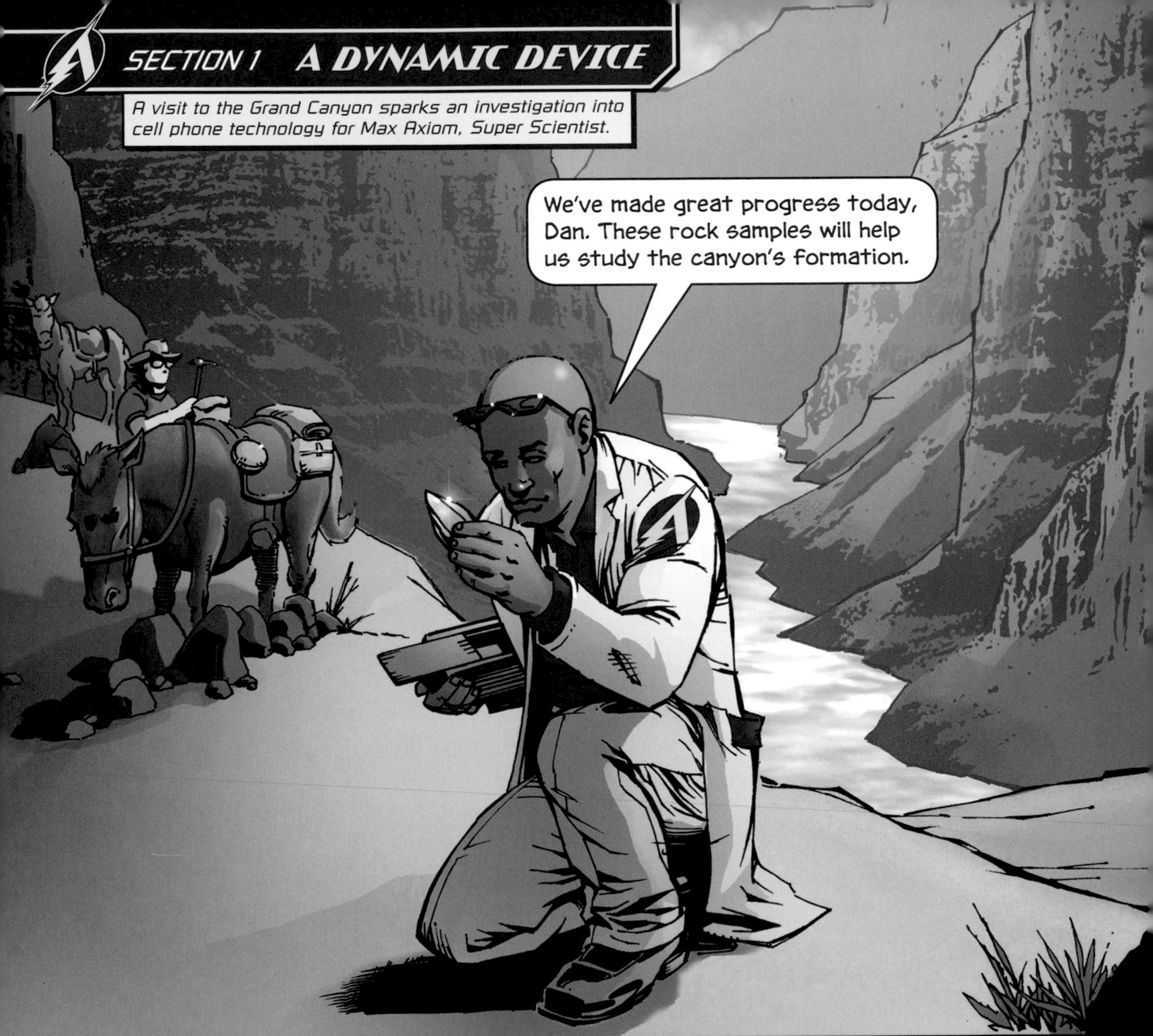
We've made great progress today, Dan. These rock samples will help us study the canyon's formation.

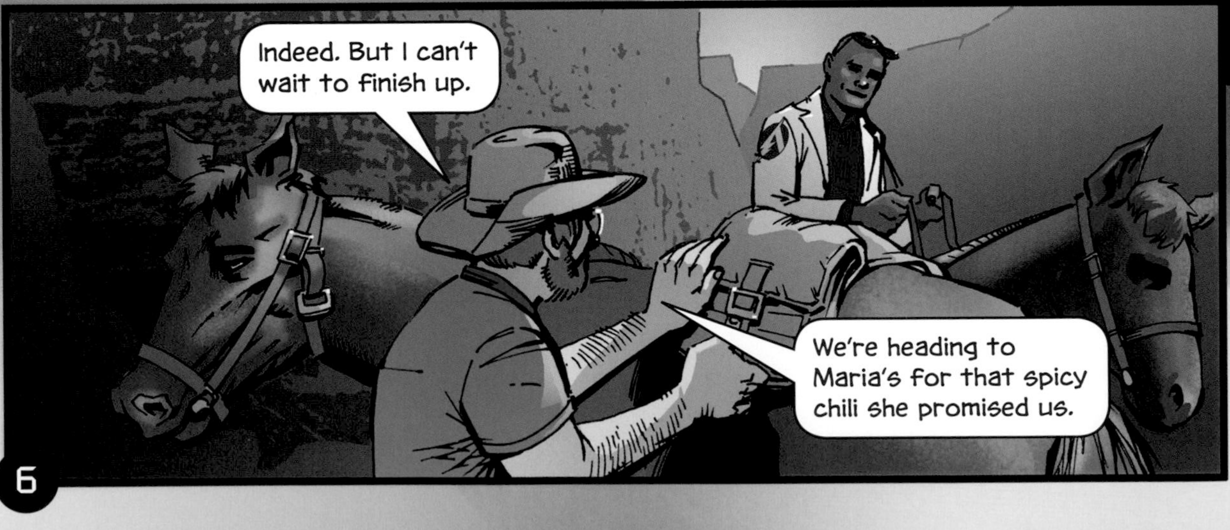
Indeed. But I can't wait to finish up.
We're heading to Maria's for that spicy chili she promised us.

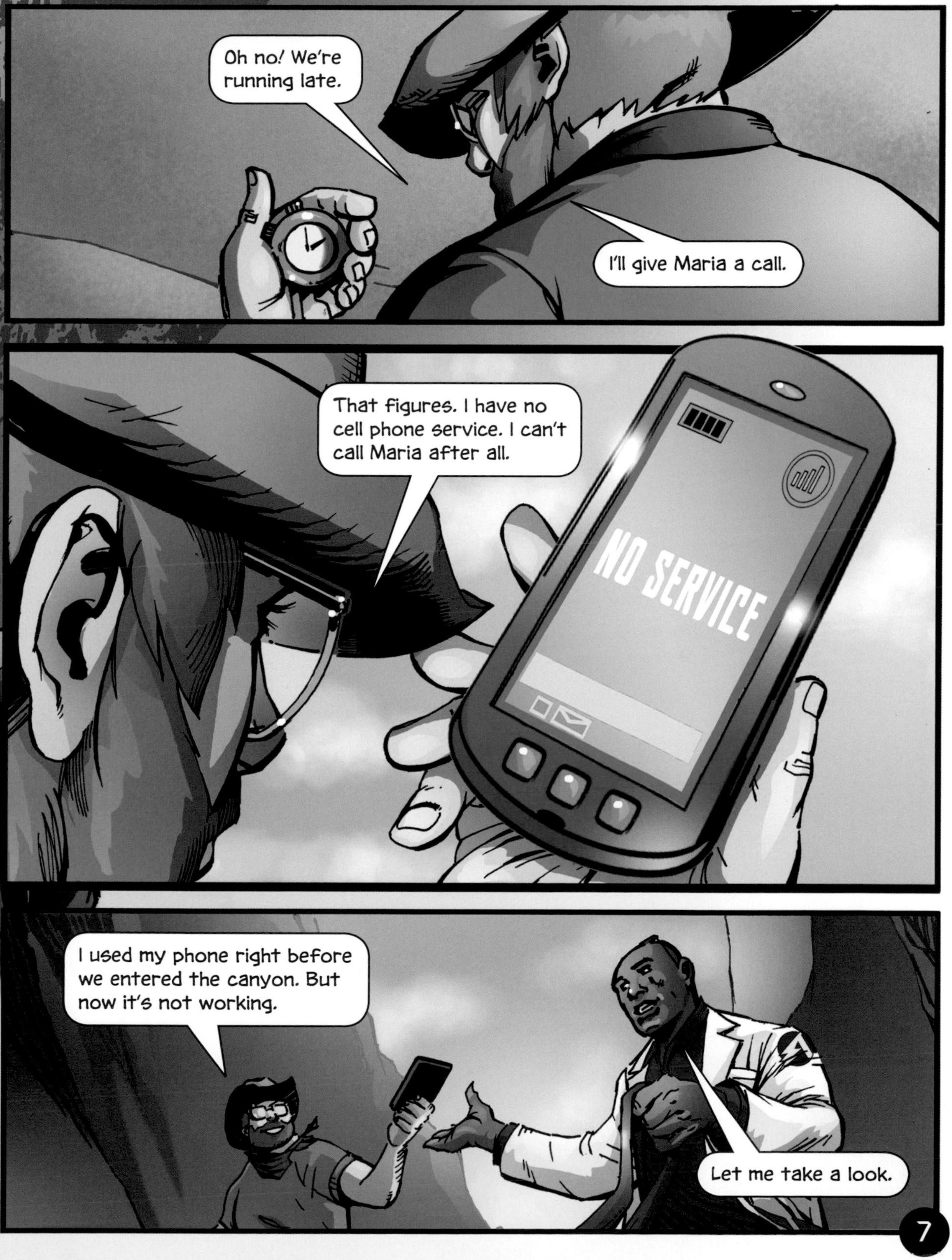
Oh no! We're running late.
I'll give Maria a call.
That figures. I have no cell phone service. I can't call Maria after all.
NO SERVICE
I used my phone right before we entered the canyon. But now it's not working.
Let me take a look.

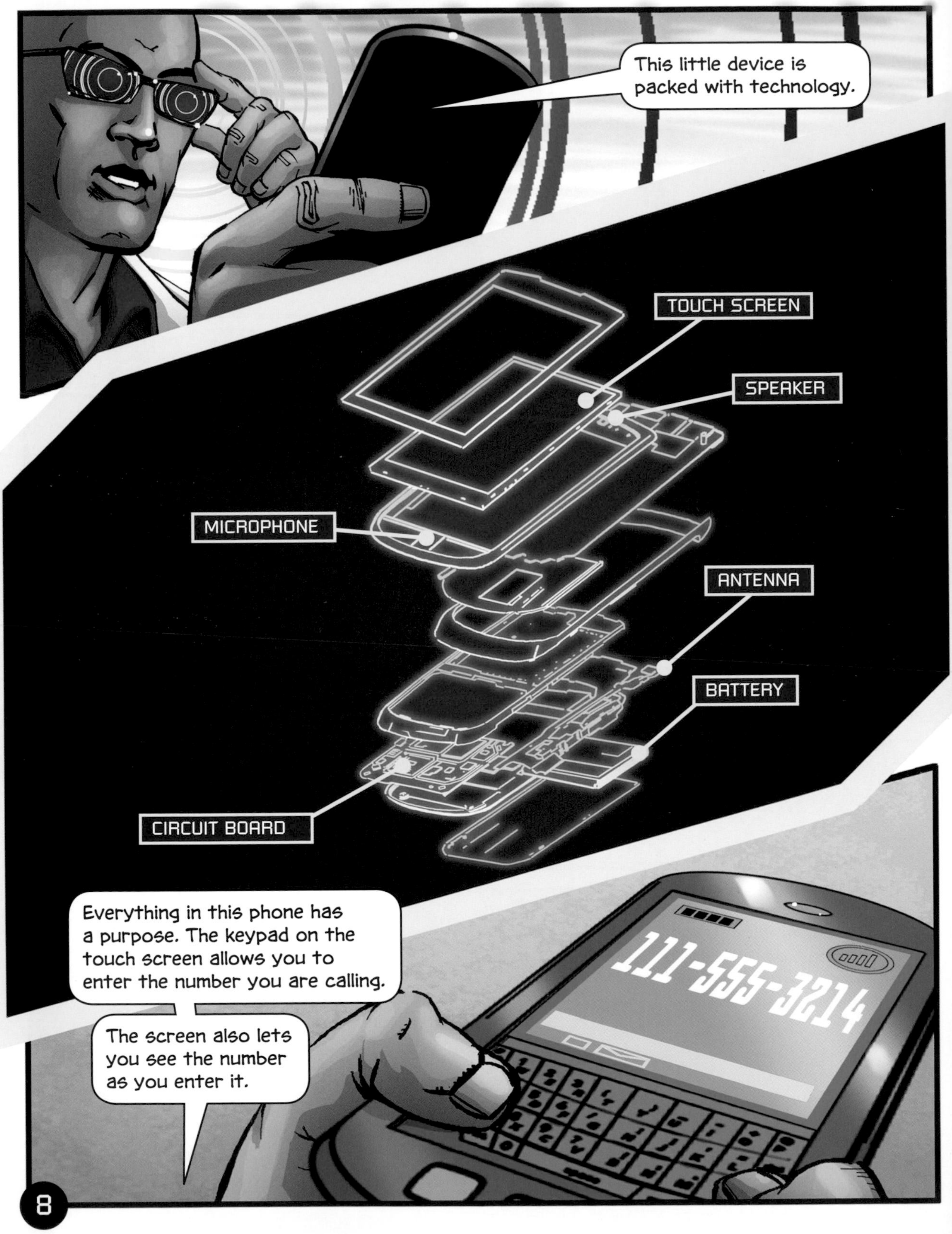
This little device is packed with technology.
TOUCH SCREEN
SPEAKER
MICROPHONE
ANTENNA
BATTERY
CIRCUIT BOARD
Everything in this phone has a purpose. The keypad on the touch screen allows you to enter the number you are calling.
The screen also lets you see the number as you enter it.
111-555-3214

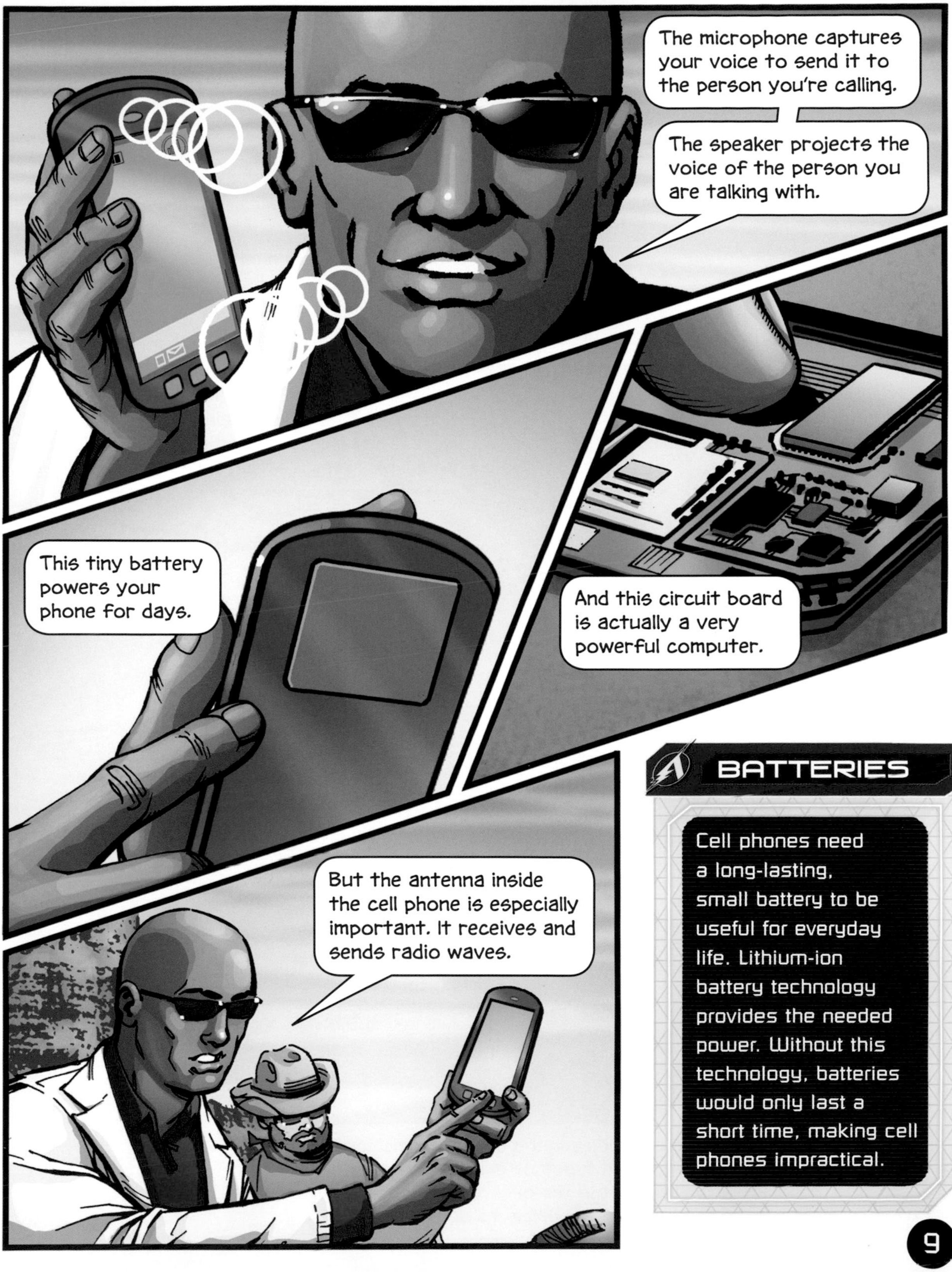
The microphone captures your voice to send it to the person you're calling.
The speaker projects the voice of the person you are talking with.
This tiny battery powers your phone for days.
And this circuit board is actually a very powerful computer.
But the antenna inside the cell phone is especially important. It receives and sends radio waves.

BATTERIES

Cell phones need a long-lasting, small battery to be useful for everyday life. Lithium-ion battery technology provides the needed power. Without this technology, batteries would only last a short time, making cell phones impractical.

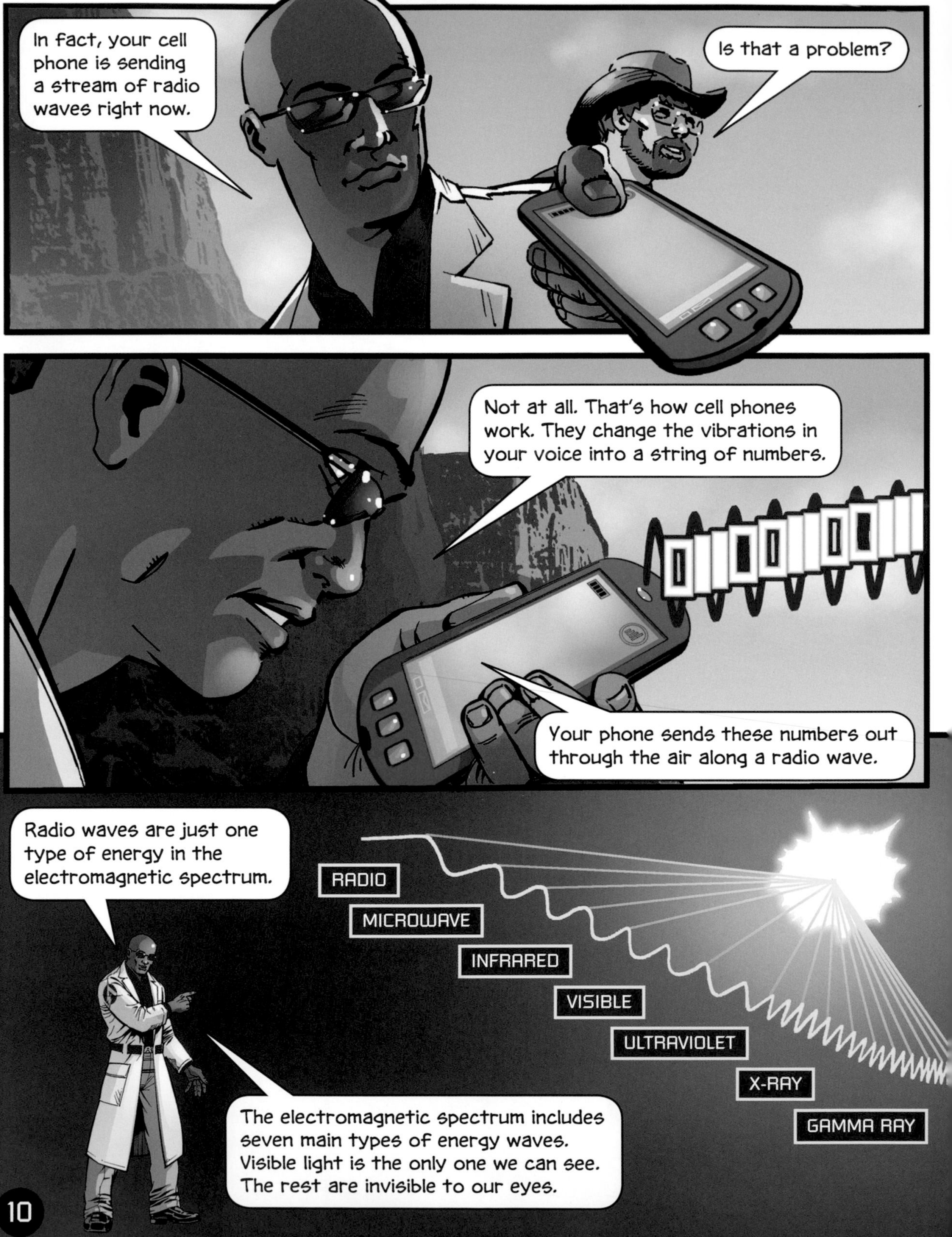

In fact, your cell phone is sending a stream of radio waves right now.
Is that a problem?
Not at all. That's how cell phones work. They change the vibrations in your voice into a string of numbers.
Your phone sends these numbers out through the air along a radio wave.
Radio waves are just one type of energy in the electromagnetic spectrum.
RADIO
MICROWAVE
INFRARED
VISIBLE
ULTRAVIOLET
X-RAY
GAMMA RAY
The electromagnetic spectrum includes seven main types of energy waves. Visible light is the only one we can see. The rest are invisible to our eyes.

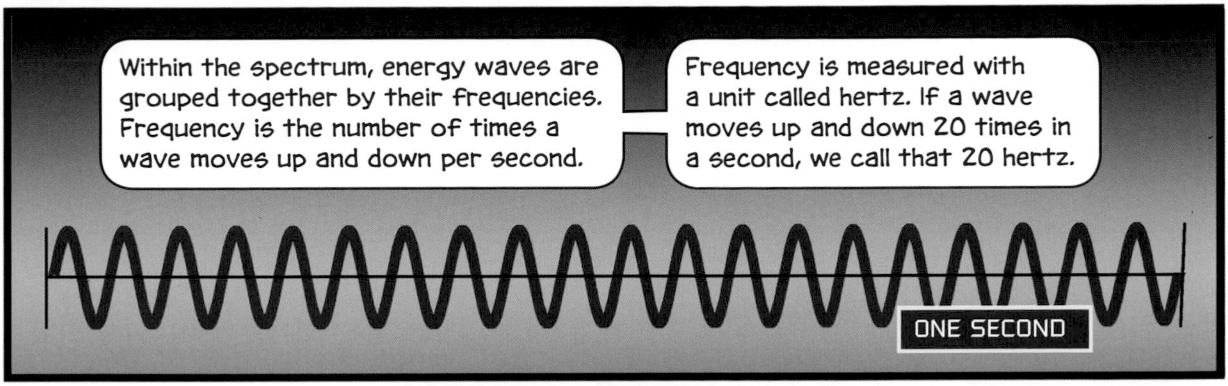
Within the spectrum, energy waves are grouped together by their frequencies. Frequency is the number of times a wave moves up and down per second.
Frequency is measured with a unit called hertz. If a wave moves up and down 20 times in a second, we call that 20 hertz.
ONE SECOND

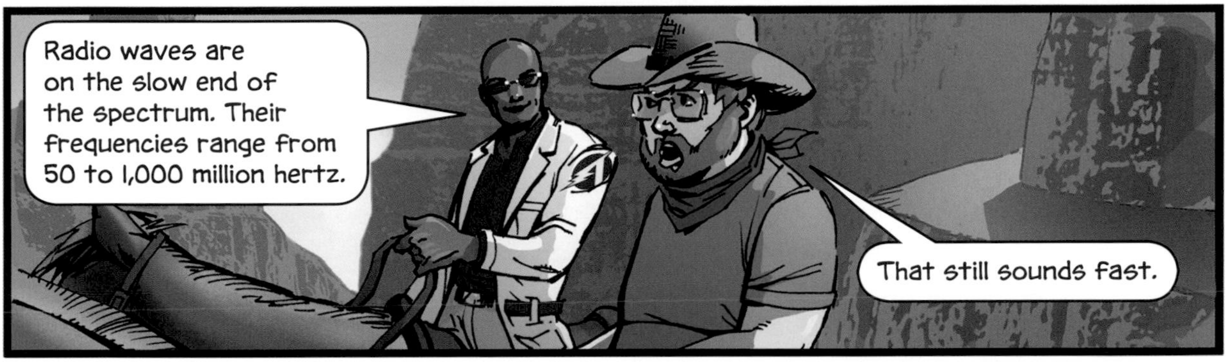
Radio waves are on the slow end of the spectrum. Their frequencies range from 50 to 1,000 million hertz.
That still sounds fast.

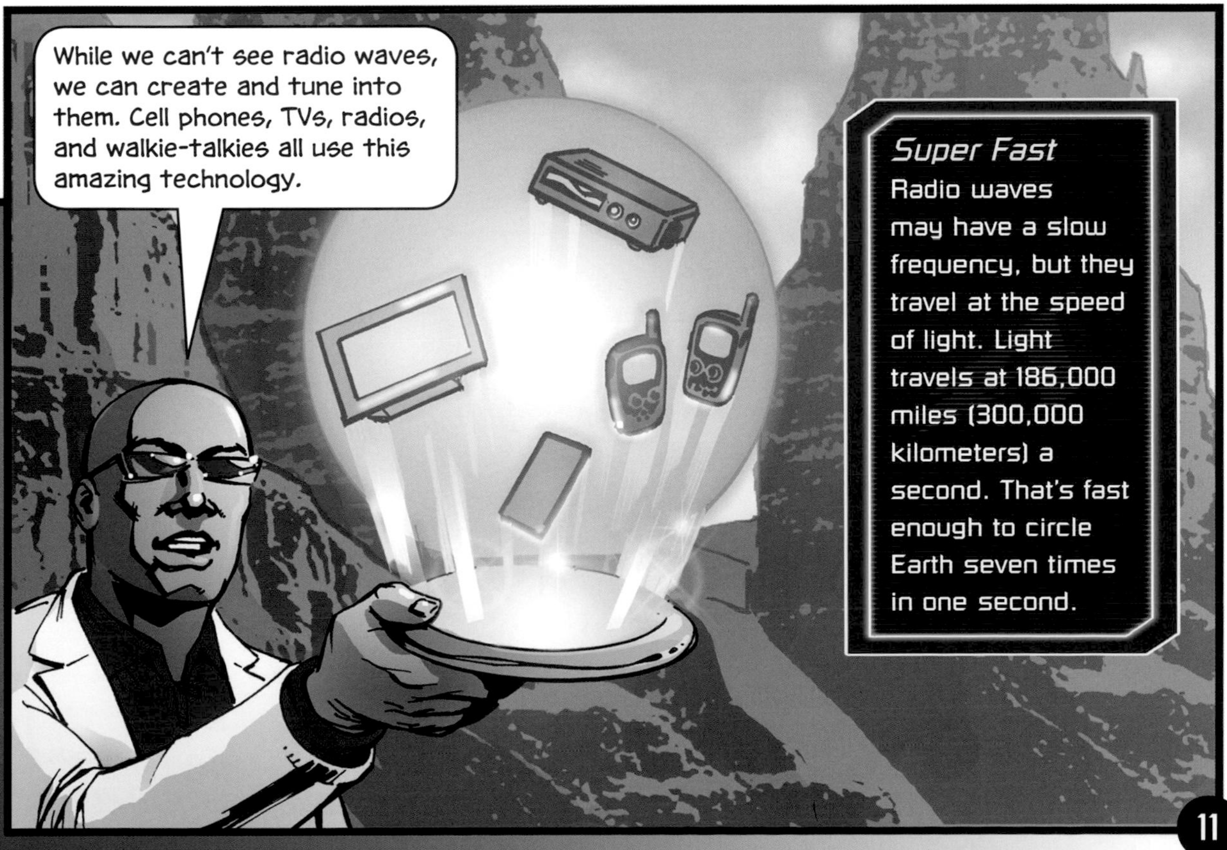
While we can't see radio waves, we can create and tune into them. Cell phones, TVs, radios, and walkie-talkies all use this amazing technology.
Super Fast
Radio waves may have a slow frequency, but they travel at the speed of light. Light travels at 186,000 miles (300,000 kilometers) a second. That's fast enough to circle Earth seven times in one second.

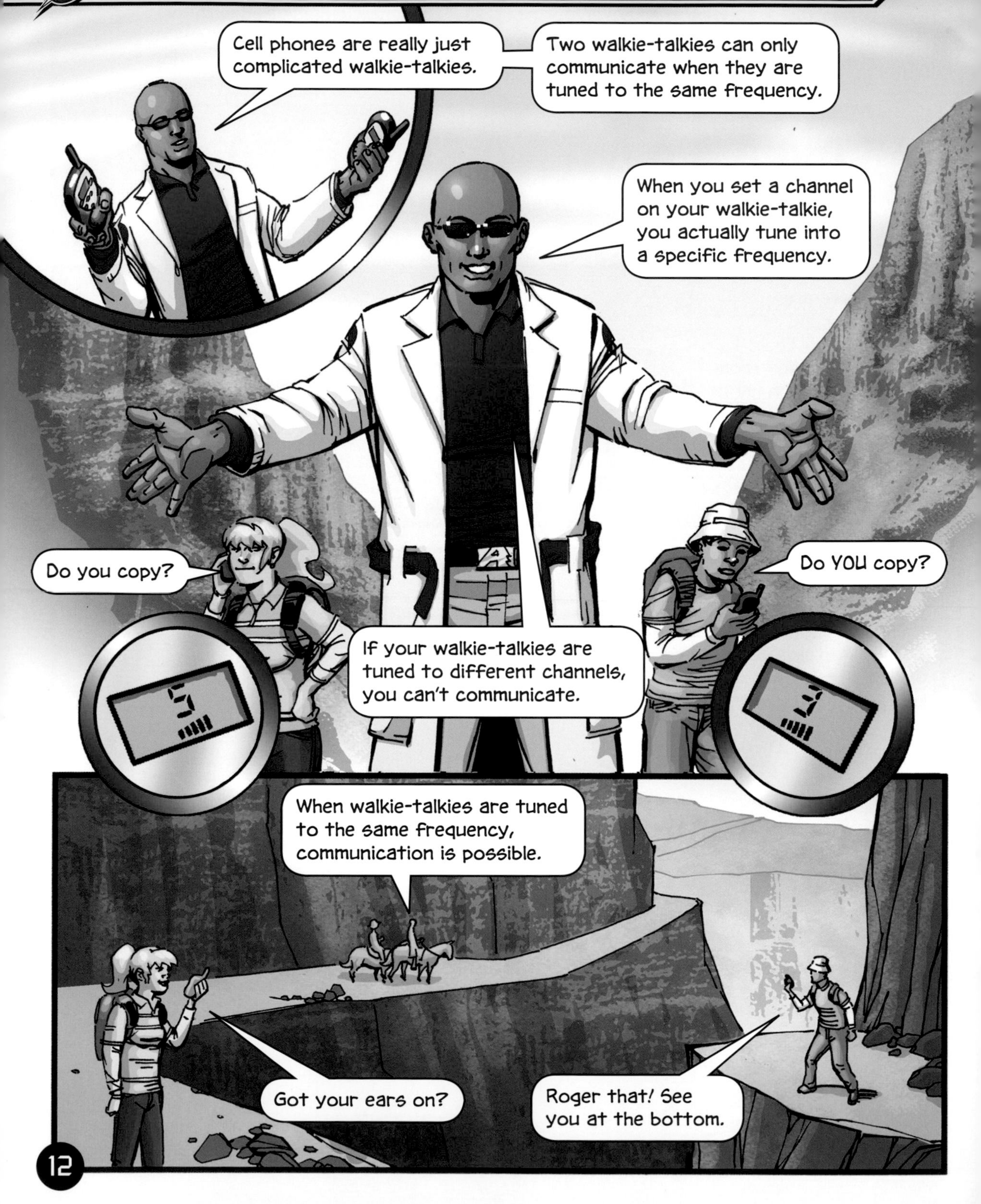
Cell phones are really just complicated walkie-talkies.
Two walkie-talkies can only communicate when they are tuned to the same frequency.
When you set a channel on your walkie-talkie, you actually tune into a specific frequency.
Do you copy?
Do YOU copy?
If your walkie-talkies are tuned to different channels, you can't communicate.
When walkie-talkies are tuned to the same frequency, communication is possible.
Got your ears on?
Roger that! See you at the bottom.

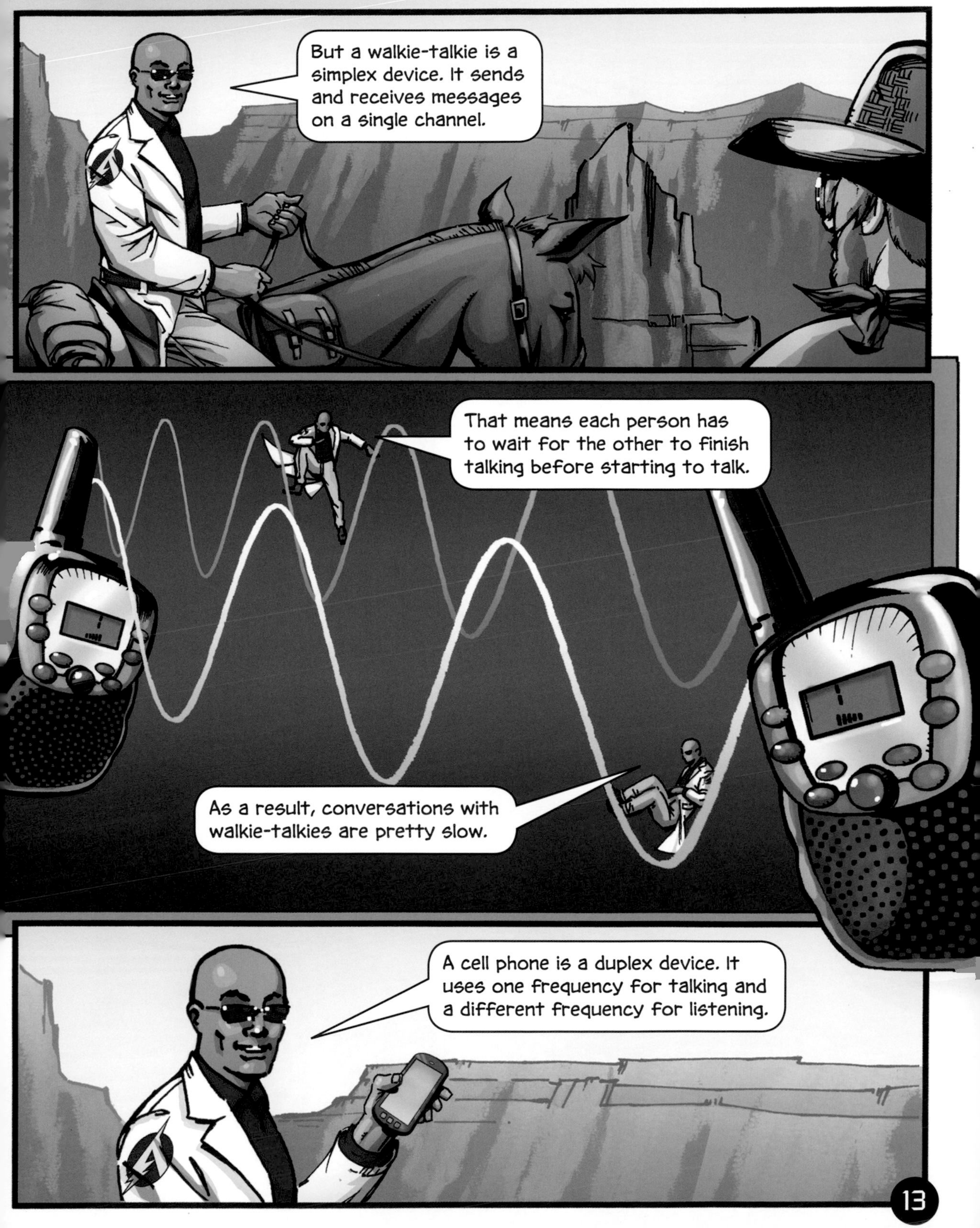
But a walkie-talkie is a simplex device. It sends and receives messages on a single channel.
That means each person has to wait for the other to finish talking before starting to talk.
As a result, conversations with walkie-talkies are pretty slow.
A cell phone is a duplex device. It uses one frequency for talking and a different frequency for listening.

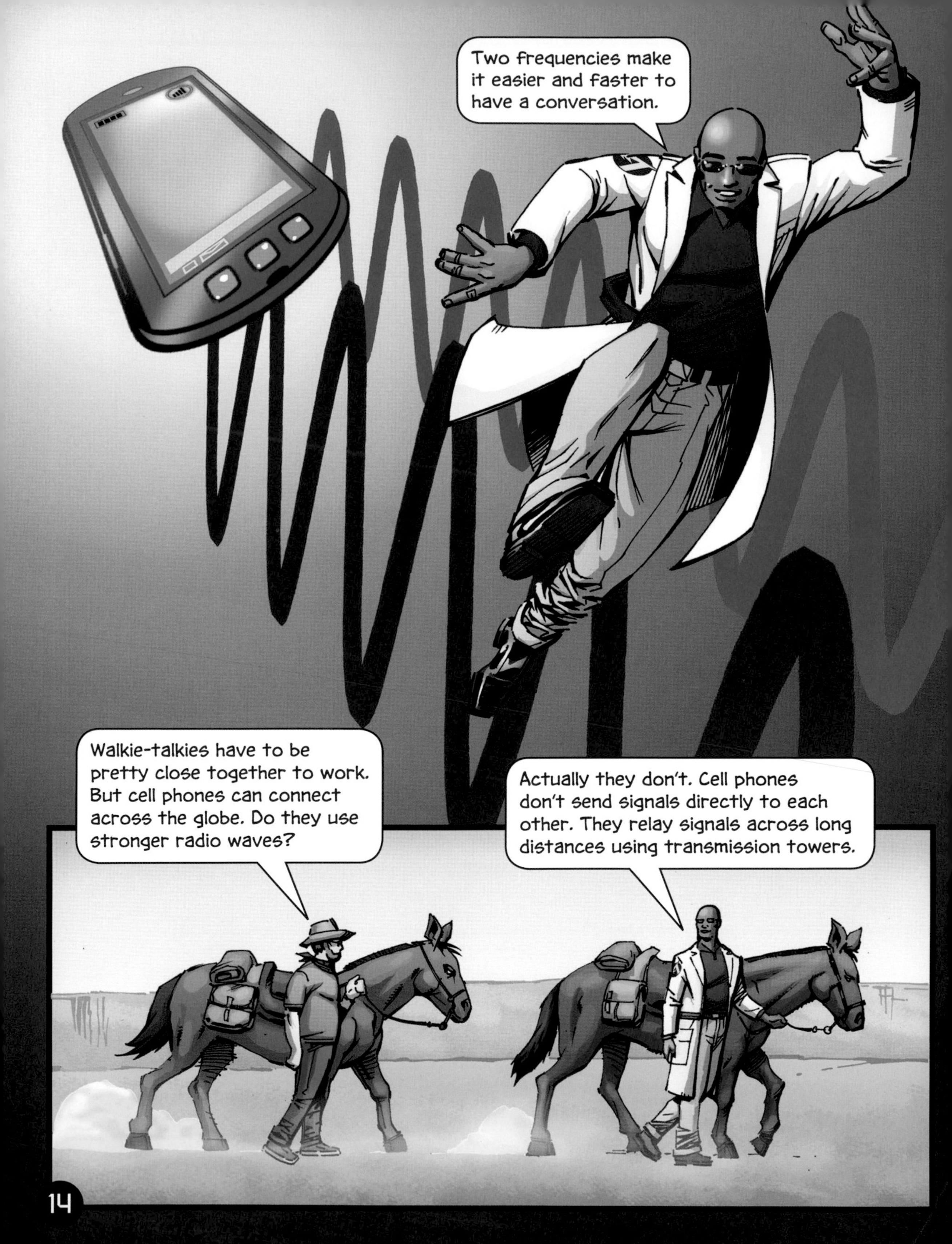
Two frequencies make it easier and faster to have a conversation.
Walkie-talkies have to be pretty close together to work. But cell phones can connect across the globe. Do they use stronger radio waves?
Actually they don't. Cell phones don't send signals directly to each other. They relay signals across long distances using transmission towers.

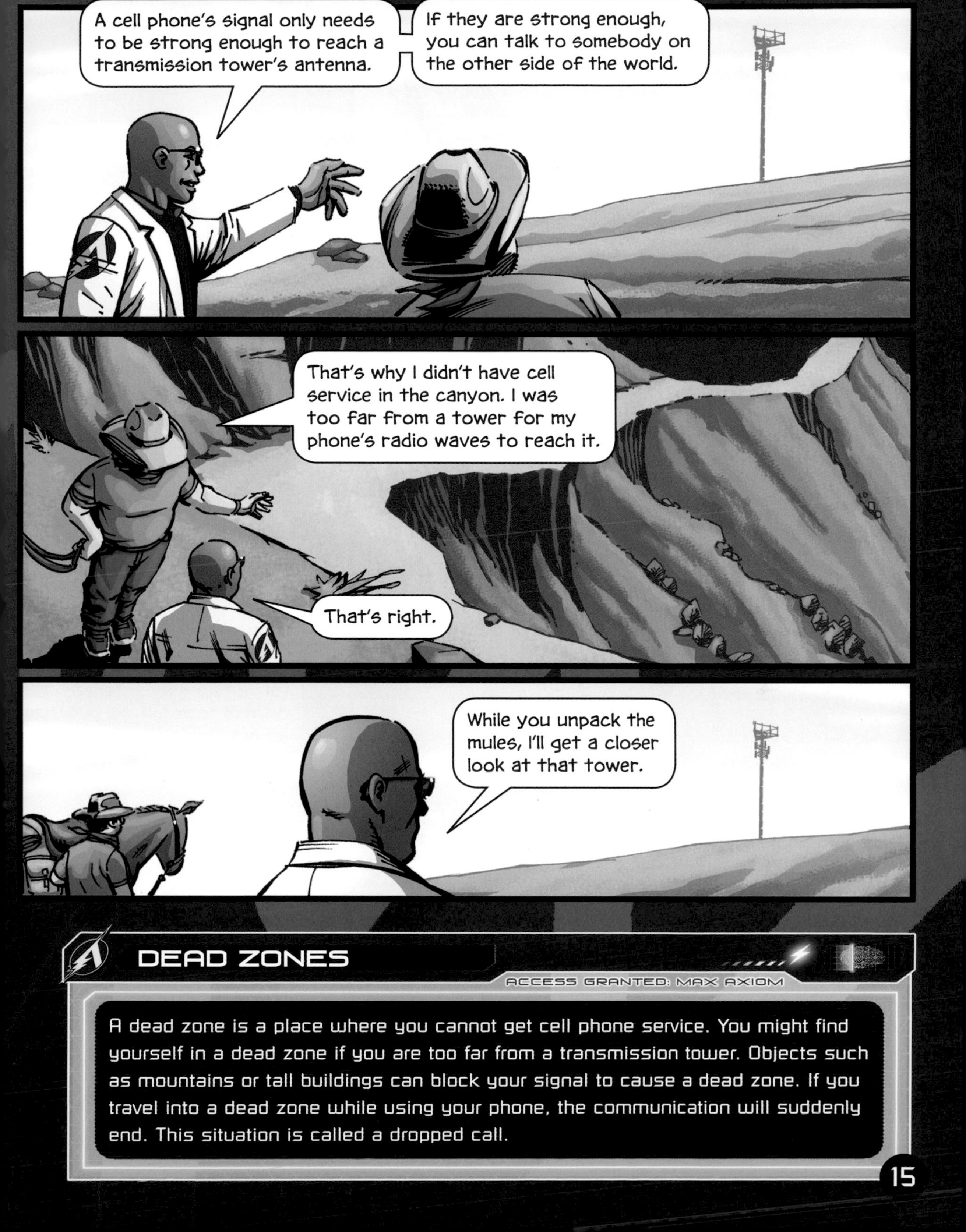

A cell phone's signal only needs to be strong enough to reach a transmission tower's antenna.
If they are strong enough, you can talk to somebody on the other side of the world.
That's why I didn't have cell service in the canyon. I was too far from a tower for my phone's radio waves to reach it.
That's right.
While you unpack the mules, I'll get a closer look at that tower.

DEAD ZONES

ACCESS GRANTED: MAX AXIOM

A dead zone is a place where you cannot get cell phone service. You might find yourself in a dead zone if you are too far from a transmission tower. Objects such as mountains or tall buildings can block your signal to cause a dead zone. If you travel into a dead zone while using your phone, the communication will suddenly end. This situation is called a dropped call.

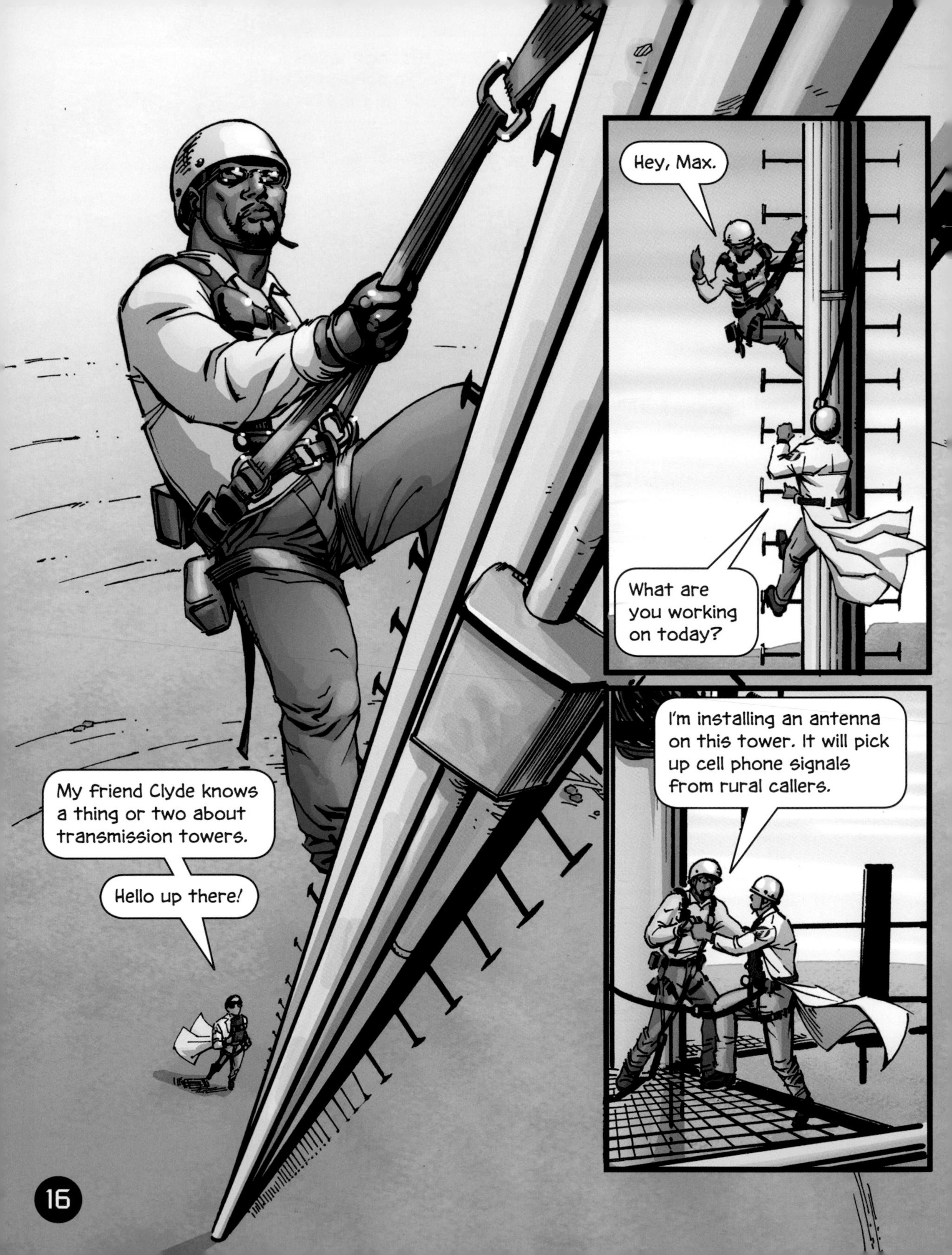
My friend Clyde knows a thing or two about transmission towers.
Hello up there!
Hey, Max.
What are you working on today?
I'm installing an antenna on this tower. It will pick up cell phone signals from rural callers.

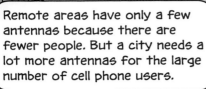

Remote areas have only a few antennas because there are fewer people. But a city needs a lot more antennas for the large number of cell phone users.

Antennas all over the city pick up radio waves from nearby cell phones. Here, take a look.

As you can see, antennas are harder to spot in the cities. They usually aren't placed on top of towers.

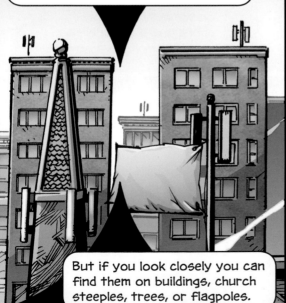

But if you look closely you can find them on buildings, church steeples, trees, or flagpoles.

Thanks, Clyde! I'm off to see some of these antennas close up.

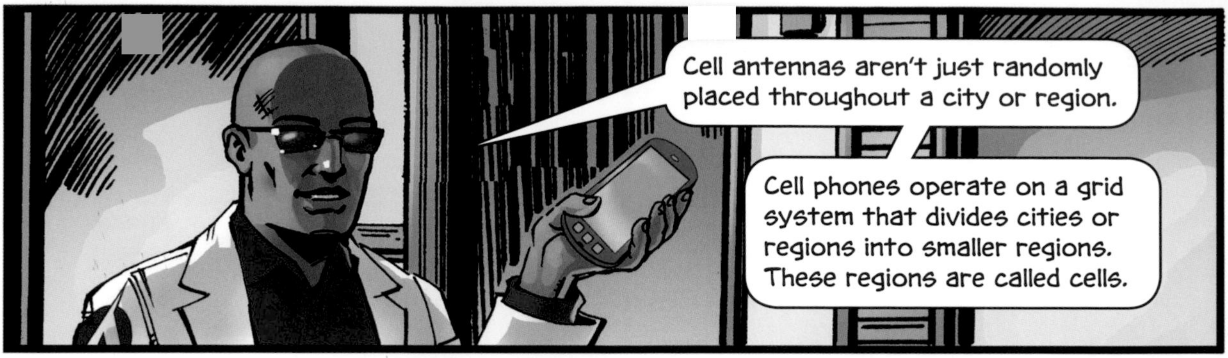
Cell antennas aren't just randomly placed throughout a city or region.
Cell phones operate on a grid system that divides cities or regions into smaller regions. These regions are called cells.

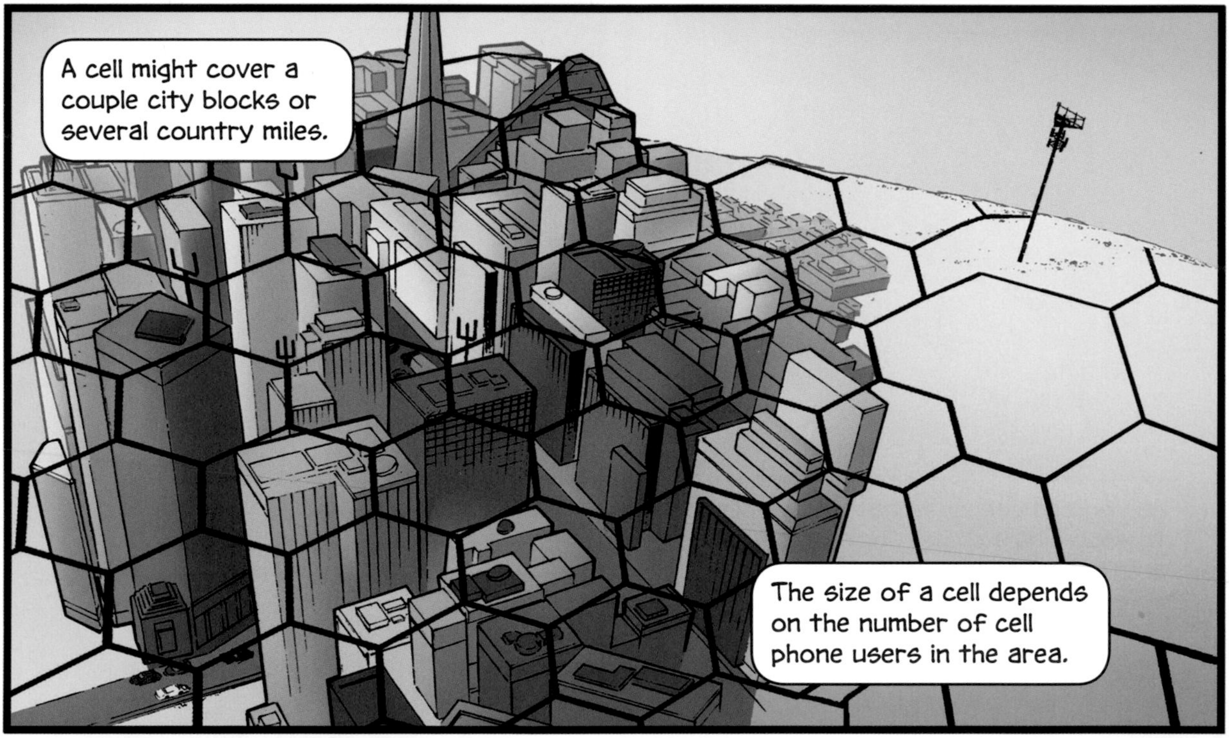
A cell might cover a couple city blocks or several country miles.
The size of a cell depends on the number of cell phone users in the area.

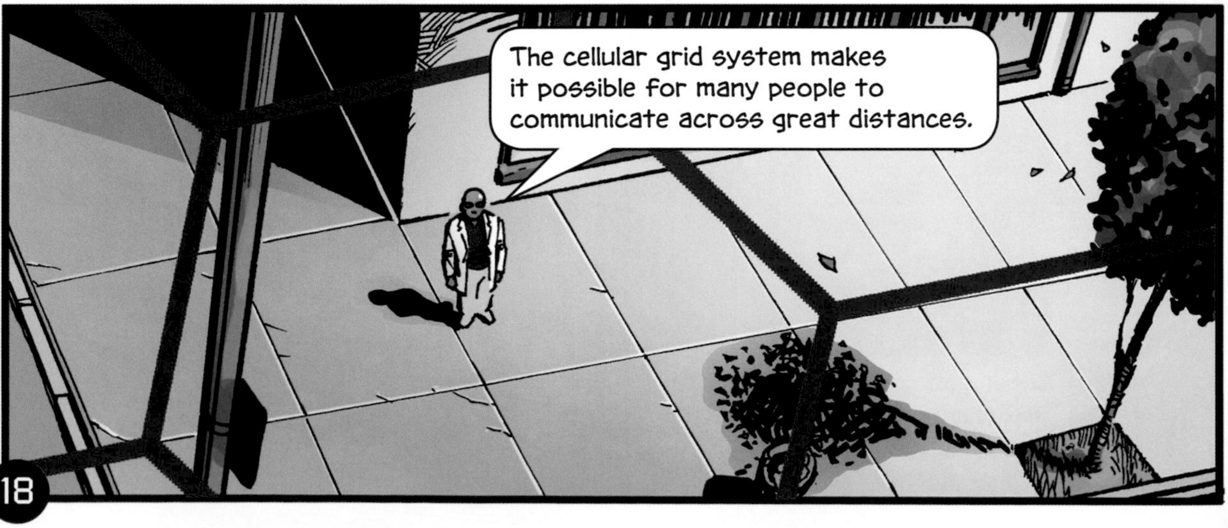
The cellular grid system makes it possible for many people to communicate across great distances.

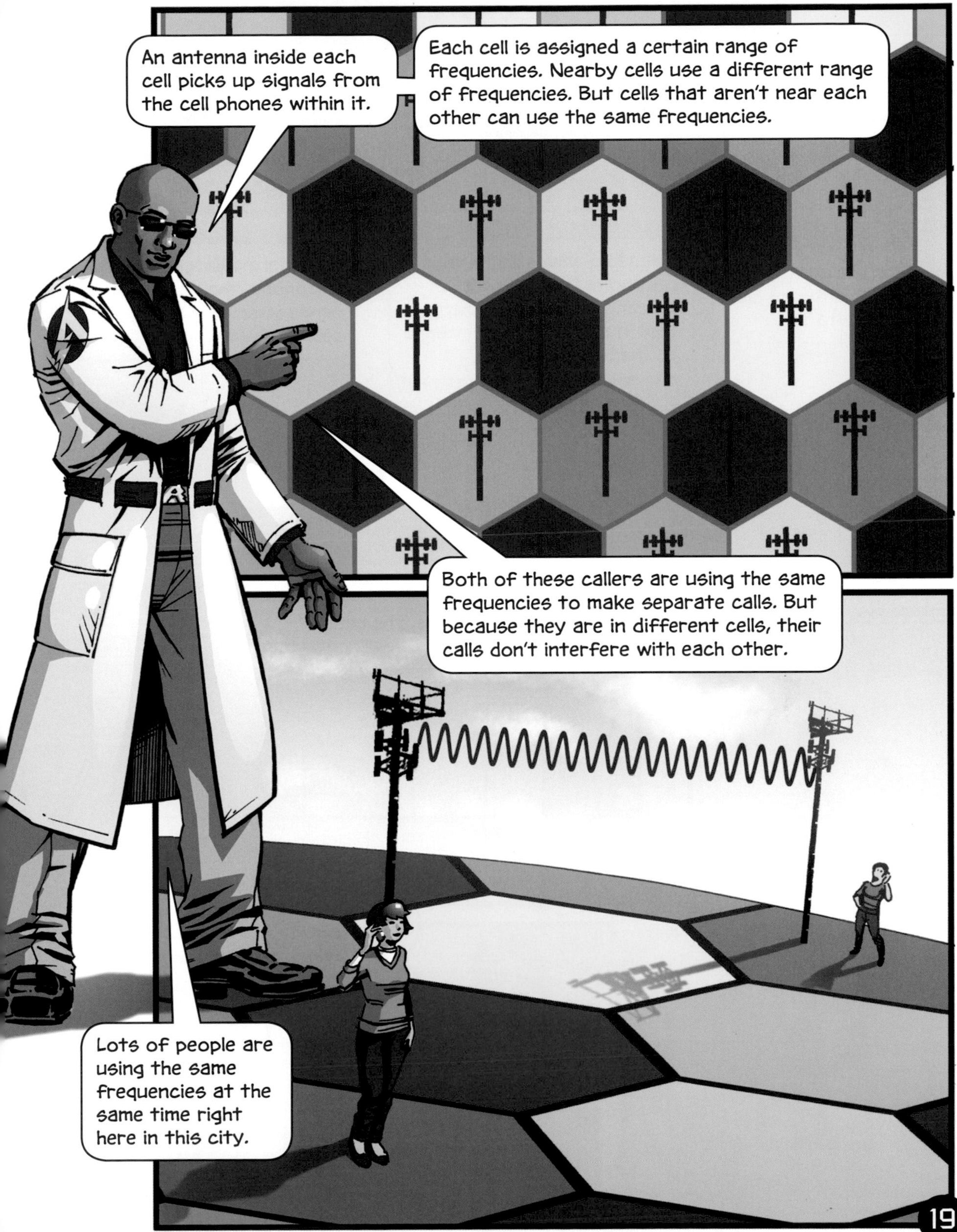
An antenna inside each cell picks up signals from the cell phones within it.
Each cell is assigned a certain range of frequencies. Nearby cells use a different range of frequencies. But cells that aren't near each other can use the same frequencies.
Both of these callers are using the same frequencies to make separate calls. But because they are in different cells, their calls don't interfere with each other.
Lots of people are using the same frequencies at the same time right here in this city.

To make a call, you need a phone and a nearby antenna.

But a lot more goes on behind the scenes to make a connection.

Each cell contains a cellular antenna and a base station.

The radio waves from your cell phone travel to the antenna in your cell. Then they travel from the antenna to the base station.

If you are calling another cell phone, the base station sends your call through the cellular system.

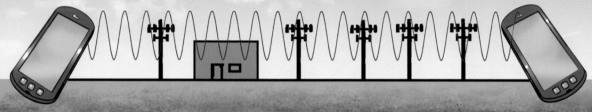

If you call someone's landline phone, the base station sends your call through the landline system.

Either way, your call zips through these channels in just a few seconds.

But your phone is at work even before you dial a number or hit send.

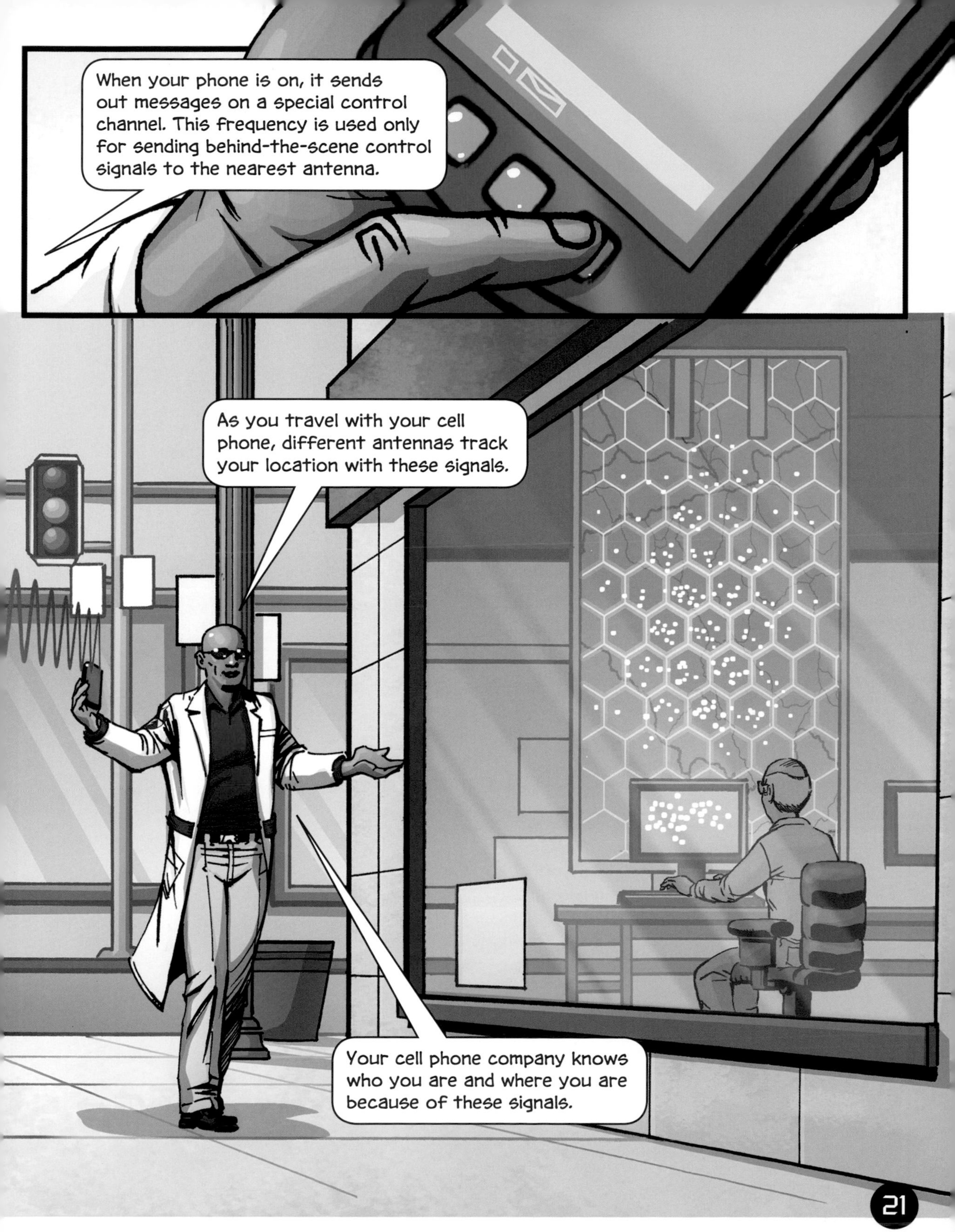
When your phone is on, it sends out messages on a special control channel. This frequency is used only for sending behind-the-scene control signals to the nearest antenna.
As you travel with your cell phone, different antennas track your location with these signals.
Your cell phone company knows who you are and where you are because of these signals.

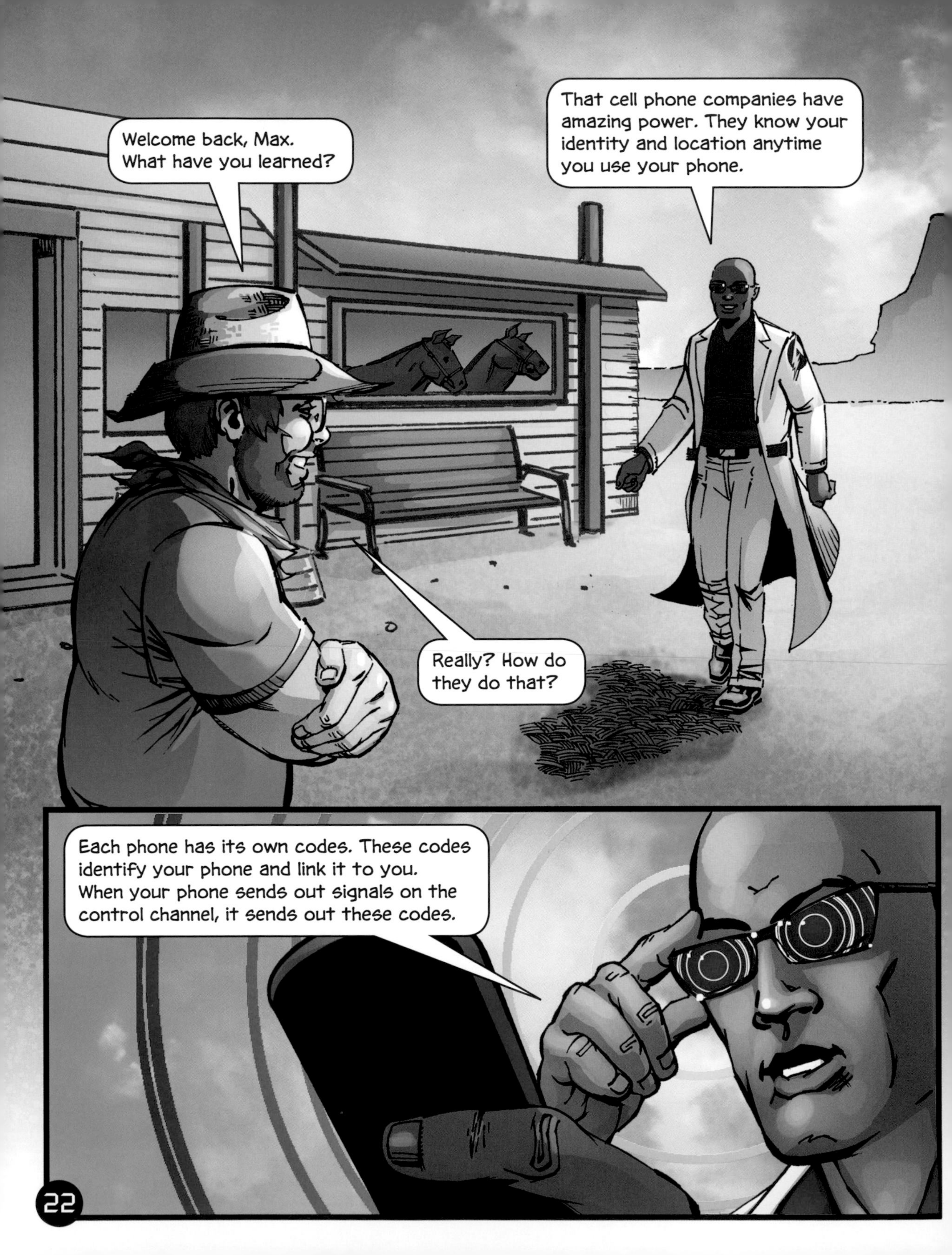
Welcome back, Max. What have you learned?
That cell phone companies have amazing power. They know your identity and location anytime you use your phone.
Really? How do they do that?
Each phone has its own codes. These codes identify your phone and link it to you. When your phone sends out signals on the control channel, it sends out these codes.

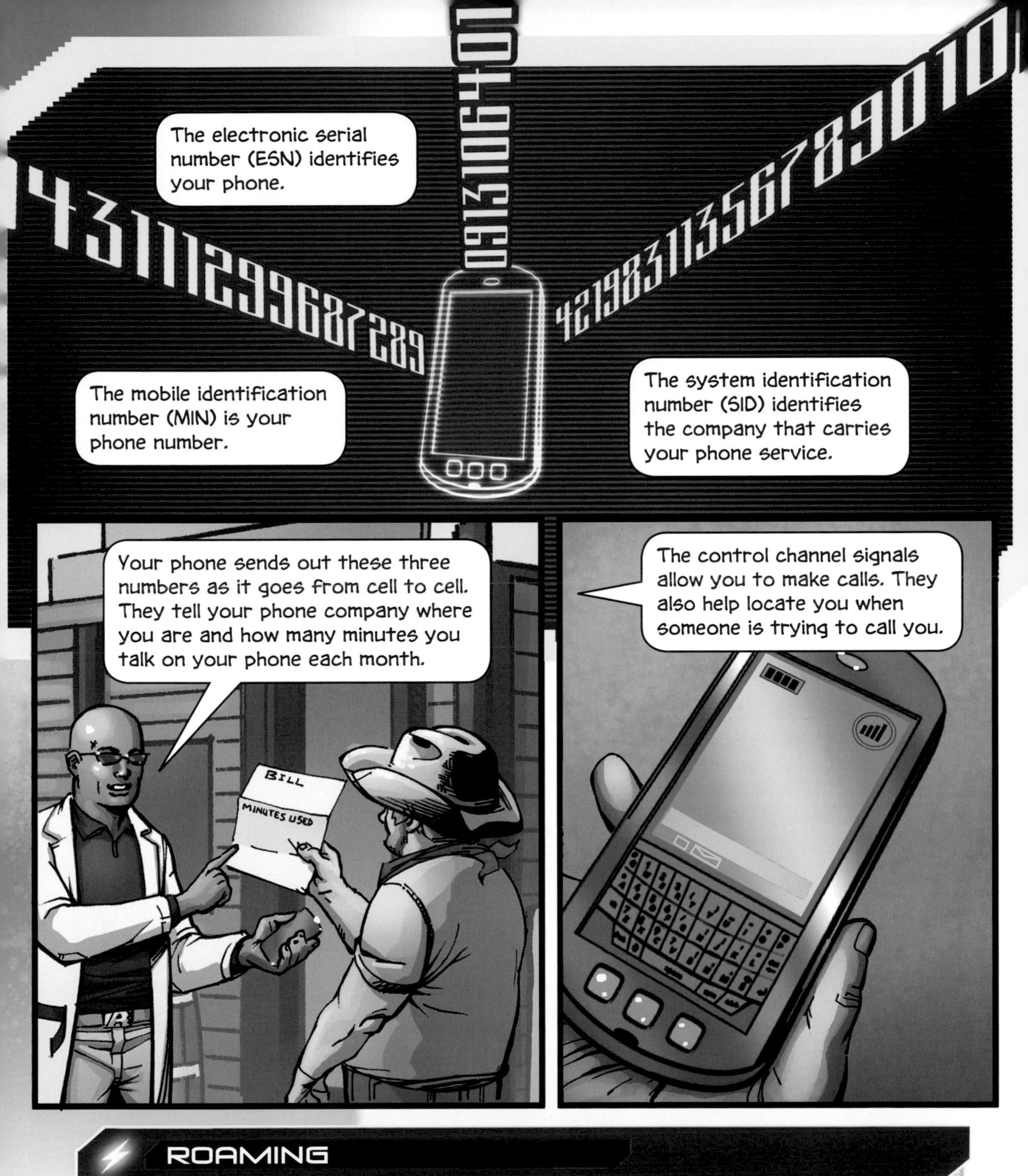
The electronic serial number (ESN) identifies your phone.
The mobile identification number (MIN) is your phone number.
The system identification number (SID) identifies the company that carries your phone service.
Your phone sends out these three numbers as it goes from cell to cell. They tell your phone company where you are and how many minutes you talk on your phone each month.
BILL
MINUTES USED
The control channel signals allow you to make calls. They also help locate you when someone is trying to call you.

ROAMING

Even if you travel in areas where your cell phone company doesn't operate, other companies will carry your phone calls. But they usually charge you extra money to do it. This charge is for what phone companies call "roaming."

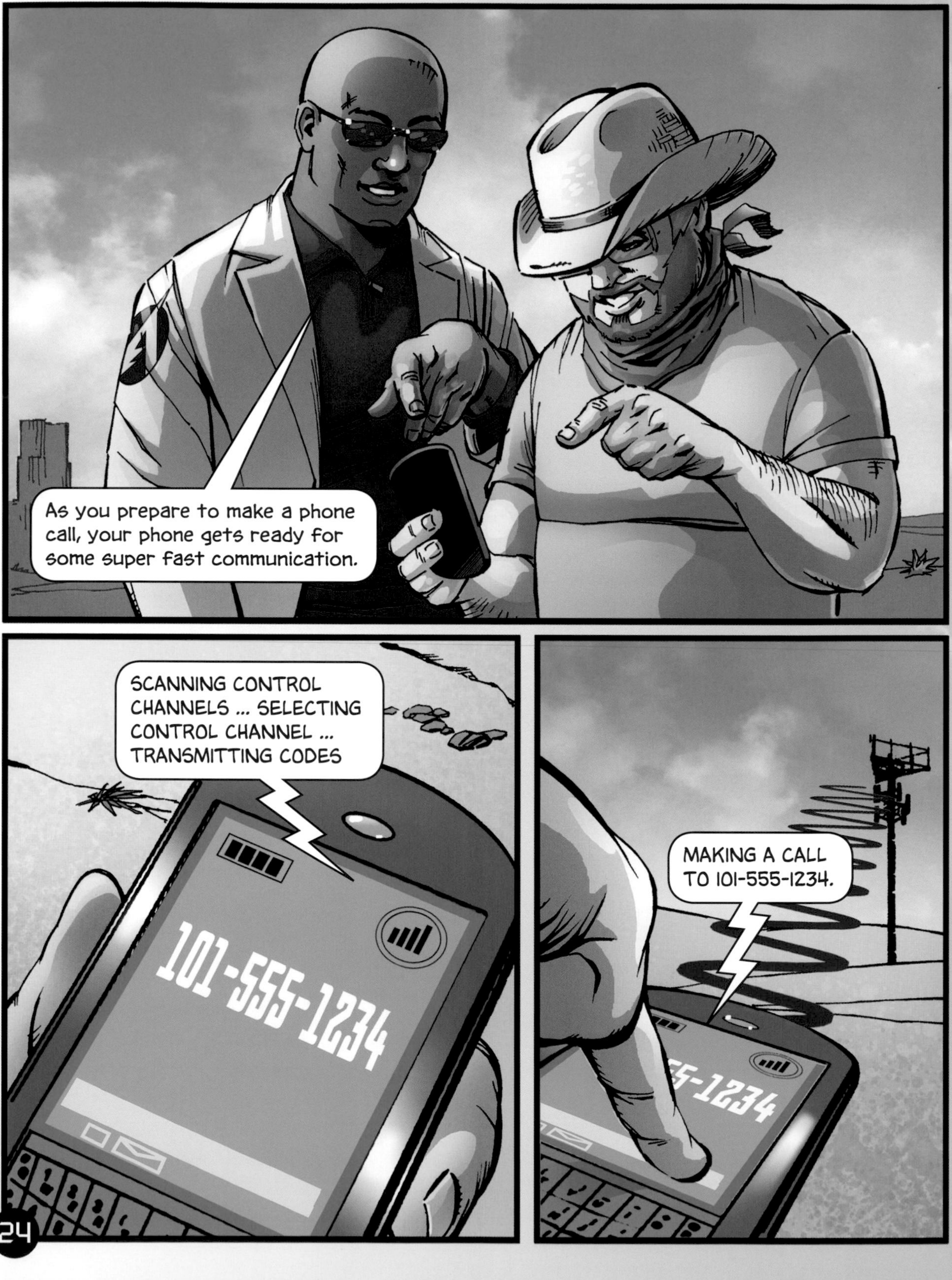
As you prepare to make a phone call, your phone gets ready for some super fast communication.
SCANNING CONTROL CHANNELS ... SELECTING CONTROL CHANNEL ... TRANSMITTING CODES
101-555-1234
MAKING A CALL TO 101-555-1234.
55-1234

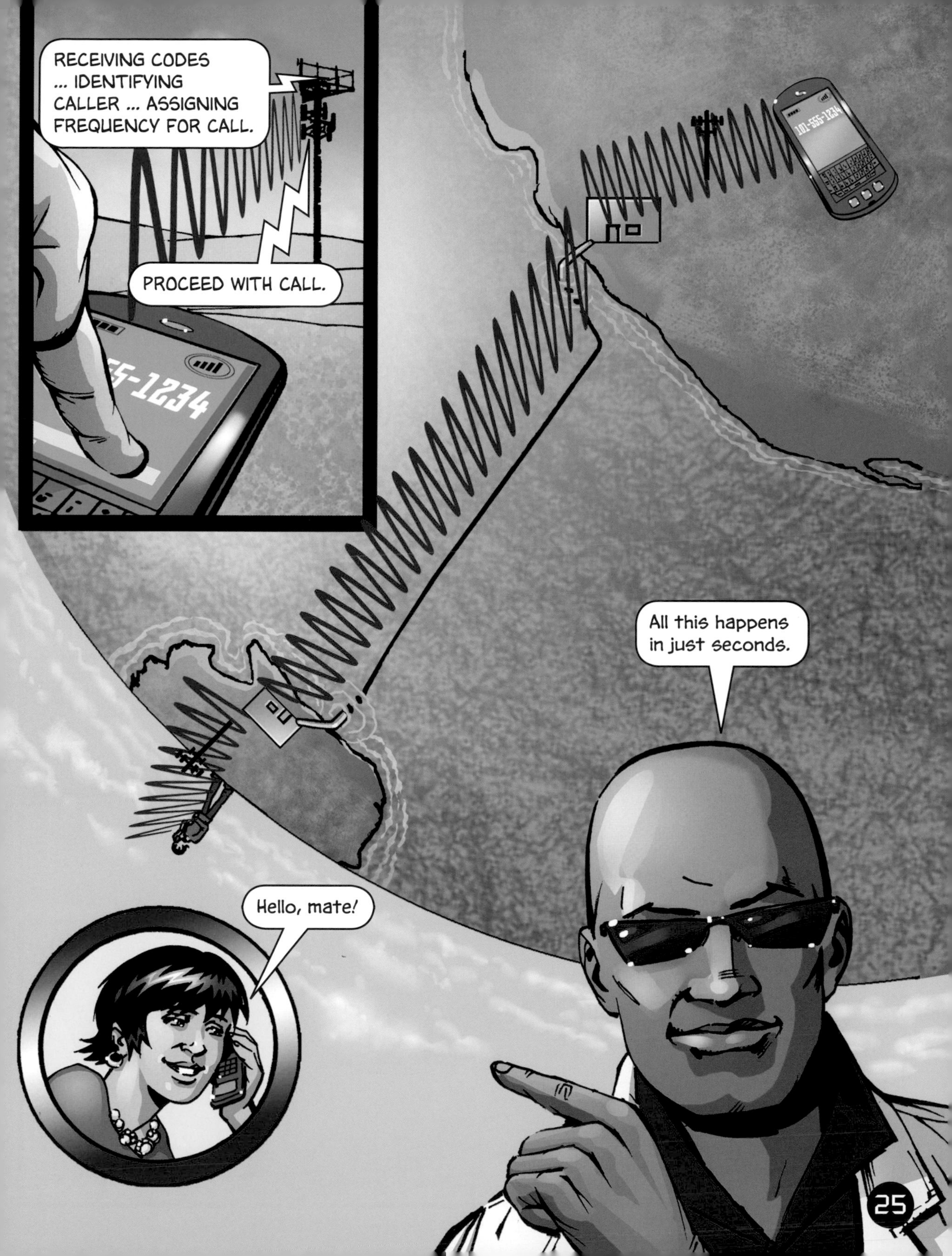

RECEIVING CODES ... IDENTIFYING CALLER ... ASSIGNING FREQUENCY FOR CALL.
PROCEED WITH CALL.
101-555-1234
All this happens in just seconds.
Hello, mate!

SECTION 4 | MAKING THE CALL

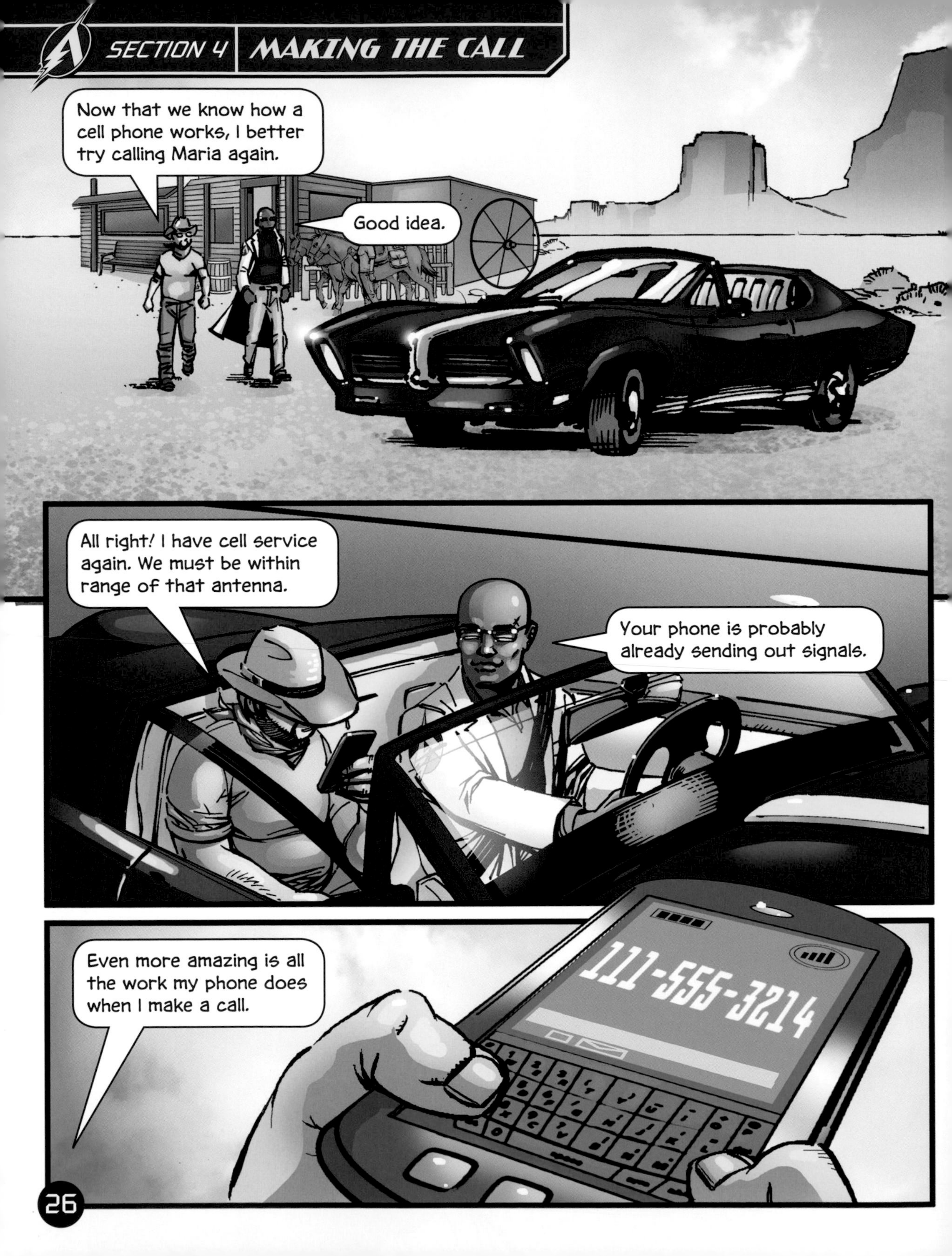

Now that we know how a cell phone works, I better try calling Maria again.
Good idea.
All right! I have cell service again. We must be within range of that antenna.
Your phone is probably already sending out signals.
Even more amazing is all the work my phone does when I make a call.
111-555-3214

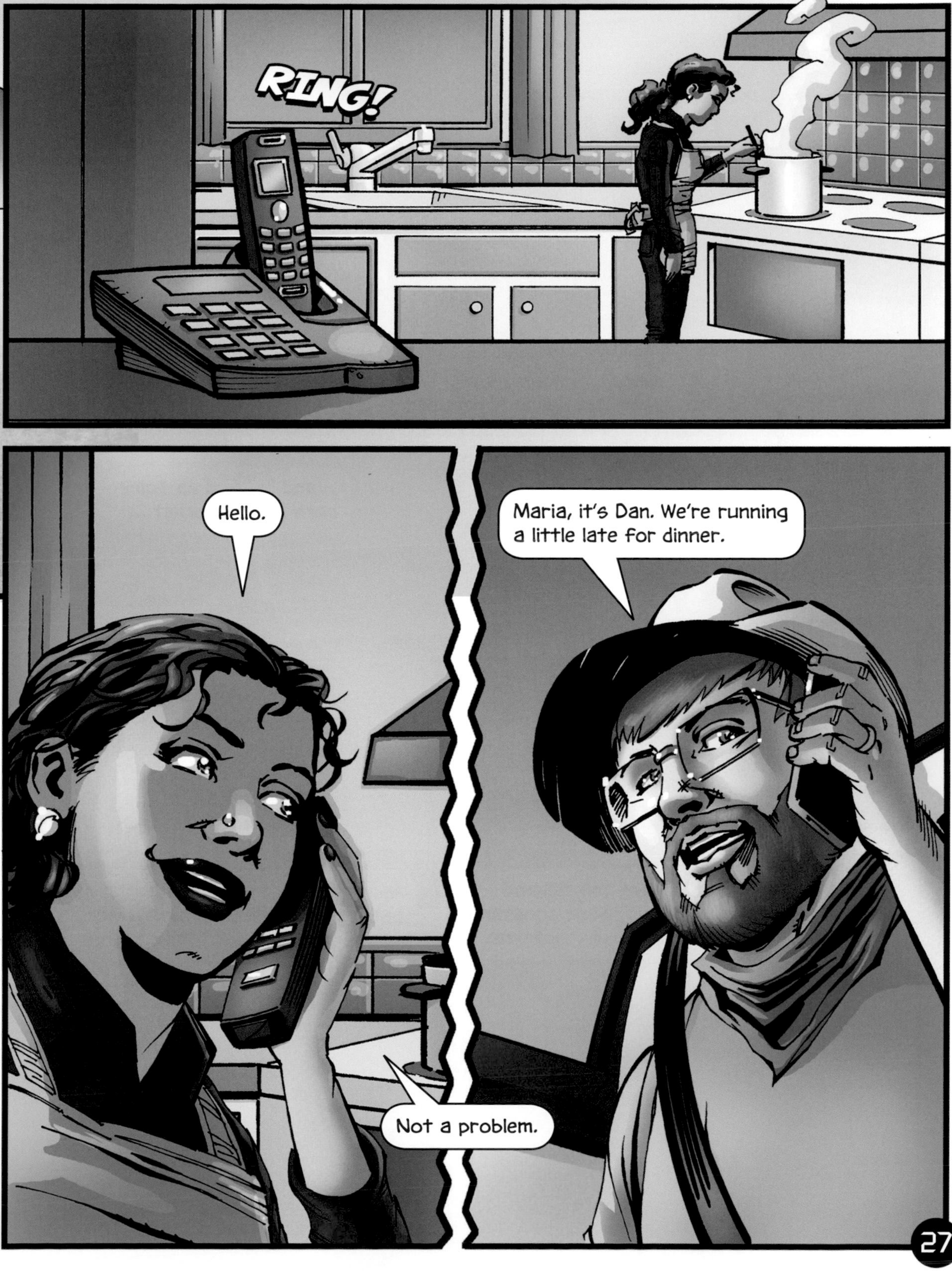
RING!
Hello.
Maria, it's Dan. We're running a little late for dinner.
Not a problem.

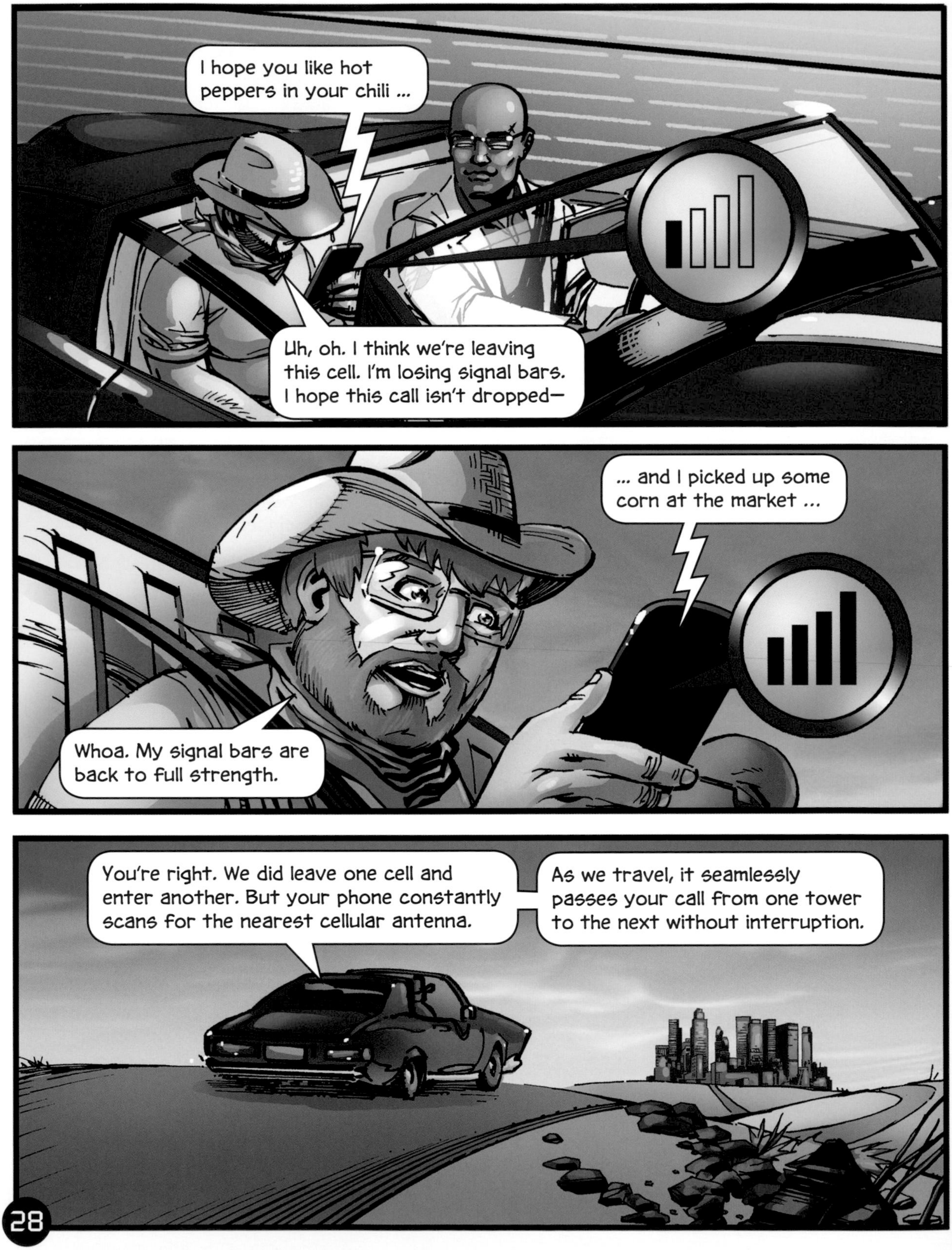

I hope you like hot peppers in your chili ...
Uh, oh. I think we're leaving this cell. I'm losing signal bars. I hope this call isn't dropped—
... and I picked up some corn at the market ...
Whoa. My signal bars are back to full strength.
You're right. We did leave one cell and enter another. But your phone constantly scans for the nearest cellular antenna.
As we travel, it seamlessly passes your call from one tower to the next without interruption.

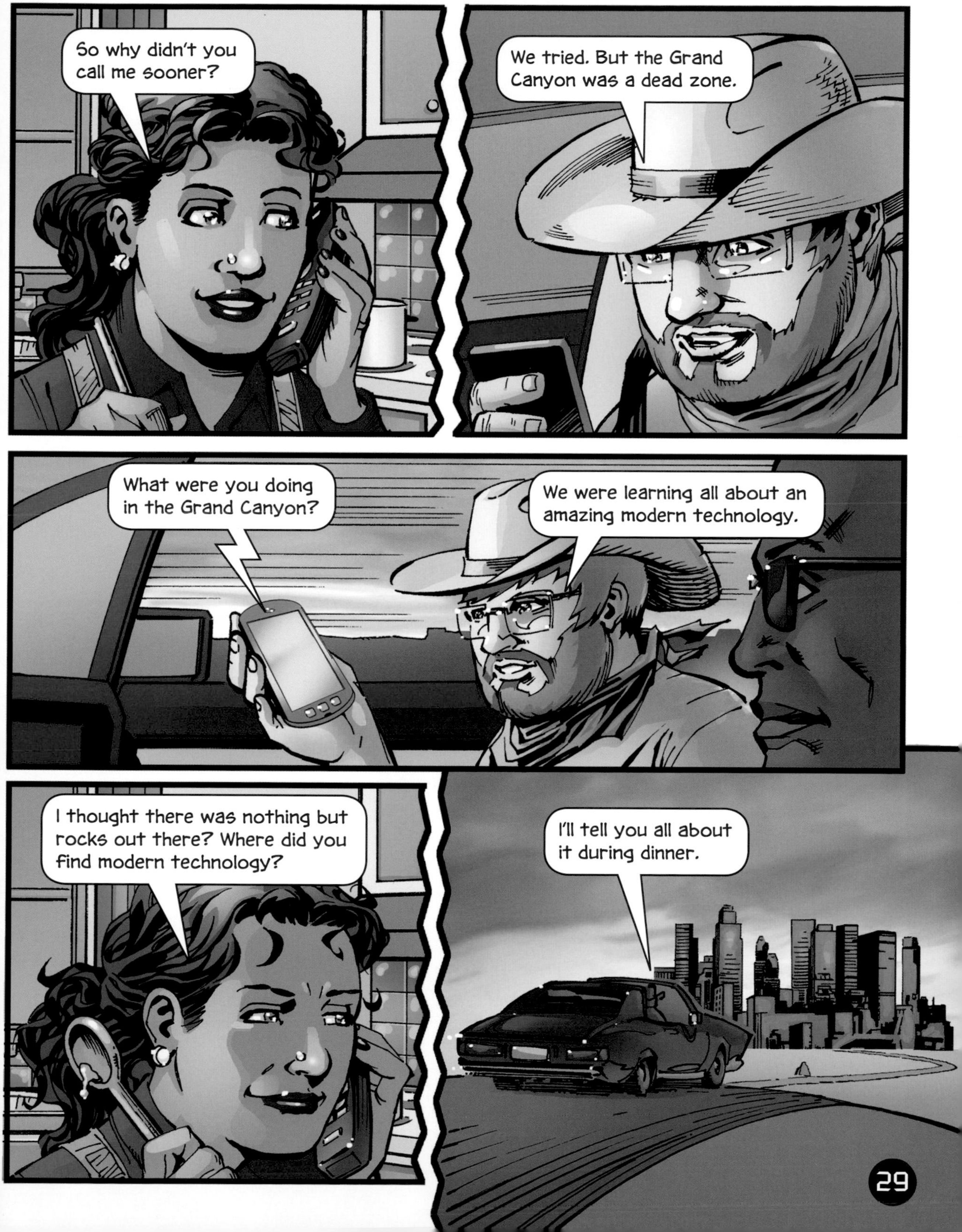
So why didn't you call me sooner?
We tried. But the Grand Canyon was a dead zone.
What were you doing in the Grand Canyon?
We were learning all about an amazing modern technology.
I thought there was nothing but rocks out there? Where did you find modern technology?
I'll tell you all about it during dinner.

MORE ABOUT
CELL PHONES

Satellite phones are another type of mobile phone. Instead of using antennas to carry signals, they beam signals to a satellite high above Earth. One satellite can do the work of thousands of cellular antennas. Satellite phones are bulky and expensive today. But they may replace cell phones someday.

Are cell phones hazardous to your health? Electromagnetic radiation is produced by the waves used to send cell phone messages. This radiation affects electrical activity in the brain. Some researchers suspect, but have yet to prove, that this radiation can cause cancer in the ears and brain.

The first successful cell phone was invented by Motorola in 1973. Early cell phones were neither small nor cheap. They were the size of a brick and sold for nearly $4,000!

New ways to use a cell phone are constantly being engineered. Most cell phone users can access the internet and take pictures with their phones. Engineers are now working on air writing. This technology will allow people to write words in the air with their phones. The words will then show up on the cell phone's screen.

The touch screen on a cell phone is an amazing technology. Some touch screens respond to the electrical currents in your finger. Others detect the location of your touch by noticing the interruption your finger causes in sound waves or visible light.

CHAPTER 2

The Dynamic World of Drones

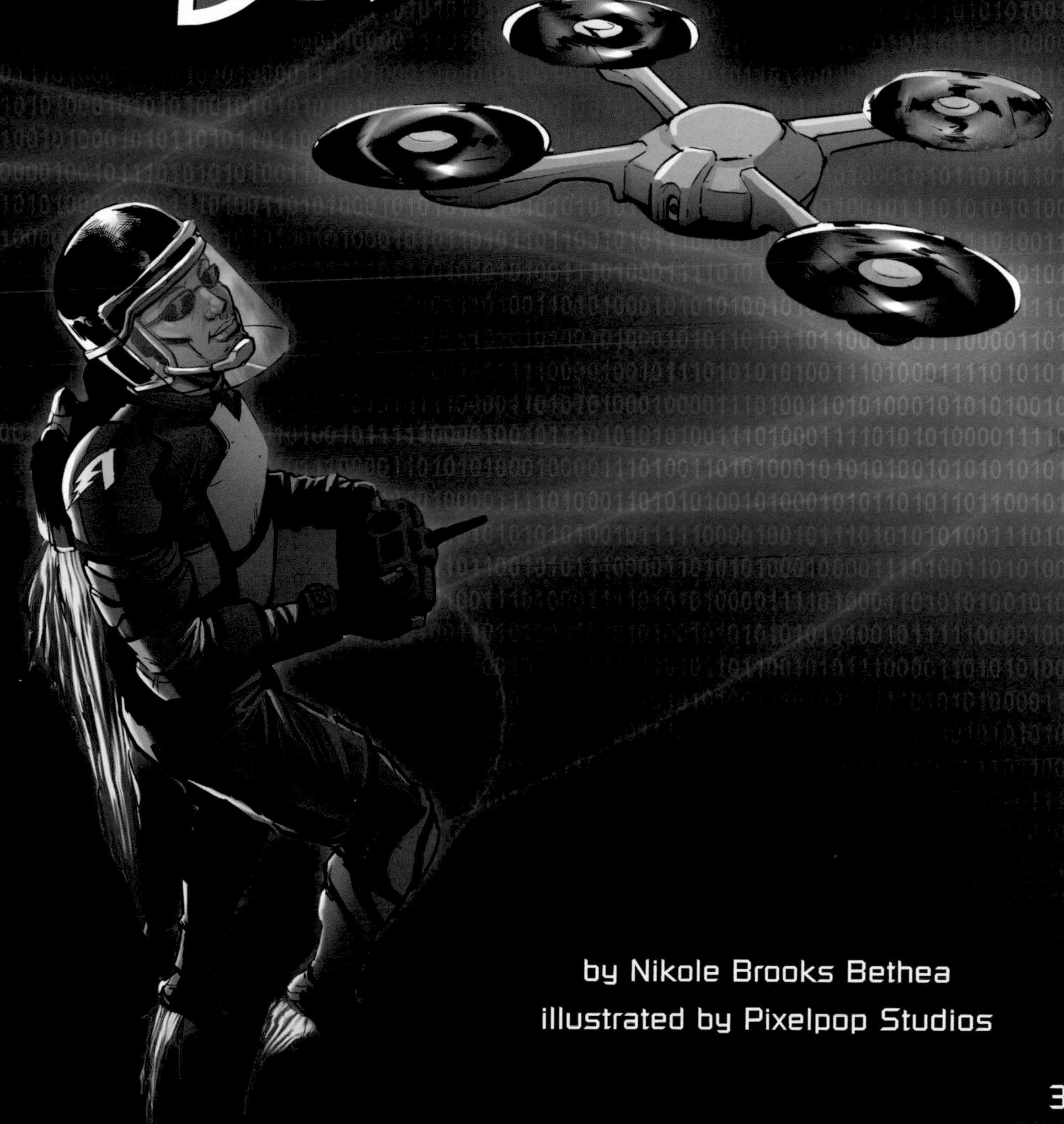

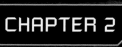

by Nikole Brooks Bethea
illustrated by Pixelpop Studios

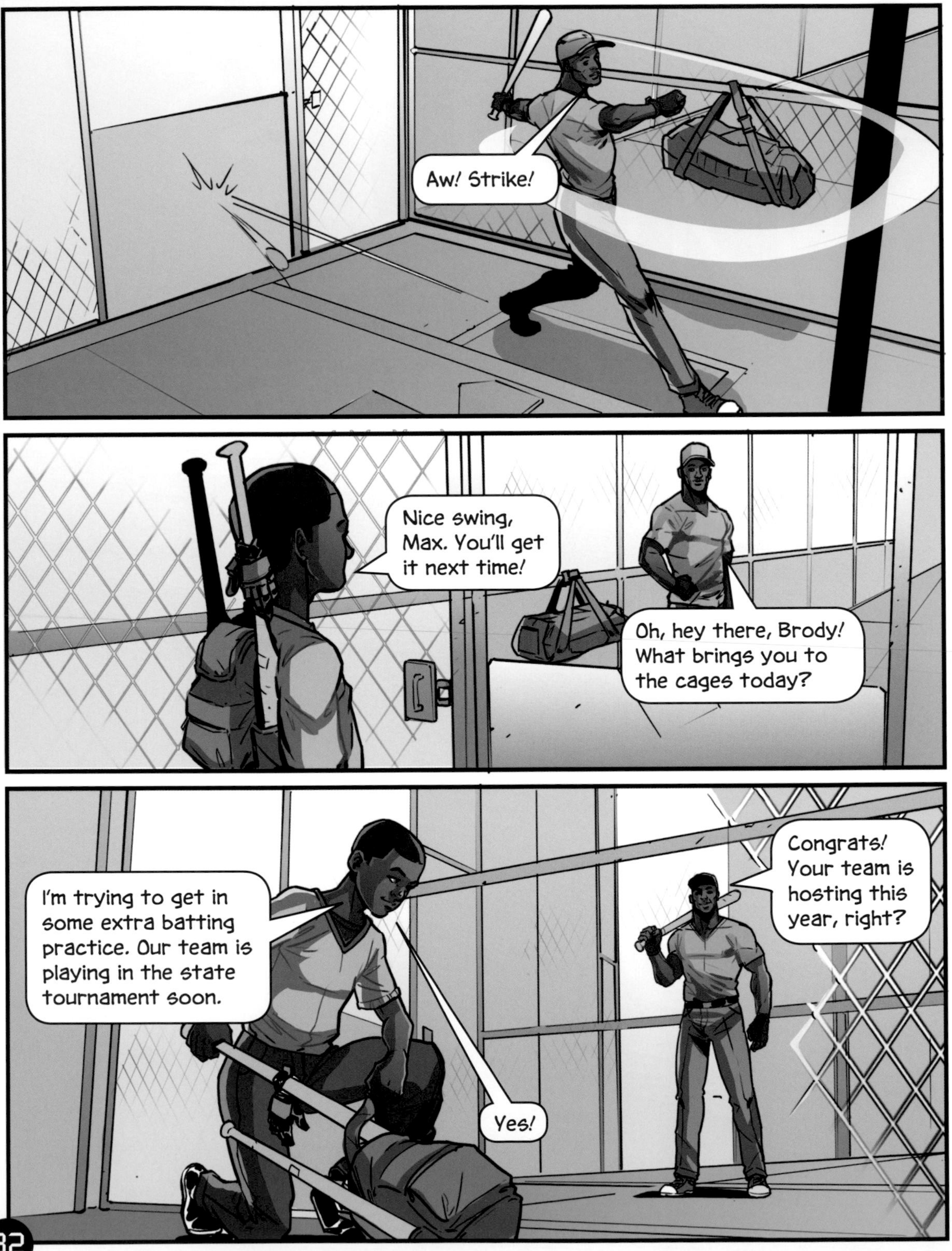
Aw! Strike!
Nice swing, Max. You'll get it next time!
Oh, hey there, Brody! What brings you to the cages today?
I'm trying to get in some extra batting practice. Our team is playing in the state tournament soon.
Congrats! Your team is hosting this year, right?
Yes!

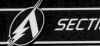

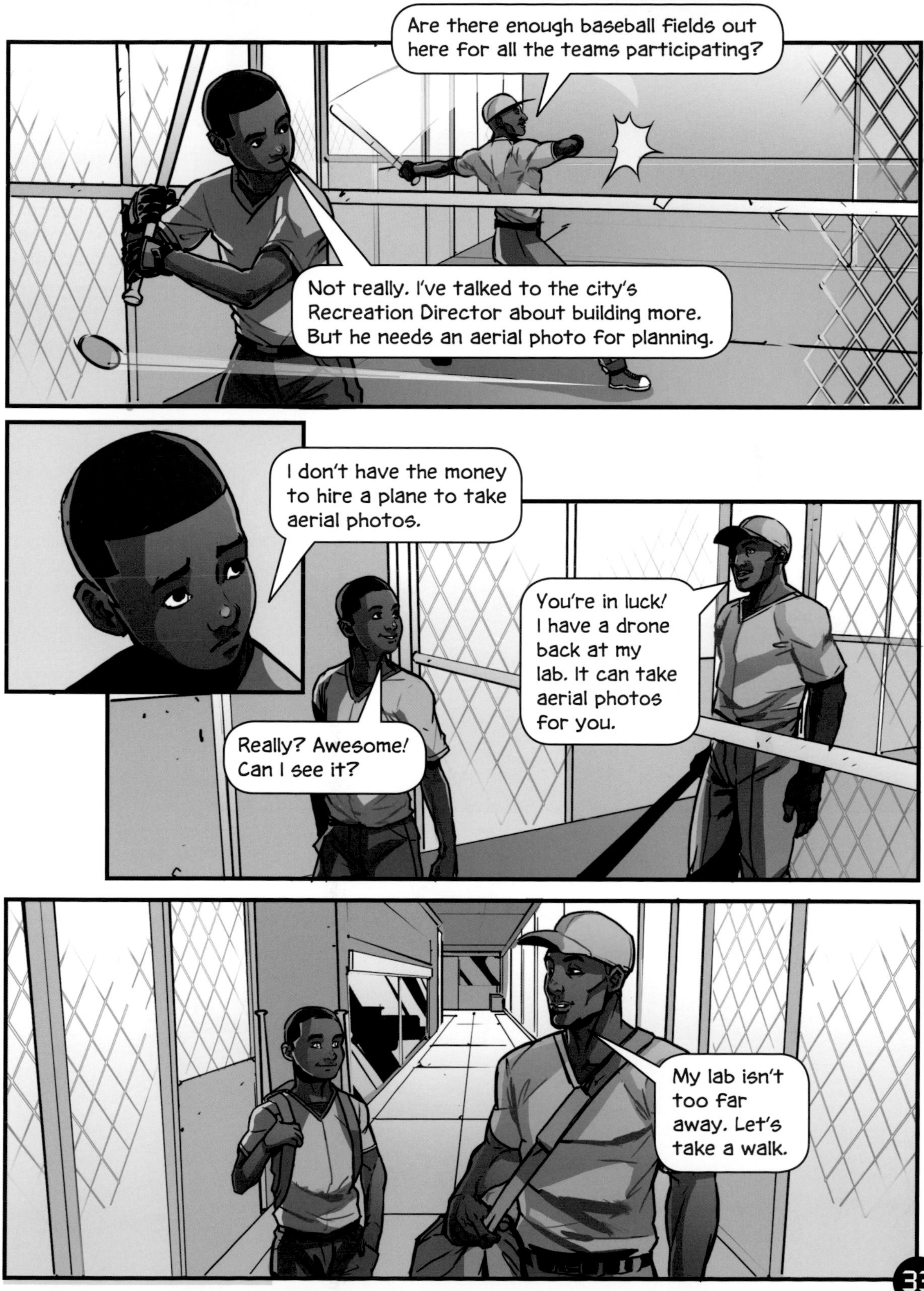
Are there enough baseball fields out here for all the teams participating?
Not really. I've talked to the city's Recreation Director about building more. But he needs an aerial photo for planning.
I don't have the money to hire a plane to take aerial photos.
You're in luck! I have a drone back at my lab. It can take aerial photos for you.
Really? Awesome! Can I see it?
My lab isn't too far away. Let's take a walk.

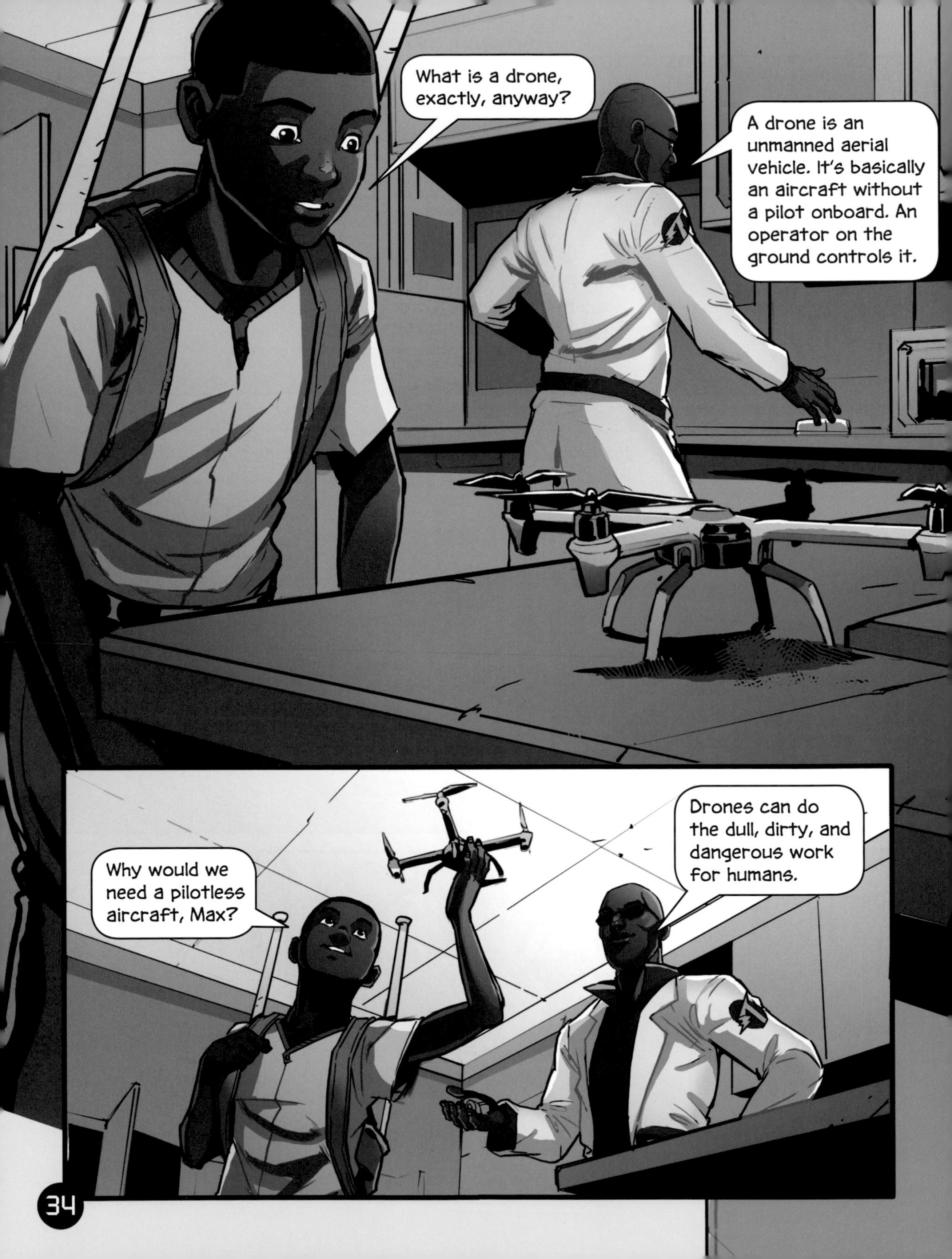
What is a drone, exactly, anyway?
A drone is an unmanned aerial vehicle. It's basically an aircraft without a pilot onboard. An operator on the ground controls it.
Why would we need a pilotless aircraft, Max?
Drones can do the dull, dirty, and dangerous work for humans.

I'm mounting the camera now. My drone also has a global positioning system, or GPS. This allows me to track its location.

My drone is a quadcopter. It's classified as a rotary drone because of these rotating blades. They provide lift and allow the drone to hover or move in any direction.

Instead of one blade like a helicopter, it has four. Is that why it's called a quadcopter?

You got it!

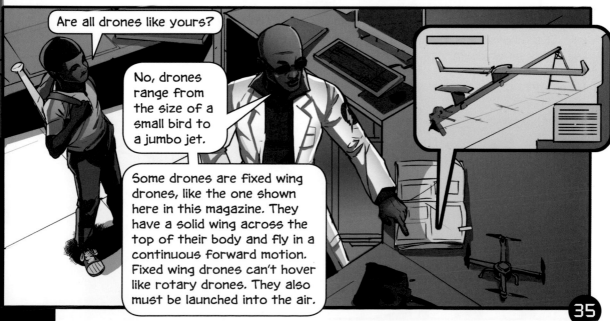

Are all drones like yours?

No, drones range from the size of a small bird to a jumbo jet.

Some drones are fixed wing drones, like the one shown here in this magazine. They have a solid wing across the top of their body and fly in a continuous forward motion. Fixed wing drones can't hover like rotary drones. They also must be launched into the air.

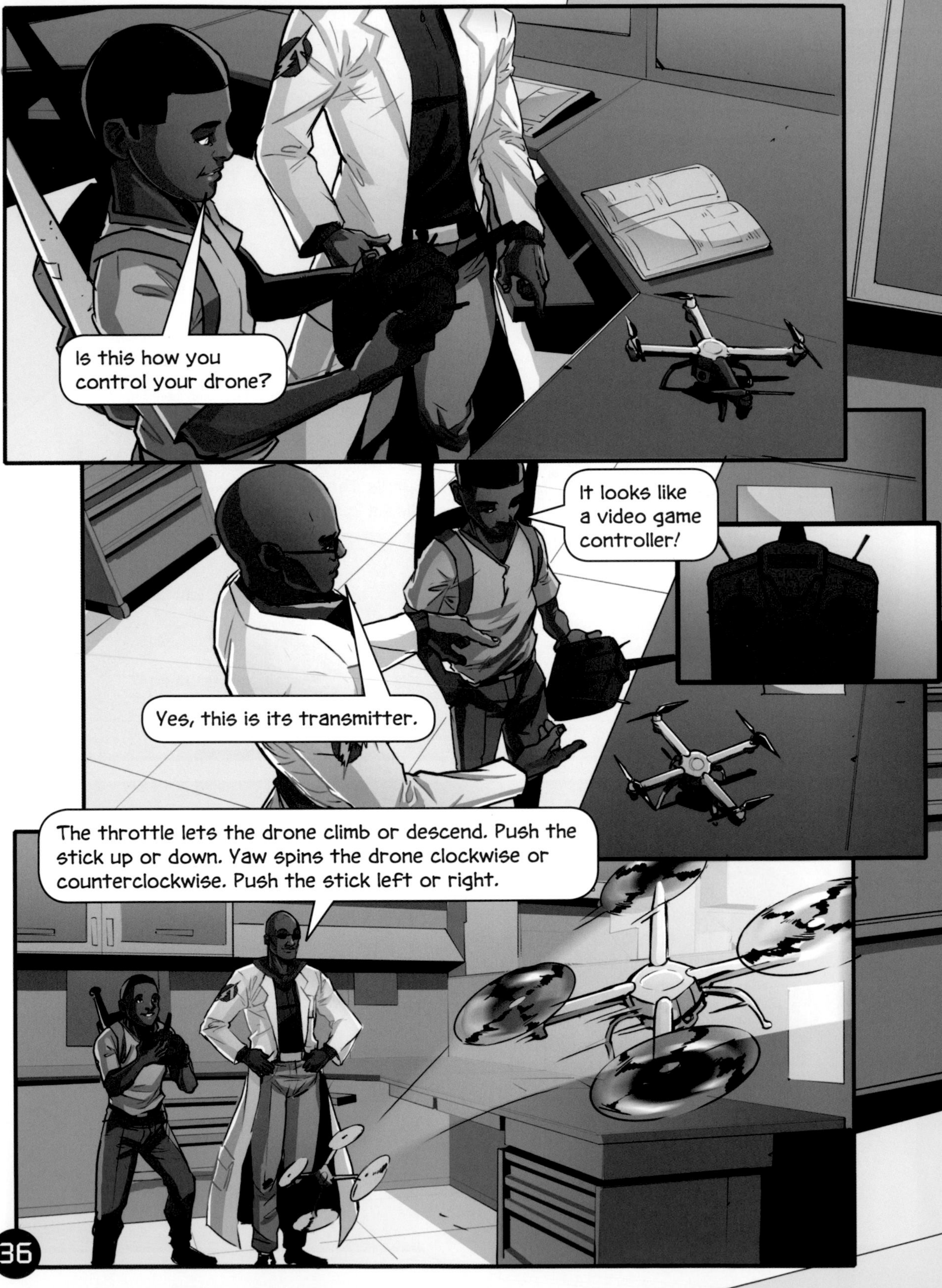
Is this how you control your drone?
It looks like a video game controller!
Yes, this is its transmitter.
The throttle lets the drone climb or descend. Push the stick up or down. Yaw spins the drone clockwise or counterclockwise. Push the stick left or right.

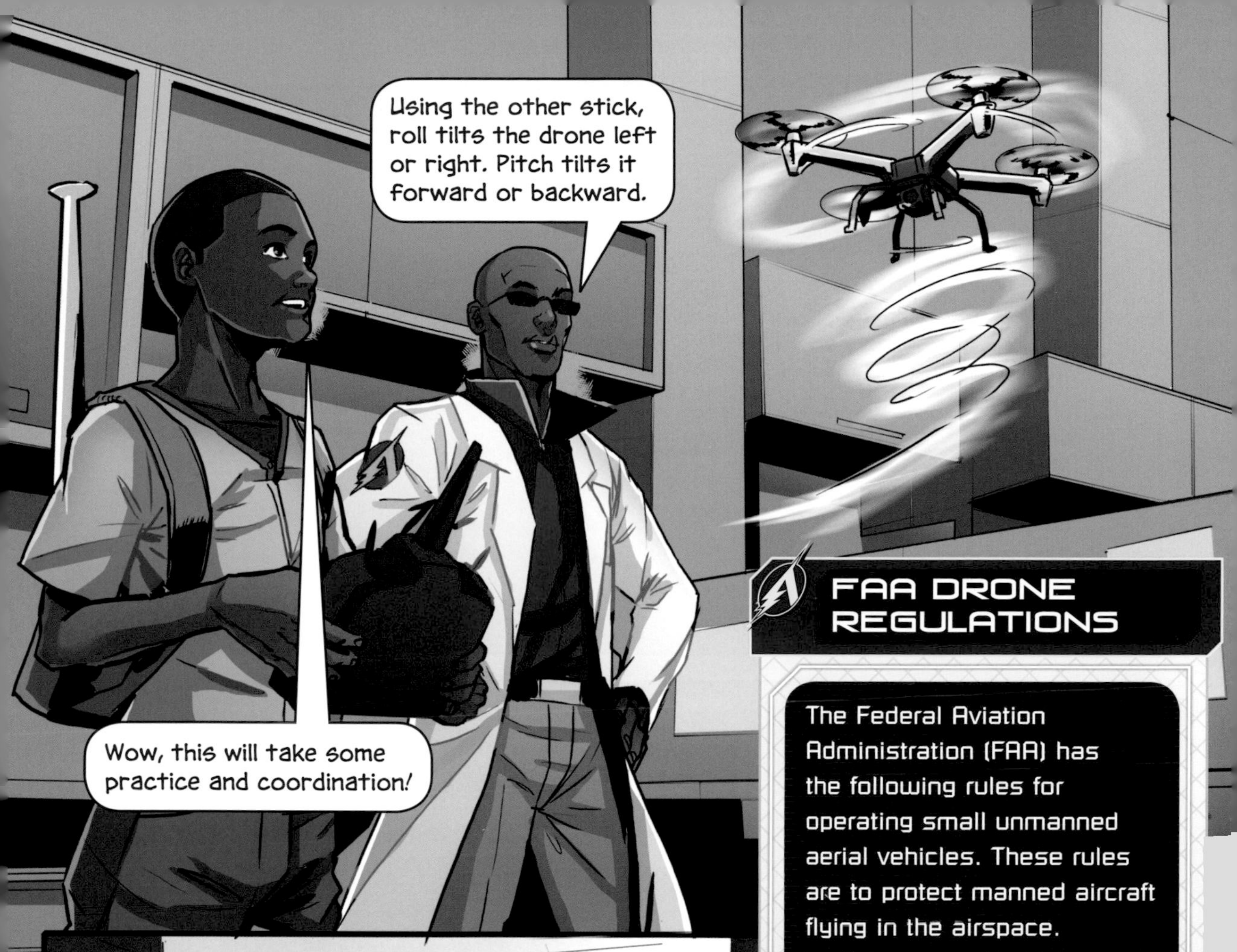
Using the other stick, roll tilts the drone left or right. Pitch tilts it forward or backward.
Wow, this will take some practice and coordination!

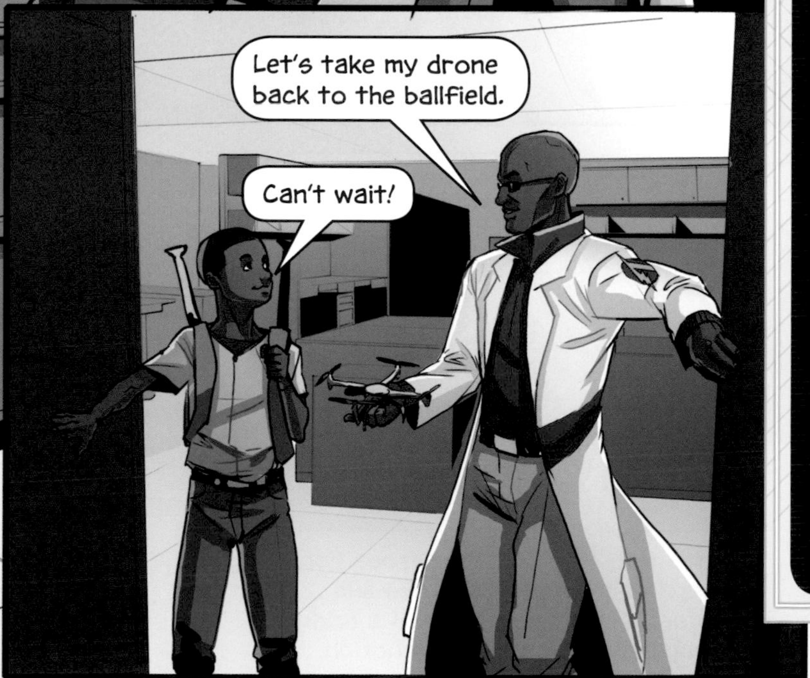
Let's take my drone back to the ballfield.
Can't wait!

FAA DRONE REGULATIONS

The Federal Aviation Administration (FAA) has the following rules for operating small unmanned aerial vehicles. These rules are to protect manned aircraft flying in the airspace.

- Drones must weigh less than 55 pounds (25 kilograms).
- The drone must remain within sight of the controller at all times.
- Drones can only be operated during daylight.
- Drones can't be operated over people or under covered structures.
- The maximum height drones can fly above ground is 400 feet (122 meters).

SECTION 2 COMMERCIAL AND SCIENTIFIC DRONES

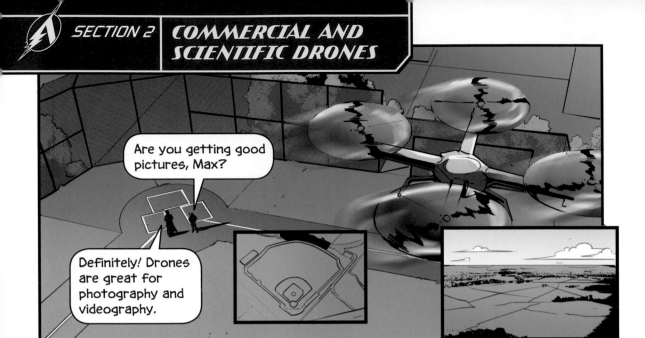

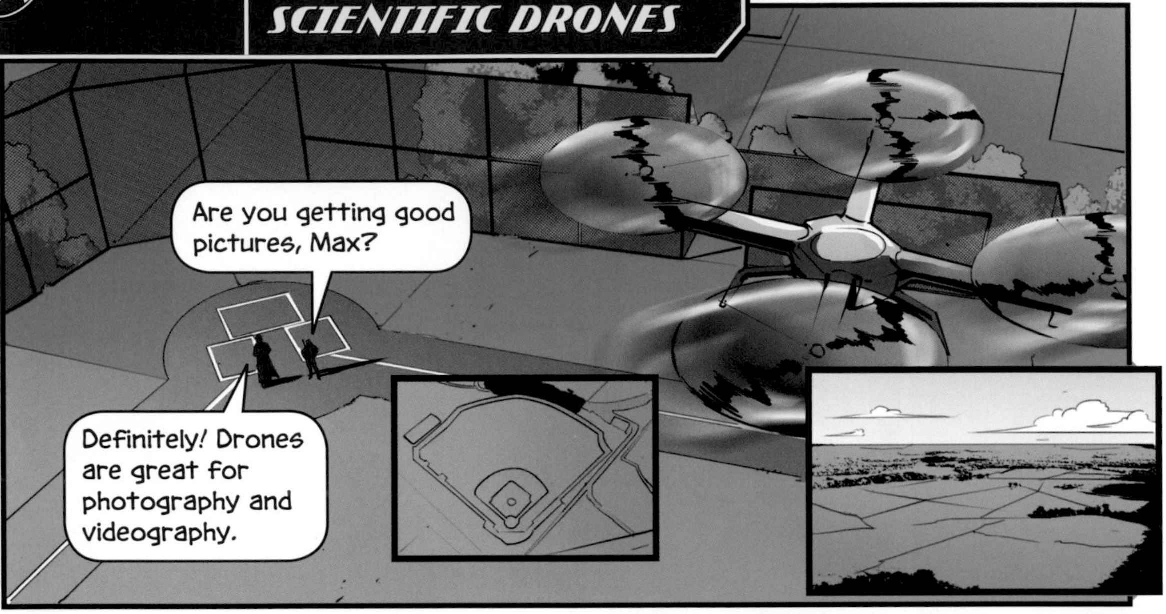
Are you getting good pictures, Max?
Definitely! Drones are great for photography and videography.

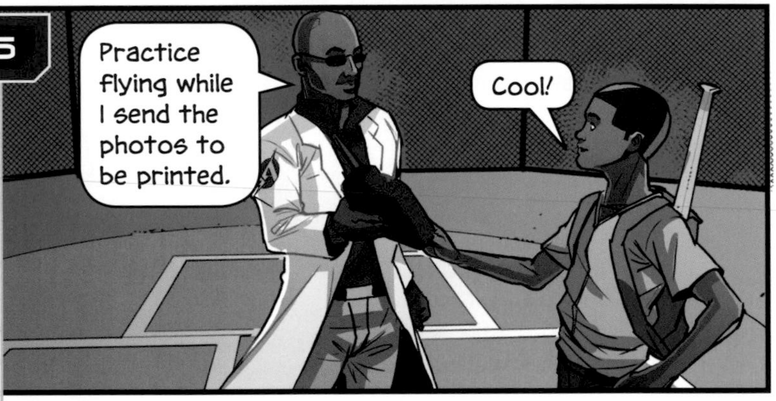
Practice flying while I send the photos to be printed.
Cool!

FOREST FIRES

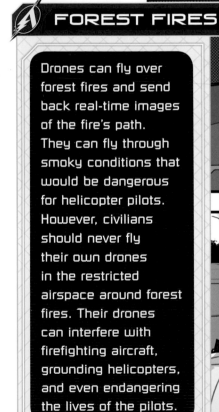

Drones can fly over forest fires and send back real-time images of the fire's path. They can fly through smoky conditions that would be dangerous for helicopter pilots. However, civilians should never fly their own drones in the restricted airspace around forest fires. Their drones can interfere with firefighting aircraft, grounding helicopters, and even endangering the lives of the pilots.

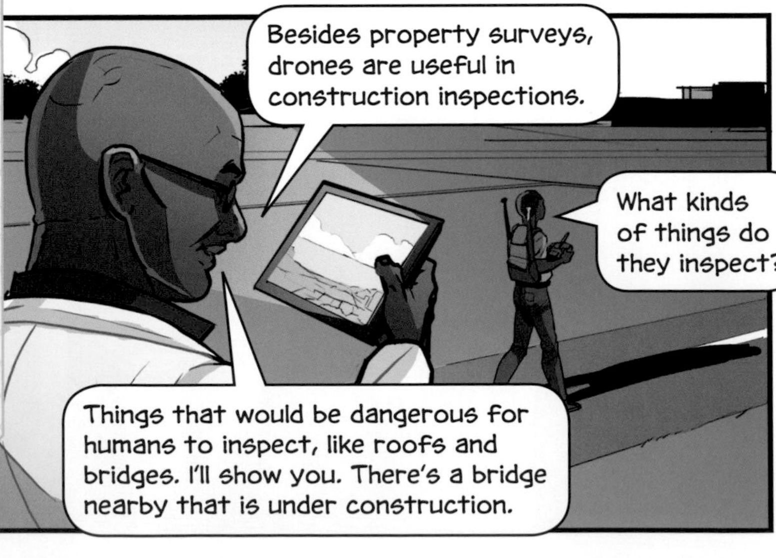
Besides property surveys, drones are useful in construction inspections.
What kinds of things do they inspect?
Things that would be dangerous for humans to inspect, like roofs and bridges. I'll show you. There's a bridge nearby that is under construction.

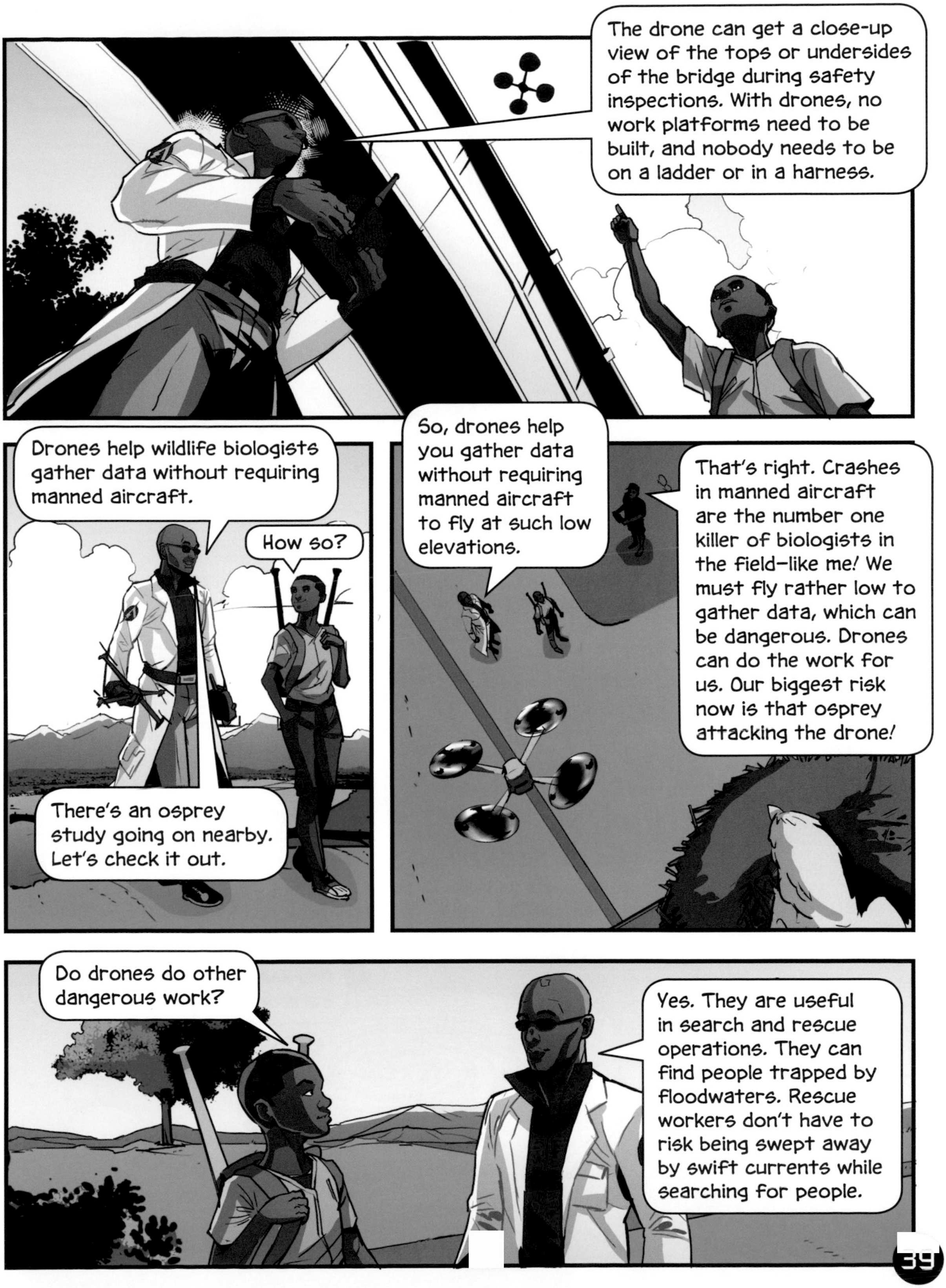

The drone can get a close-up view of the tops or undersides of the bridge during safety inspections. With drones, no work platforms need to be built, and nobody needs to be on a ladder or in a harness.
Drones help wildlife biologists gather data without requiring manned aircraft.
How so?
There's an osprey study going on nearby. Let's check it out.
So, drones help you gather data without requiring manned aircraft to fly at such low elevations.
That's right. Crashes in manned aircraft are the number one killer of biologists in the field—like me! We must fly rather low to gather data, which can be dangerous. Drones can do the work for us. Our biggest risk now is that osprey attacking the drone!
Do drones do other dangerous work?
Yes. They are useful in search and rescue operations. They can find people trapped by floodwaters. Rescue workers don't have to risk being swept away by swift currents while searching for people.

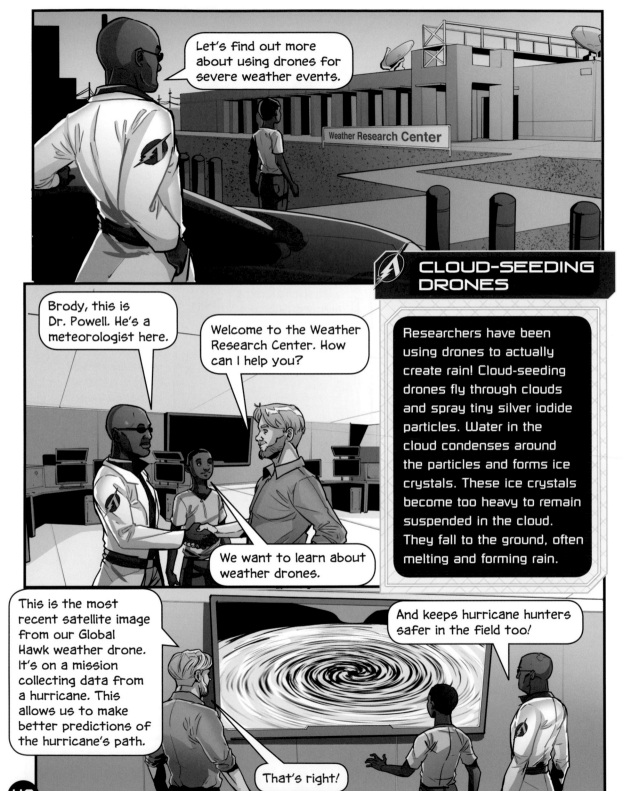

Let's find out more about using drones for severe weather events.

Weather Research Center

CLOUD-SEEDING DRONES

Researchers have been using drones to actually create rain! Cloud-seeding drones fly through clouds and spray tiny silver iodide particles. Water in the cloud condenses around the particles and forms ice crystals. These ice crystals become too heavy to remain suspended in the cloud. They fall to the ground, often melting and forming rain.

Brody, this is Dr. Powell. He's a meteorologist here.

Welcome to the Weather Research Center. How can I help you?

We want to learn about weather drones.

This is the most recent satellite image from our Global Hawk weather drone. It's on a mission collecting data from a hurricane. This allows us to make better predictions of the hurricane's path.

And keeps hurricane hunters safer in the field too!

That's right!

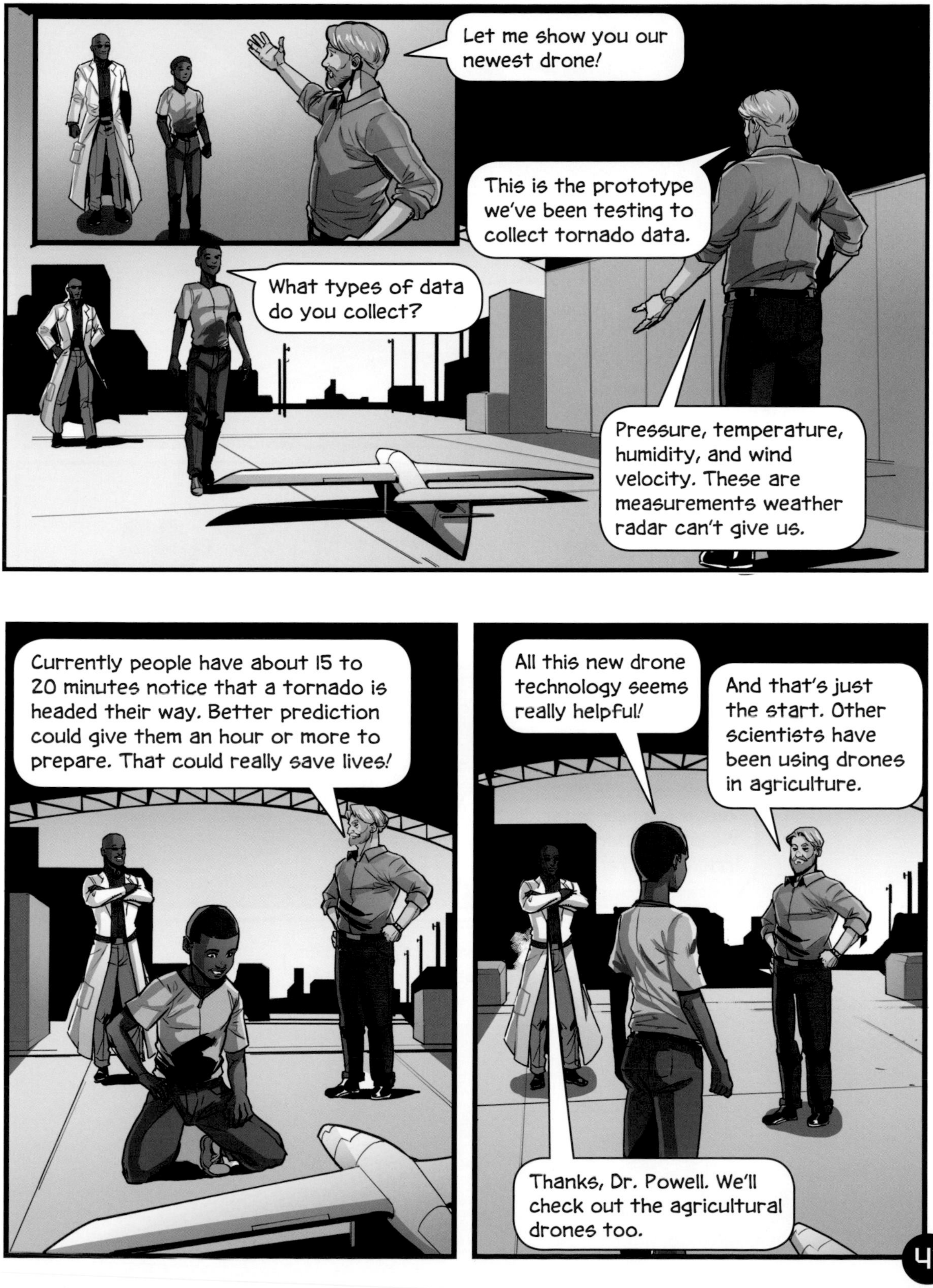
Let me show you our newest drone!
This is the prototype we've been testing to collect tornado data.
What types of data do you collect?
Pressure, temperature, humidity, and wind velocity. These are measurements weather radar can't give us.
Currently people have about 15 to 20 minutes notice that a tornado is headed their way. Better prediction could give them an hour or more to prepare. That could really save lives!
All this new drone technology seems really helpful!
And that's just the start. Other scientists have been using drones in agriculture.
Thanks, Dr. Powell. We'll check out the agricultural drones too.

Wow! I want a closer view of that!

Hi folks! I'm Jeff Ricks, the agricultural manager.

Is that drone watering the grapevines?

Yes, it's a helicopter drone. We save water by only irrigating where it's needed.

What's that one doing?

That one's a quadcopter. It's taking pictures of the crops.

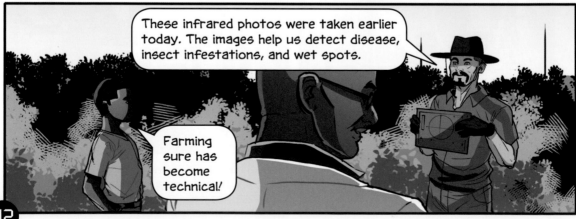

These infrared photos were taken earlier today. The images help us detect disease, insect infestations, and wet spots.

Farming sure has become technical!

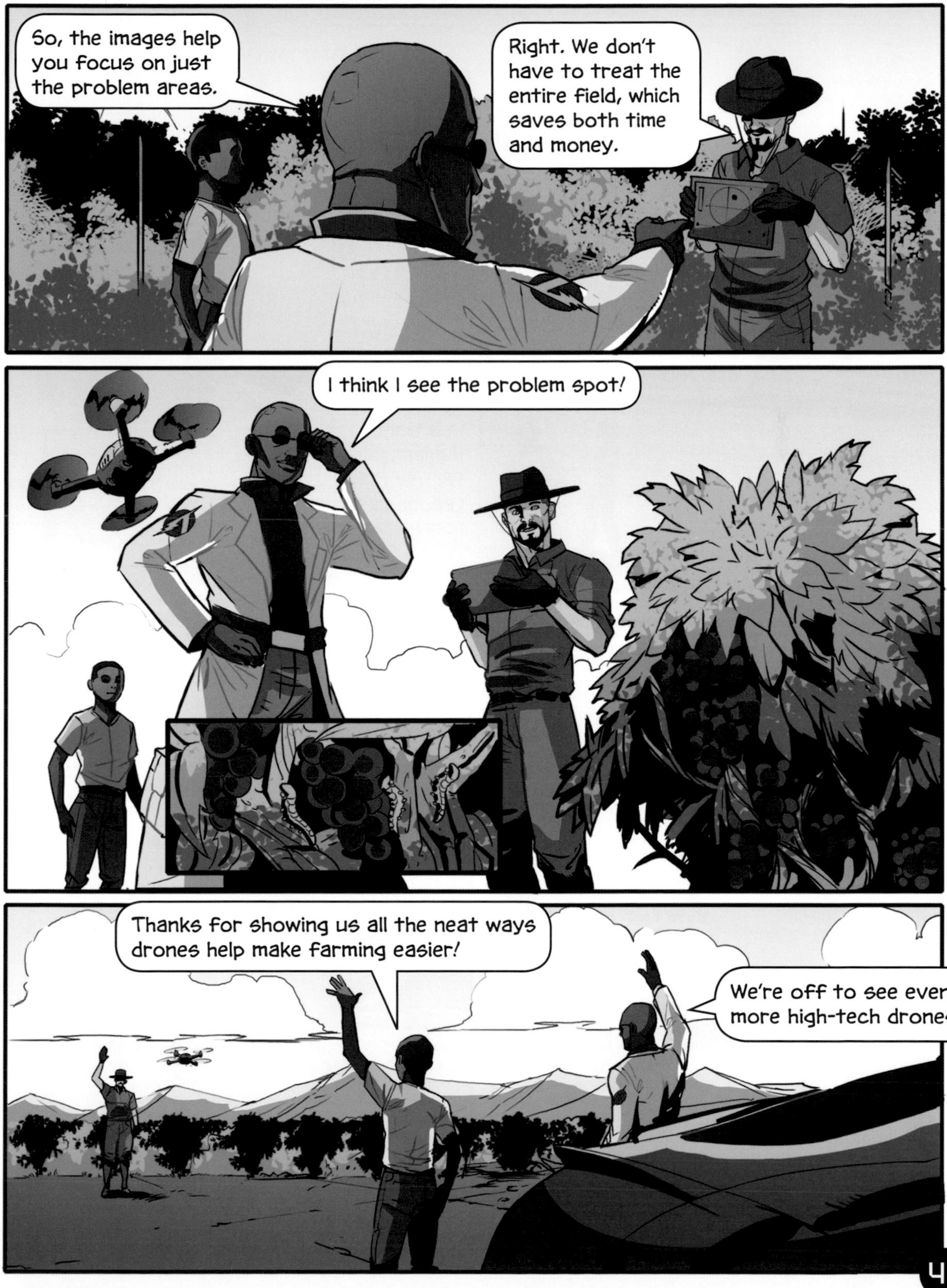
So, the images help you focus on just the problem areas.
Right. We don't have to treat the entire field, which saves both time and money.
I think I see the problem spot!
Thanks for showing us all the neat ways drones help make farming easier!
We're off to see even more high-tech drones.

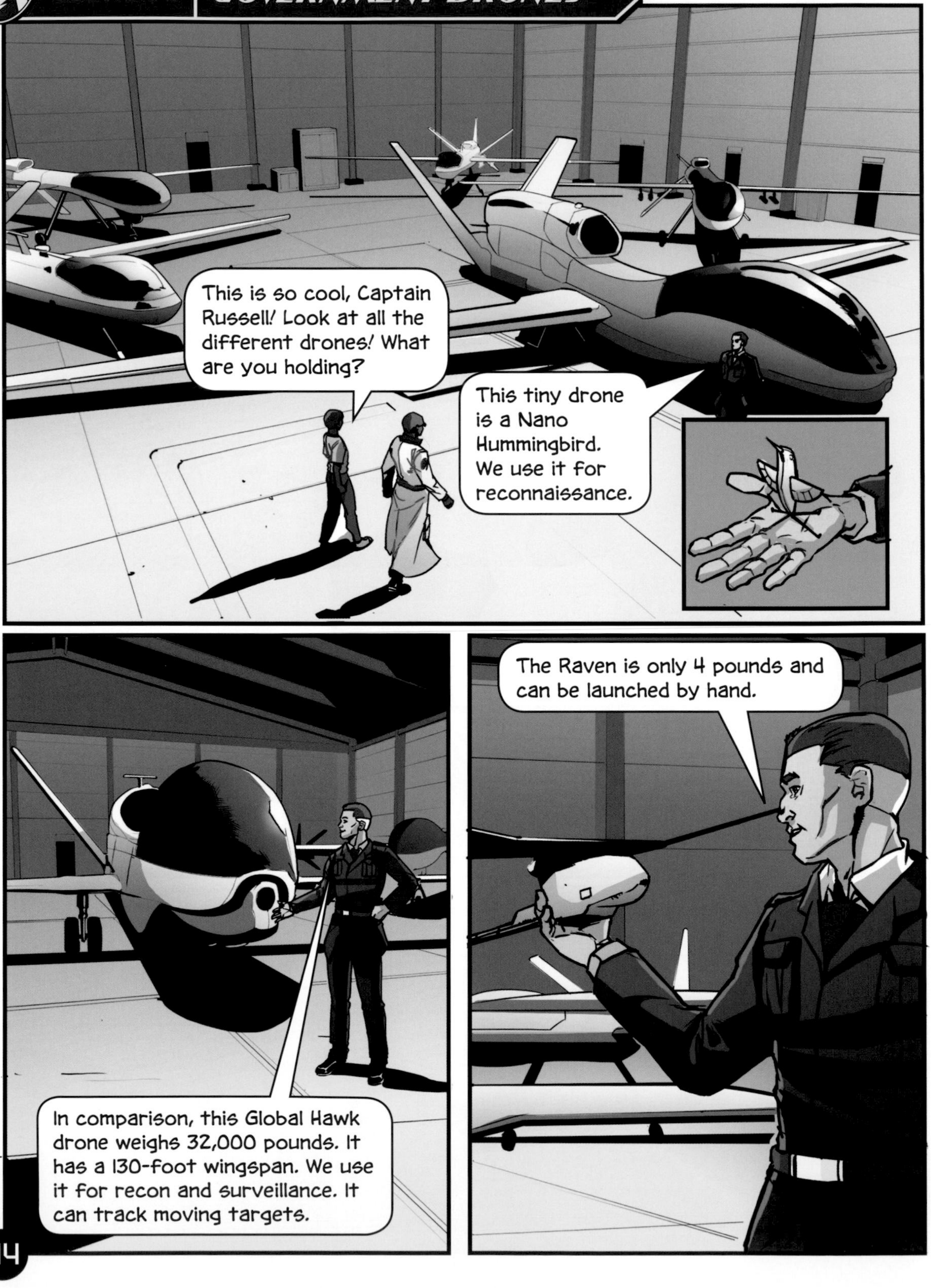
This is so cool, Captain Russell! Look at all the different drones! What are you holding?
This tiny drone is a Nano Hummingbird. We use it for reconnaissance.
In comparison, this Global Hawk drone weighs 32,000 pounds. It has a 130-foot wingspan. We use it for recon and surveillance. It can track moving targets.
The Raven is only 4 pounds and can be launched by hand.

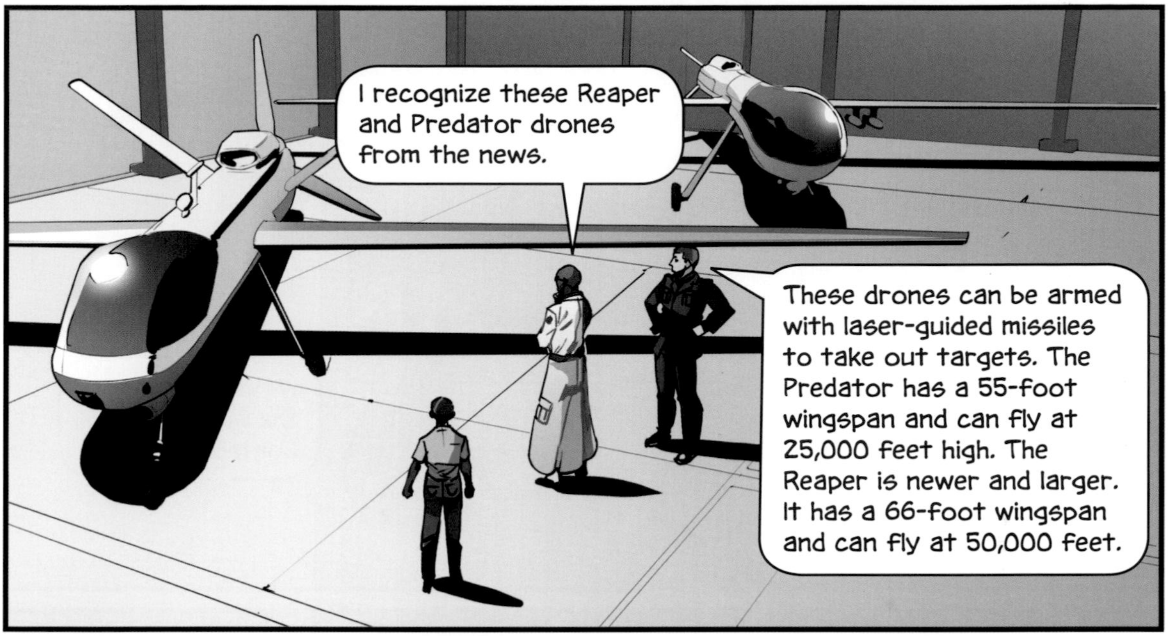
I recognize these Reaper and Predator drones from the news.
These drones can be armed with laser-guided missiles to take out targets. The Predator has a 55-foot wingspan and can fly at 25,000 feet high. The Reaper is newer and larger. It has a 66-foot wingspan and can fly at 50,000 feet.

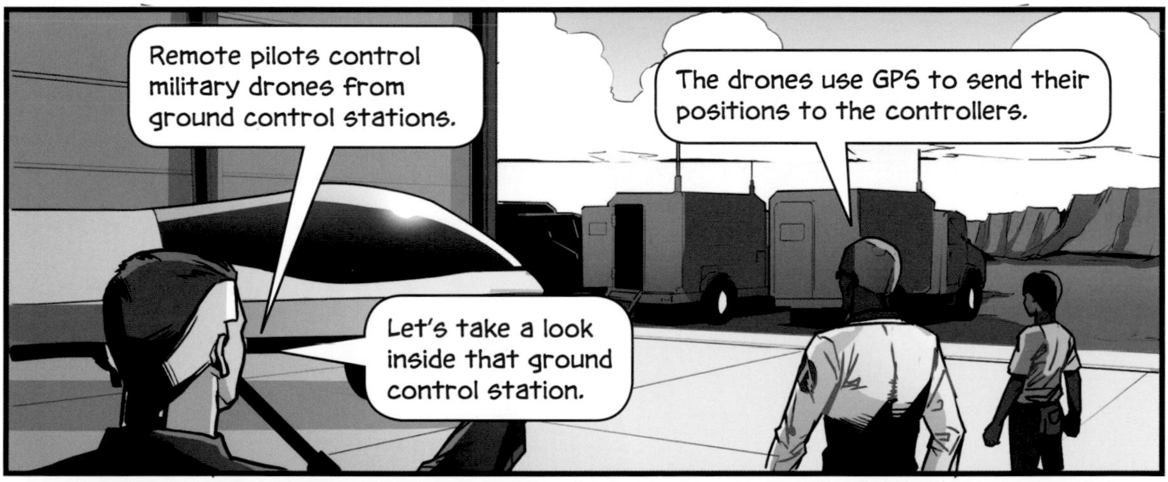
Remote pilots control military drones from ground control stations.
The drones use GPS to send their positions to the controllers.
Let's take a look inside that ground control station.

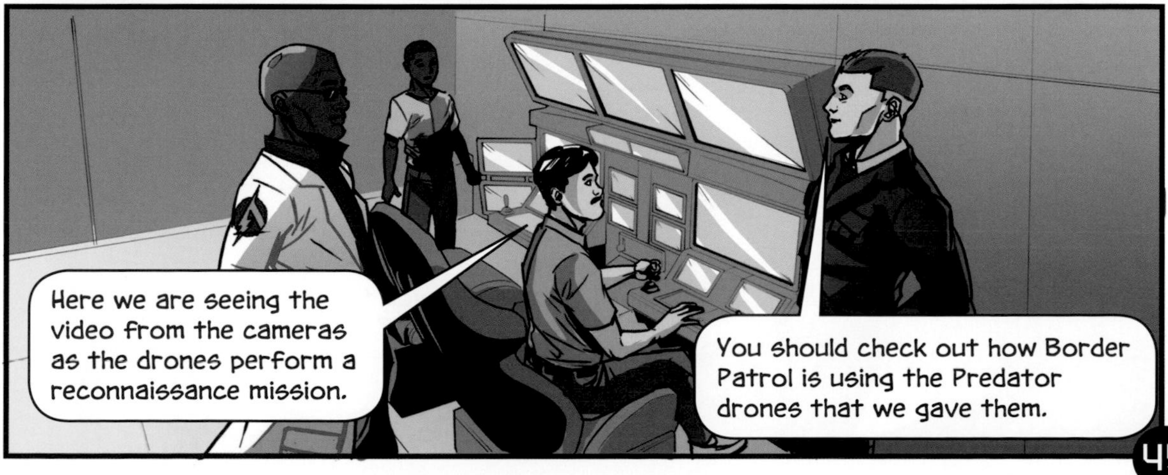
Here we are seeing the video from the cameras as the drones perform a reconnaissance mission.
You should check out how Border Patrol is using the Predator drones that we gave them.

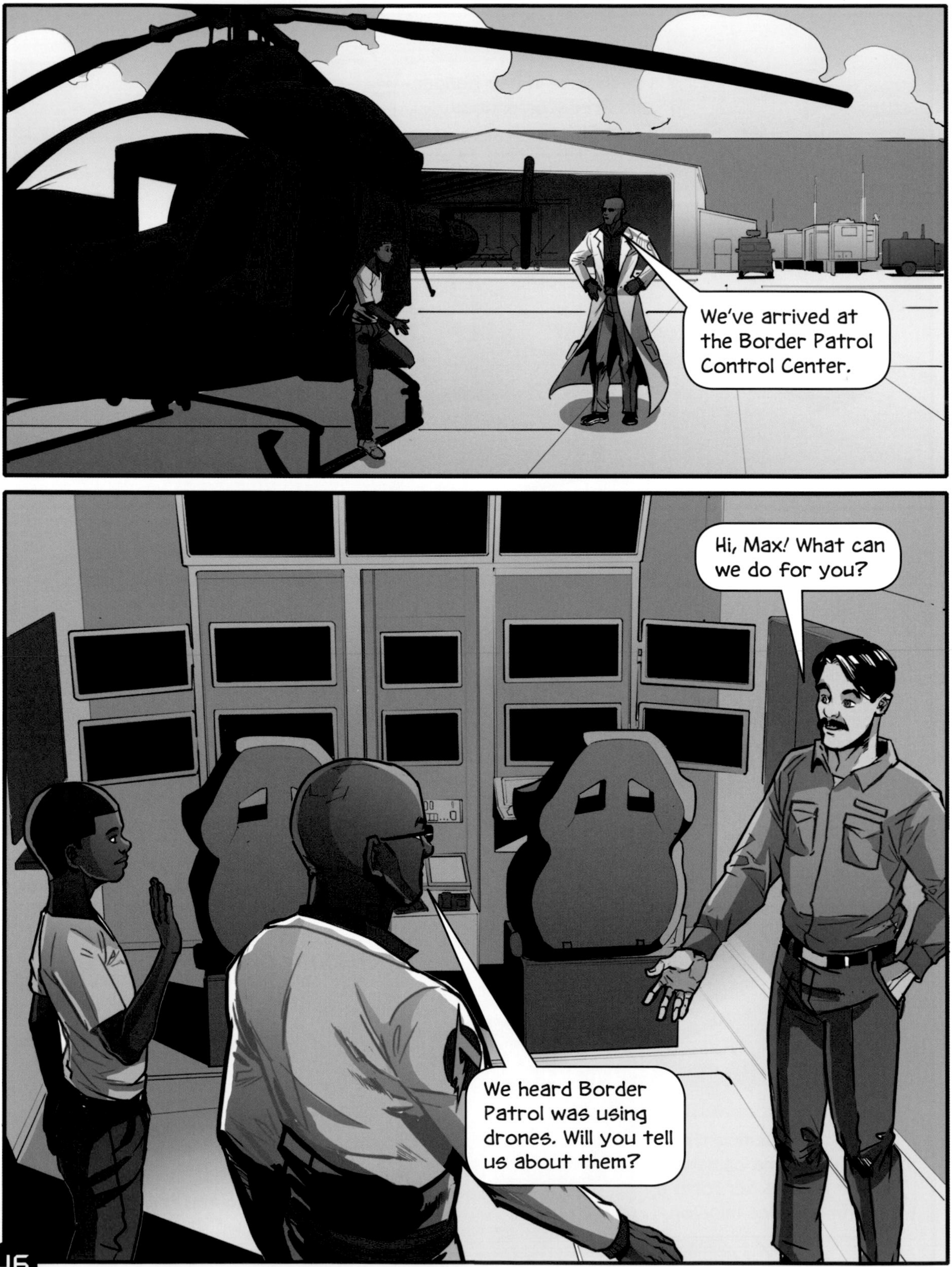
We've arrived at the Border Patrol Control Center.
Hi, Max! What can we do for you?
We heard Border Patrol was using drones. Will you tell us about them?

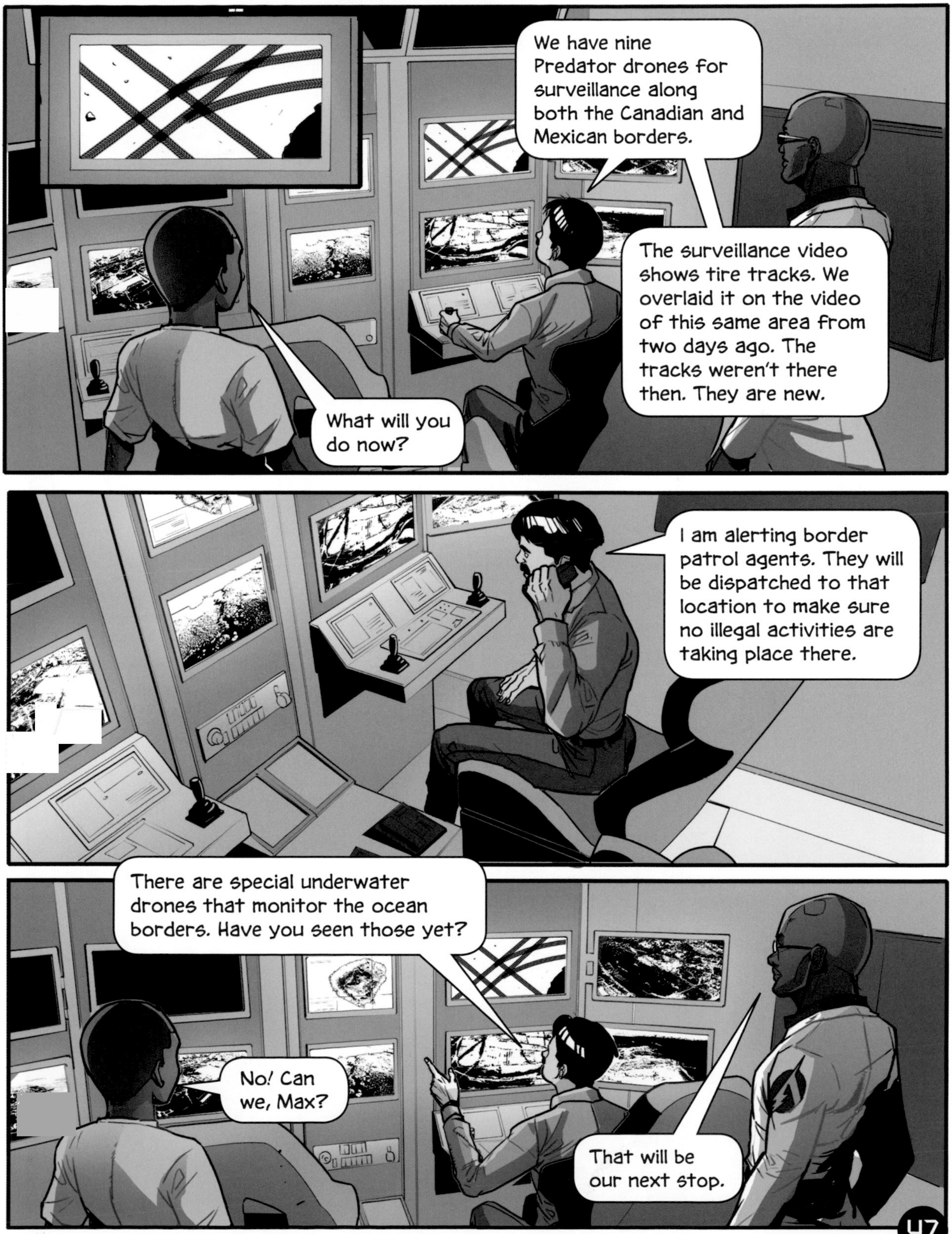
We have nine Predator drones for surveillance along both the Canadian and Mexican borders.
The surveillance video shows tire tracks. We overlaid it on the video of this same area from two days ago. The tracks weren't there then. They are new.
What will you do now?
I am alerting border patrol agents. They will be dispatched to that location to make sure no illegal activities are taking place there.
There are special underwater drones that monitor the ocean borders. Have you seen those yet?
No! Can we, Max?
That will be our next stop.

We're ready to go!

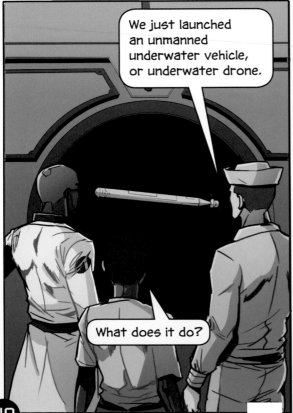

We just launched an unmanned underwater vehicle, or underwater drone.

What does it do?

It detects and removes mines so the submarine can pass safely.

The drone can also listen for other underwater vessels, and send back pictures of the sea floor.

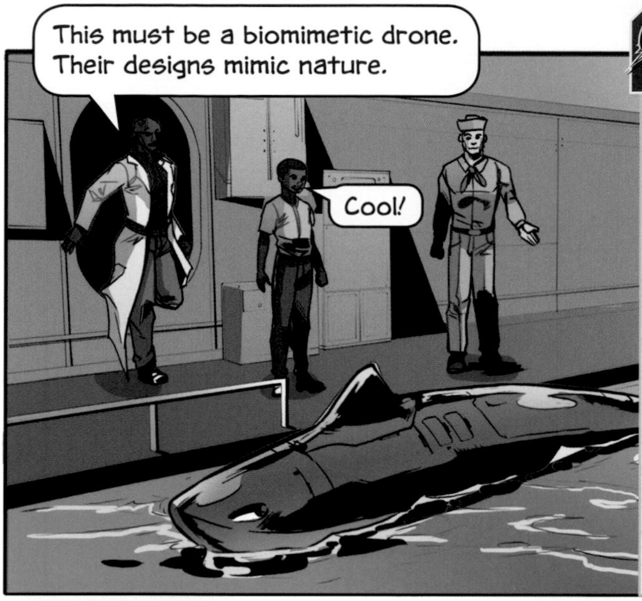
This must be a biomimetic drone. Their designs mimic nature.
Cool!

FLYING OVER FUKUSHIMA

In March 2011 the Fukushima power plant in Japan was struck by a tsunami triggered by an earthquake. A meltdown of the nuclear reactors released radiation, which made clean-up dangerous. Aerial drones were successfully used to survey the damage and monitor radiation levels. Autonomous drones are also being developed to continually monitor the buildings.

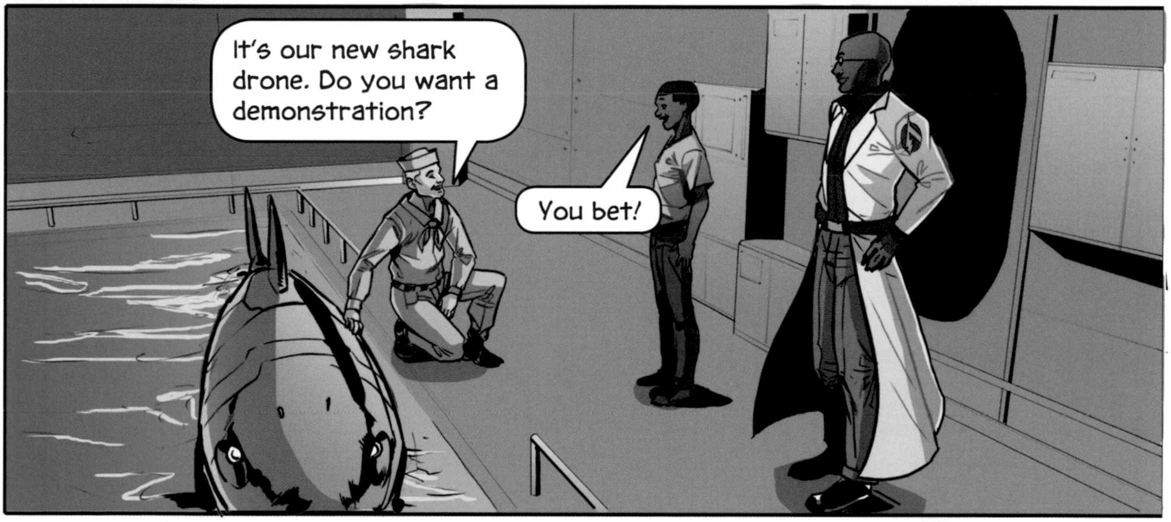
It's our new shark drone. Do you want a demonstration?
You bet!

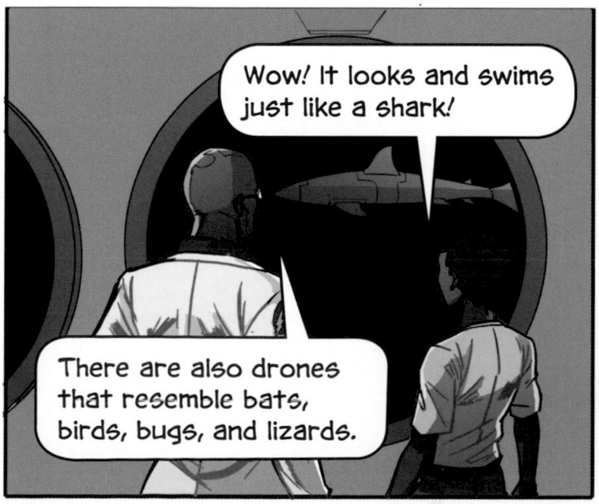
Wow! It looks and swims just like a shark!
There are also drones that resemble bats, birds, bugs, and lizards.

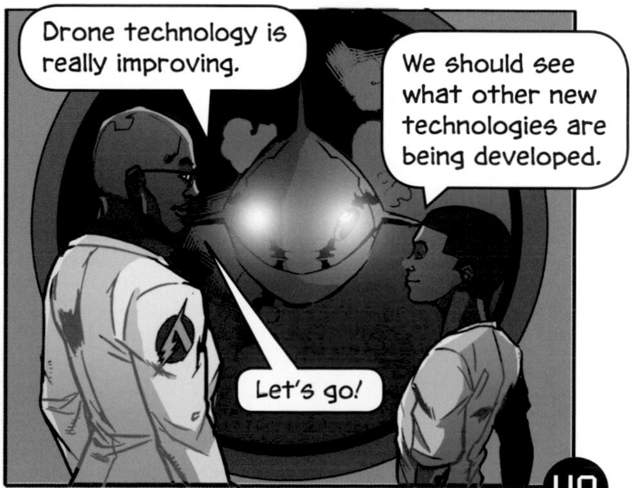
Drone technology is really improving.
We should see what other new technologies are being developed.
Let's go!

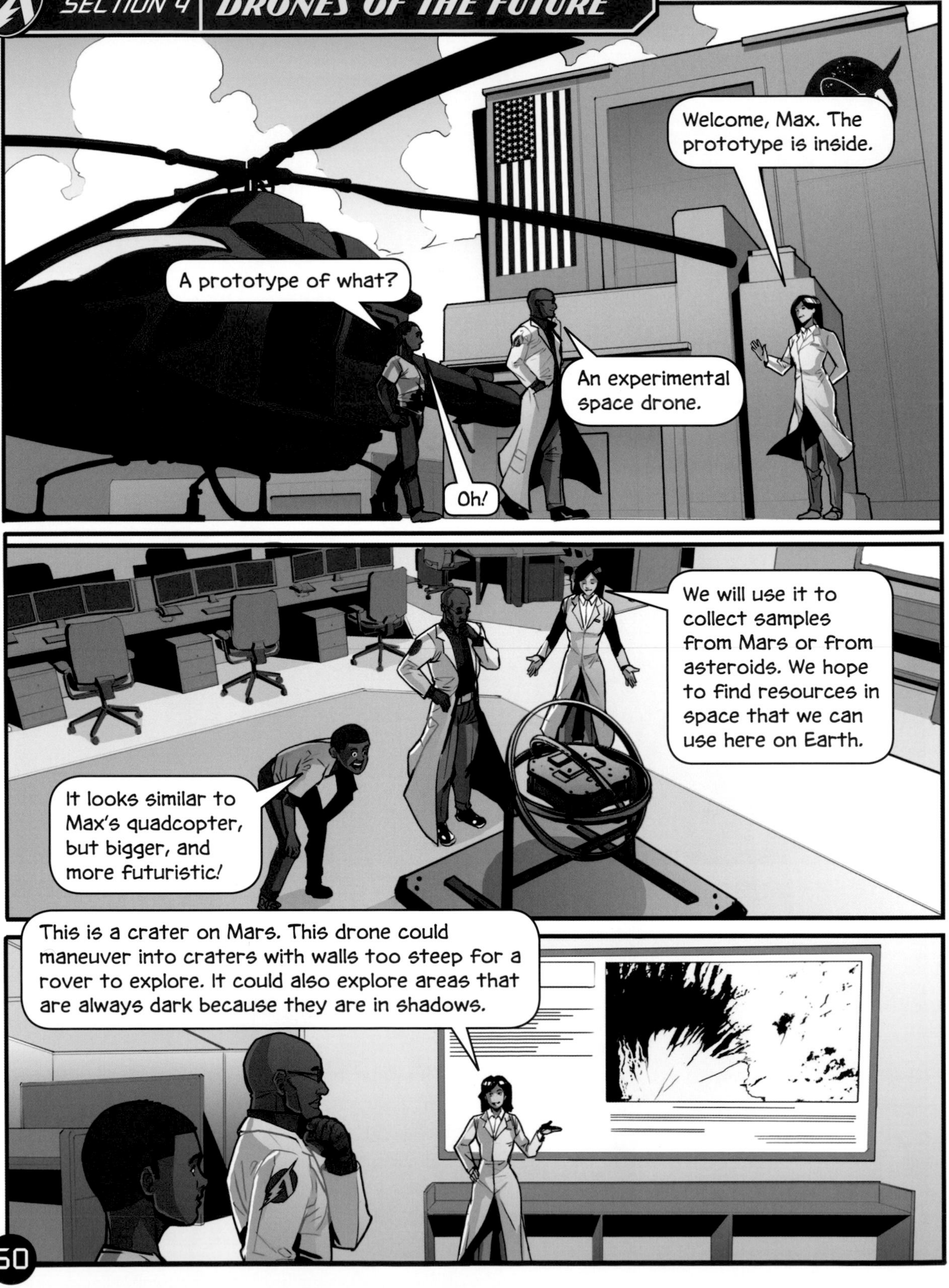
Welcome, Max. The prototype is inside.
A prototype of what?
An experimental space drone.
Oh!
We will use it to collect samples from Mars or from asteroids. We hope to find resources in space that we can use here on Earth.
It looks similar to Max's quadcopter, but bigger, and more futuristic!
This is a crater on Mars. This drone could maneuver into craters with walls too steep for a rover to explore. It could also explore areas that are always dark because they are in shadows.

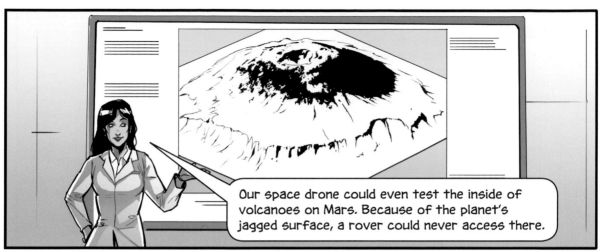

Our space drone could even test the inside of volcanoes on Mars. Because of the planet's jagged surface, a rover could never access there.

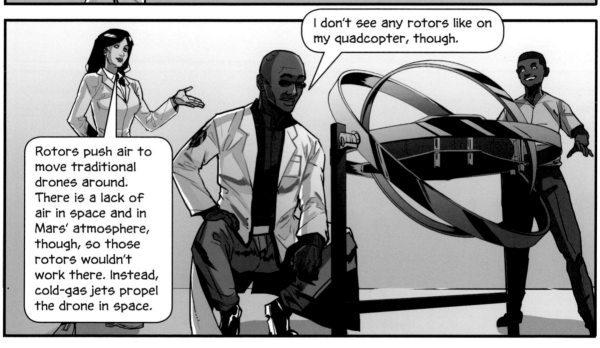

I don't see any rotors like on my quadcopter, though.

Rotors push air to move traditional drones around. There is a lack of air in space and in Mars' atmosphere, though, so those rotors wouldn't work there. Instead, cold-gas jets propel the drone in space.

Thanks for showing us your space drone. Do you know of other research showcasing drone technology?

Oh yes! Be sure to check out the experimental solar drones being studied to expand internet access.

Thanks! We will!

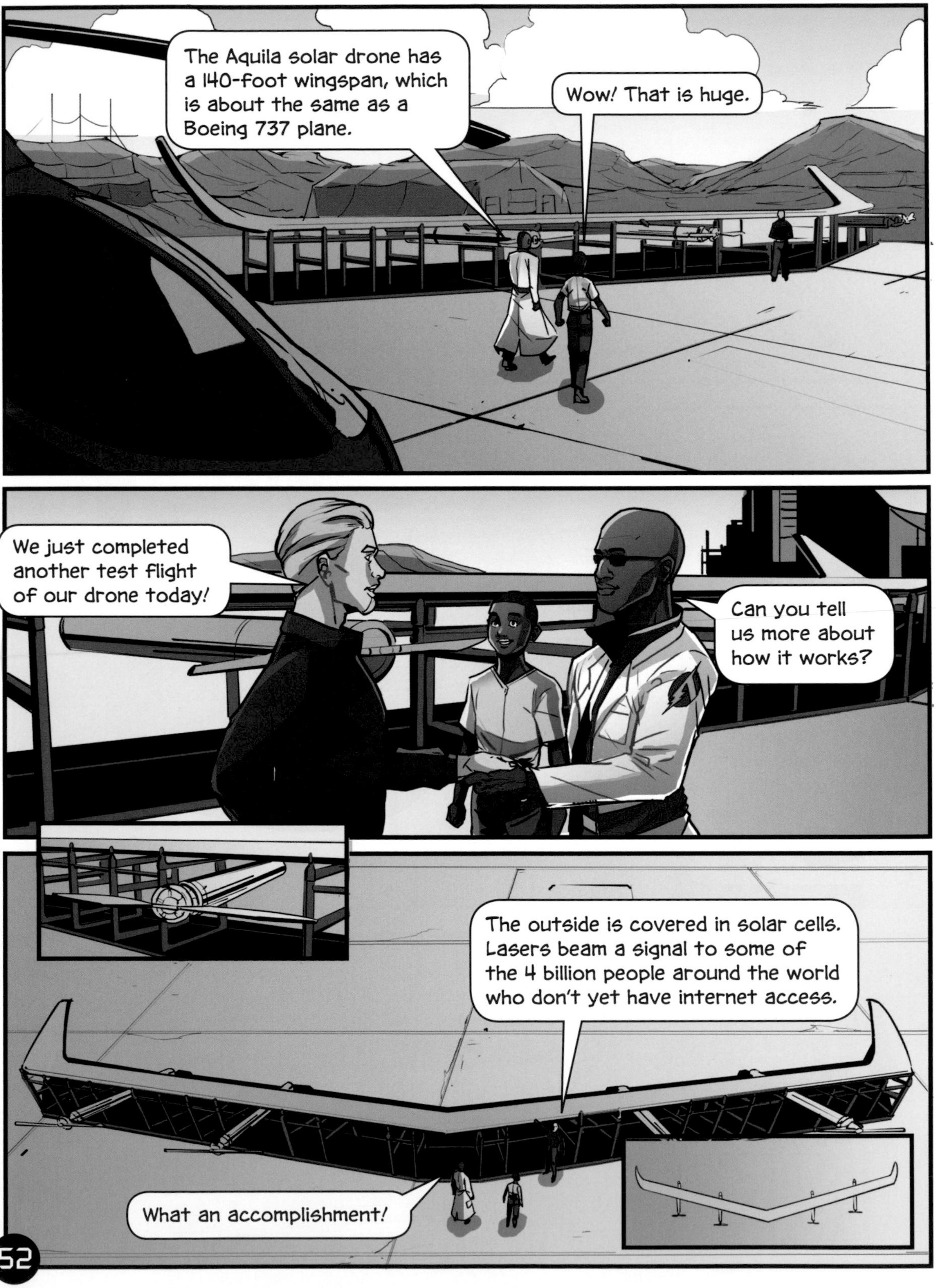
The Aquila solar drone has a 140-foot wingspan, which is about the same as a Boeing 737 plane.
Wow! That is huge.
We just completed another test flight of our drone today!
Can you tell us more about how it works?
The outside is covered in solar cells. Lasers beam a signal to some of the 4 billion people around the world who don't yet have internet access.
What an accomplishment!

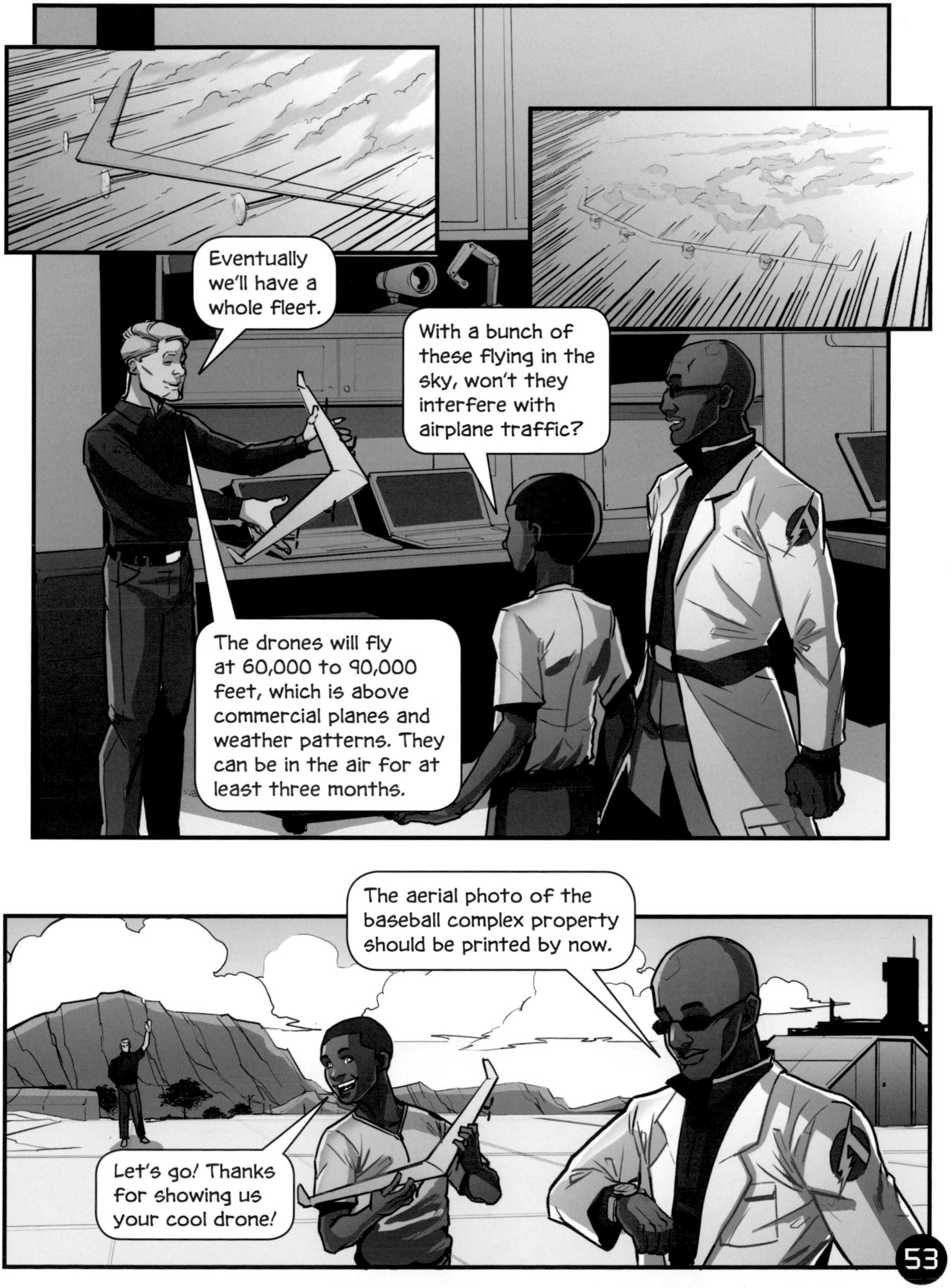
Eventually we'll have a whole fleet.
With a bunch of these flying in the sky, won't they interfere with airplane traffic?
The drones will fly at 60,000 to 90,000 feet, which is above commercial planes and weather patterns. They can be in the air for at least three months.
The aerial photo of the baseball complex property should be printed by now.
Let's go! Thanks for showing us your cool drone!

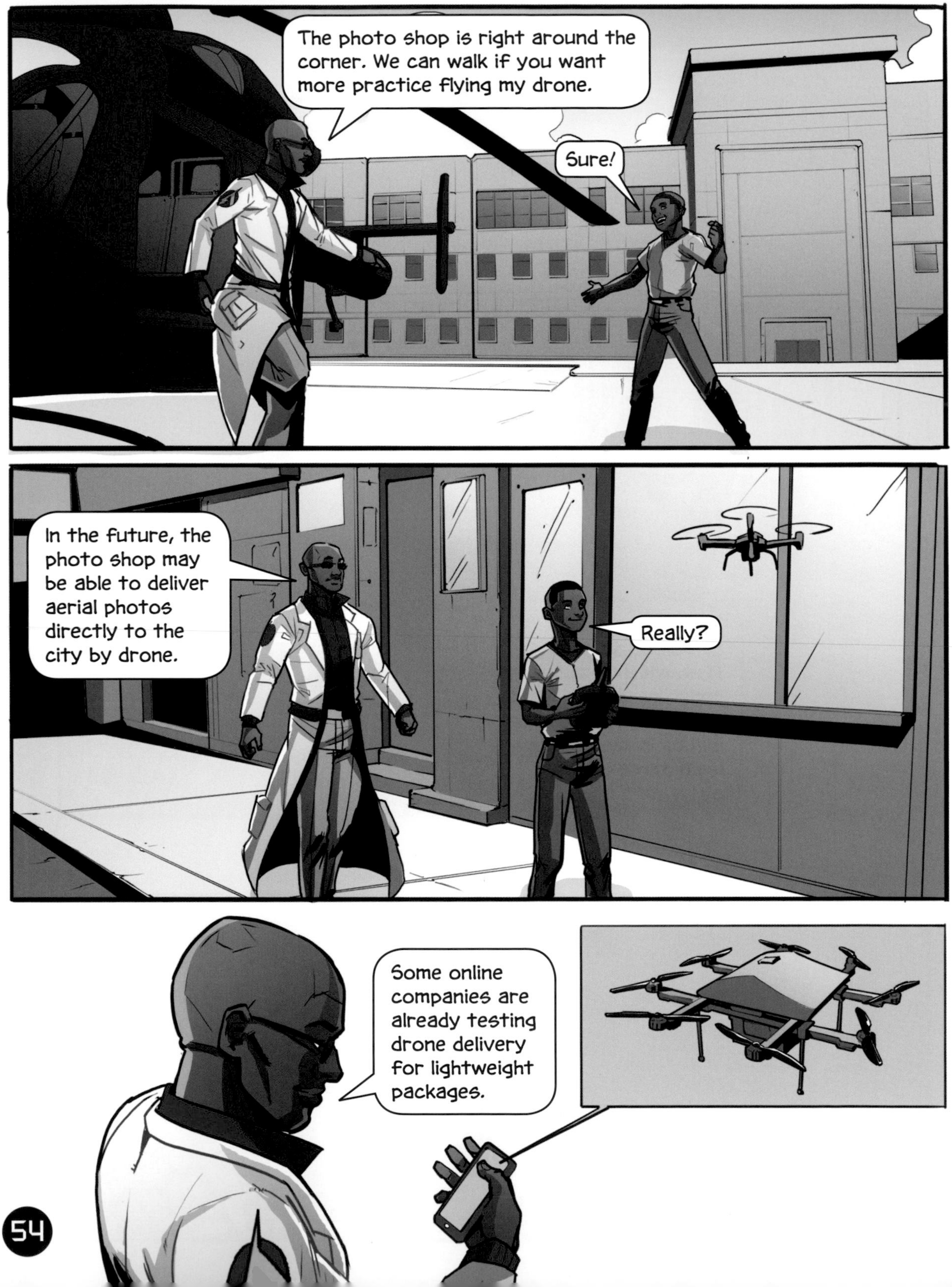
The photo shop is right around the corner. We can walk if you want more practice flying my drone.
Sure!
In the future, the photo shop may be able to deliver aerial photos directly to the city by drone.
Really?
Some online companies are already testing drone delivery for lightweight packages.

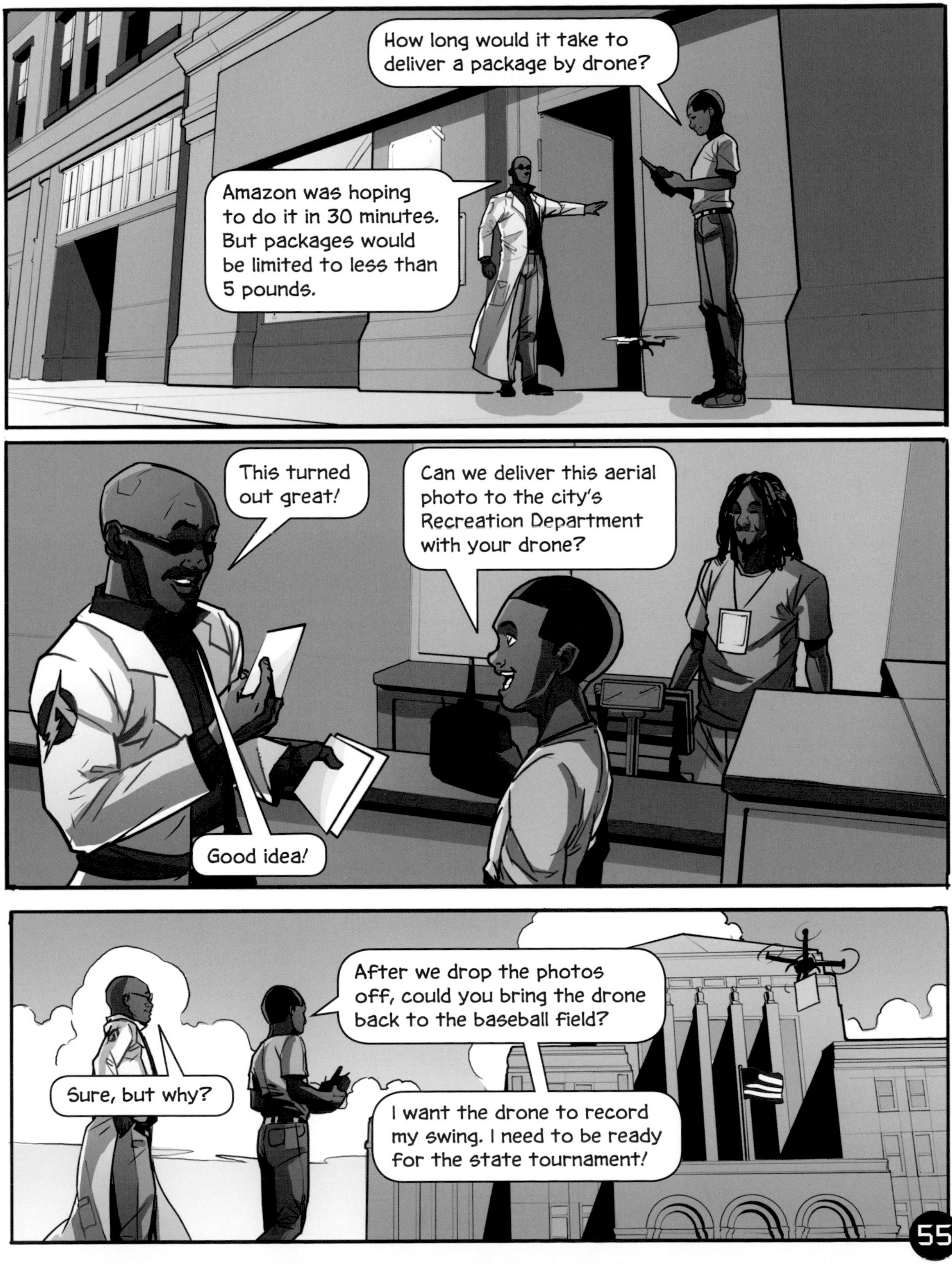
How long would it take to deliver a package by drone?
Amazon was hoping to do it in 30 minutes. But packages would be limited to less than 5 pounds.
This turned out great!
Can we deliver this aerial photo to the city's Recreation Department with your drone?
Good idea!
After we drop the photos off, could you bring the drone back to the baseball field?
Sure, but why?
I want the drone to record my swing. I need to be ready for the state tournament!

MORE ABOUT
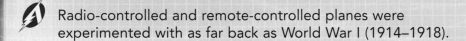
DRONES

A   Radio-controlled and remote-controlled planes were experimented with as far back as World War I (1914–1918).

A   The first drone as we know it was built by engineer Abraham Karem in the early 1980s. His drone, known as the Albatross, could fly for as long as 56 hours. His design led to the development of the Predator drone.

A   On December 1, 2013, Amazon unveiled its plan to explore drone package delivery.

A   In Rwanda, Africa, life-saving drones are delivering blood and medical supplies to clinics.

A   The United States Navy uses drones on their ships. Aerial drones can locate and follow smuggler's ships for miles without being noticed.

A   The company Skycatch uses drones with artificial intelligence to manage construction sites. Their drones can map the work zone and figure out the best way to move large equipment.

A   On October 7, 2001, the first Predator drones to be armed with missiles began missions over Afghanistan after the September 11, 2001, attacks in the United States.

A   In 2017, Super Bowl 51 featured a halftime show with 300 syncronized Shooting Star drones. The quadcopters were outfitted with LED lights. A single operator controlled all the drones.

CHAPTER 3

THE REMARKABLE WORLD OF ROBOTS

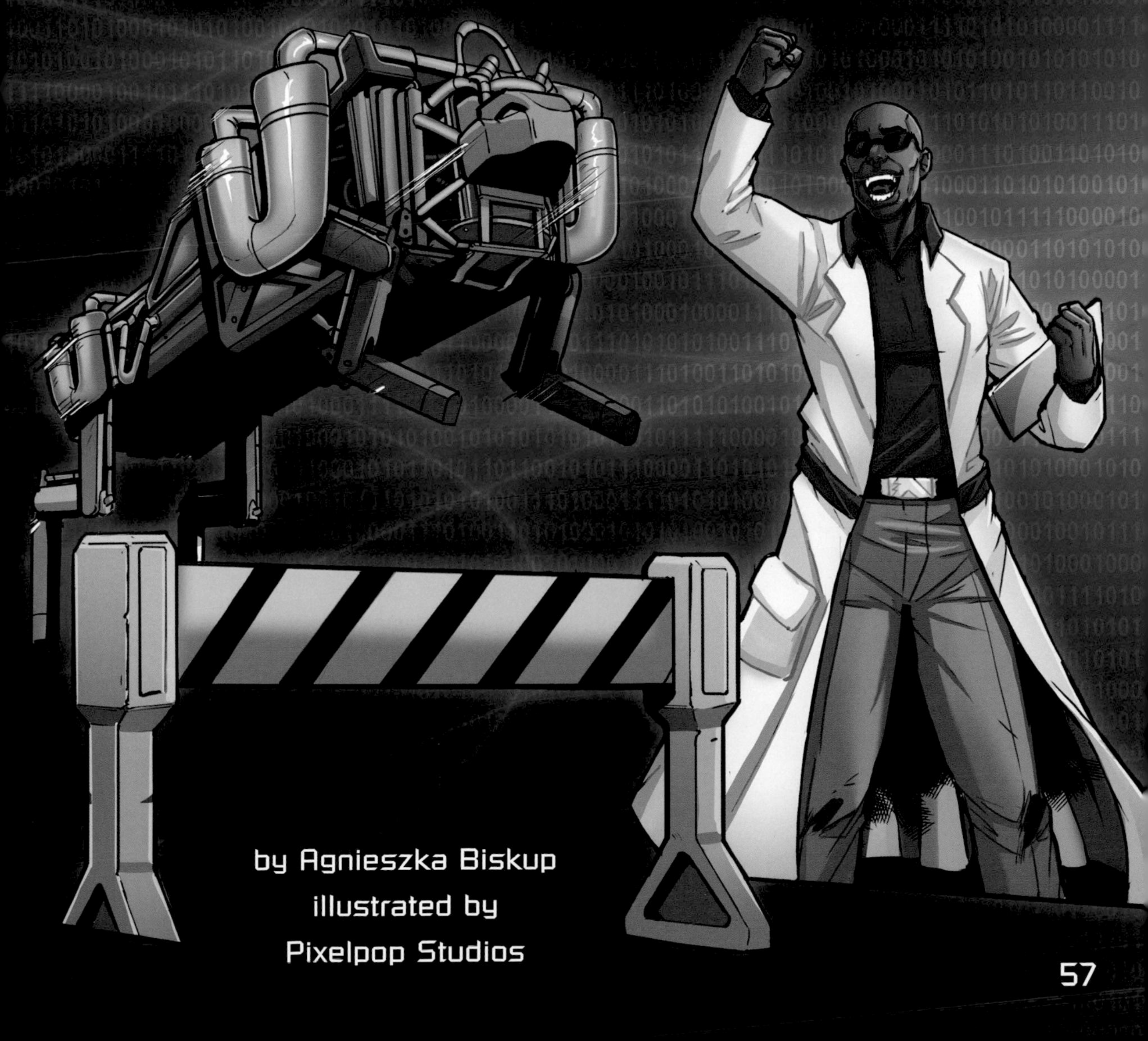

by Agnieszka Biskup
illustrated by
Pixelpop Studios

SECTION 1 | WHAT DO ROBOTS DO?

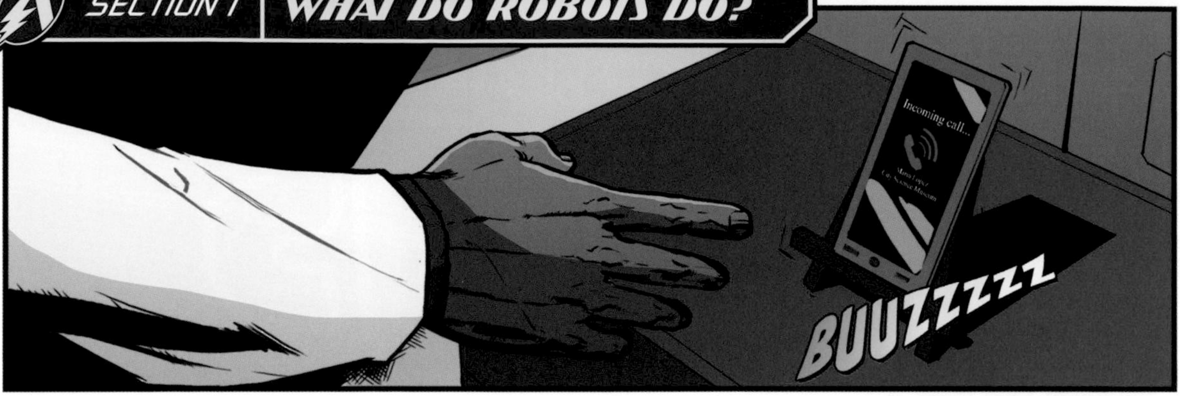
Incoming call...
BUUZZZZZ

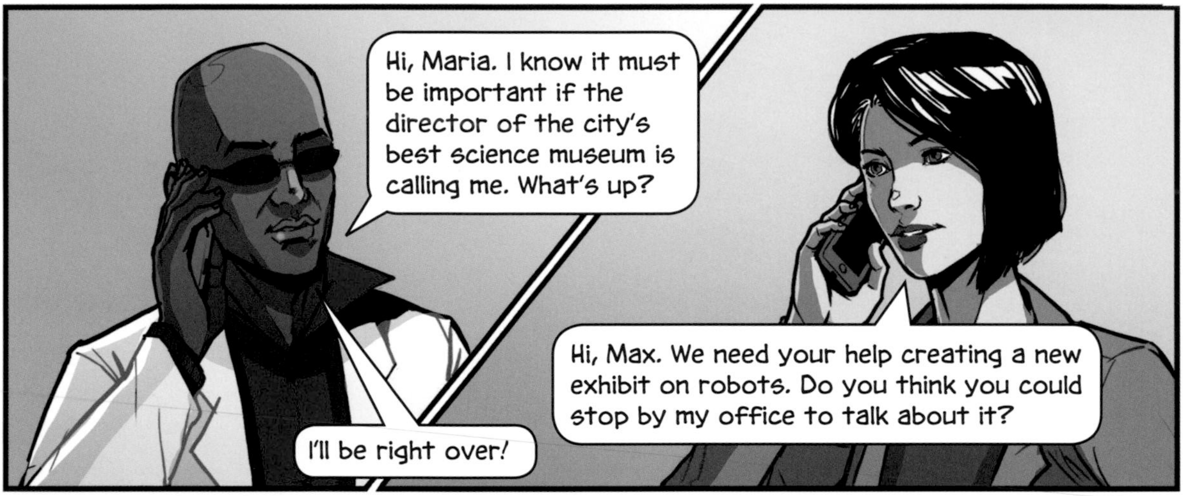
Hi, Maria. I know it must be important if the director of the city's best science museum is calling me. What's up?
Hi, Max. We need your help creating a new exhibit on robots. Do you think you could stop by my office to talk about it?
I'll be right over!

THE FIRST ROBOT

The word robot comes from the Czech word for work: *robota*. It was first used in a 1920 science fiction play by Czech writer Karel Capek called *R.U.R. (Rossum's Universal Robots)*. The first robot shown on film was in Fritz Lang's *Metropolis* (1927).

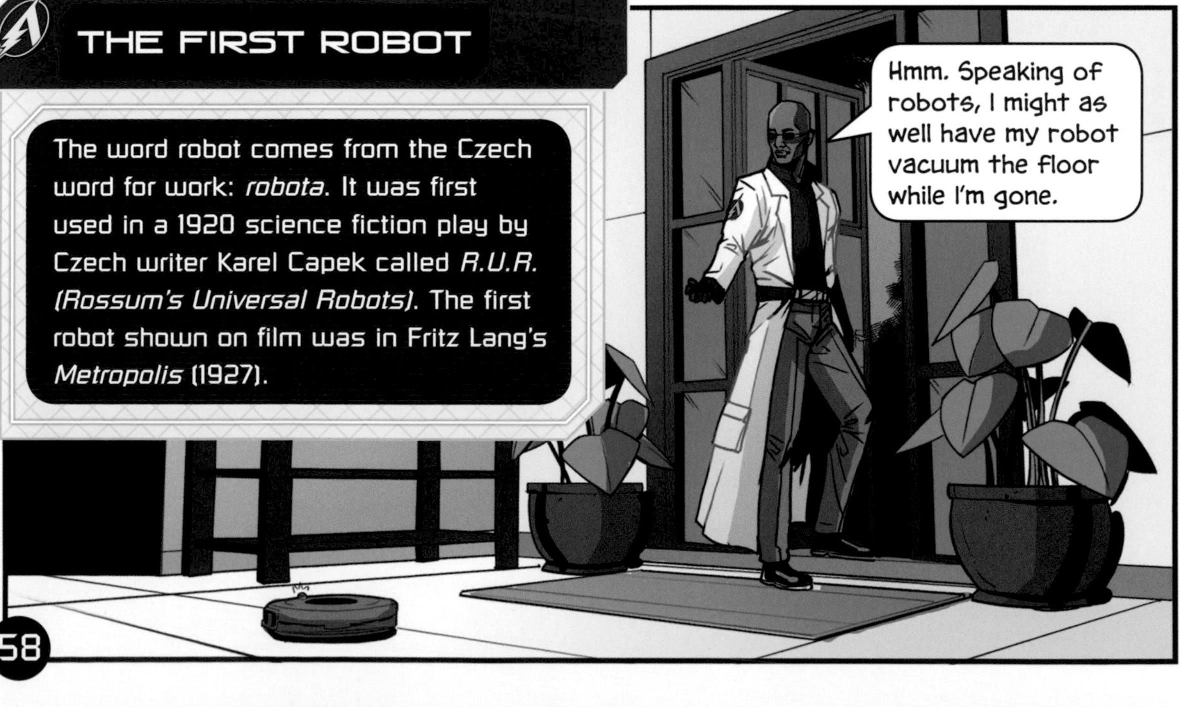
Hmm. Speaking of robots, I might as well have my robot vacuum the floor while I'm gone.

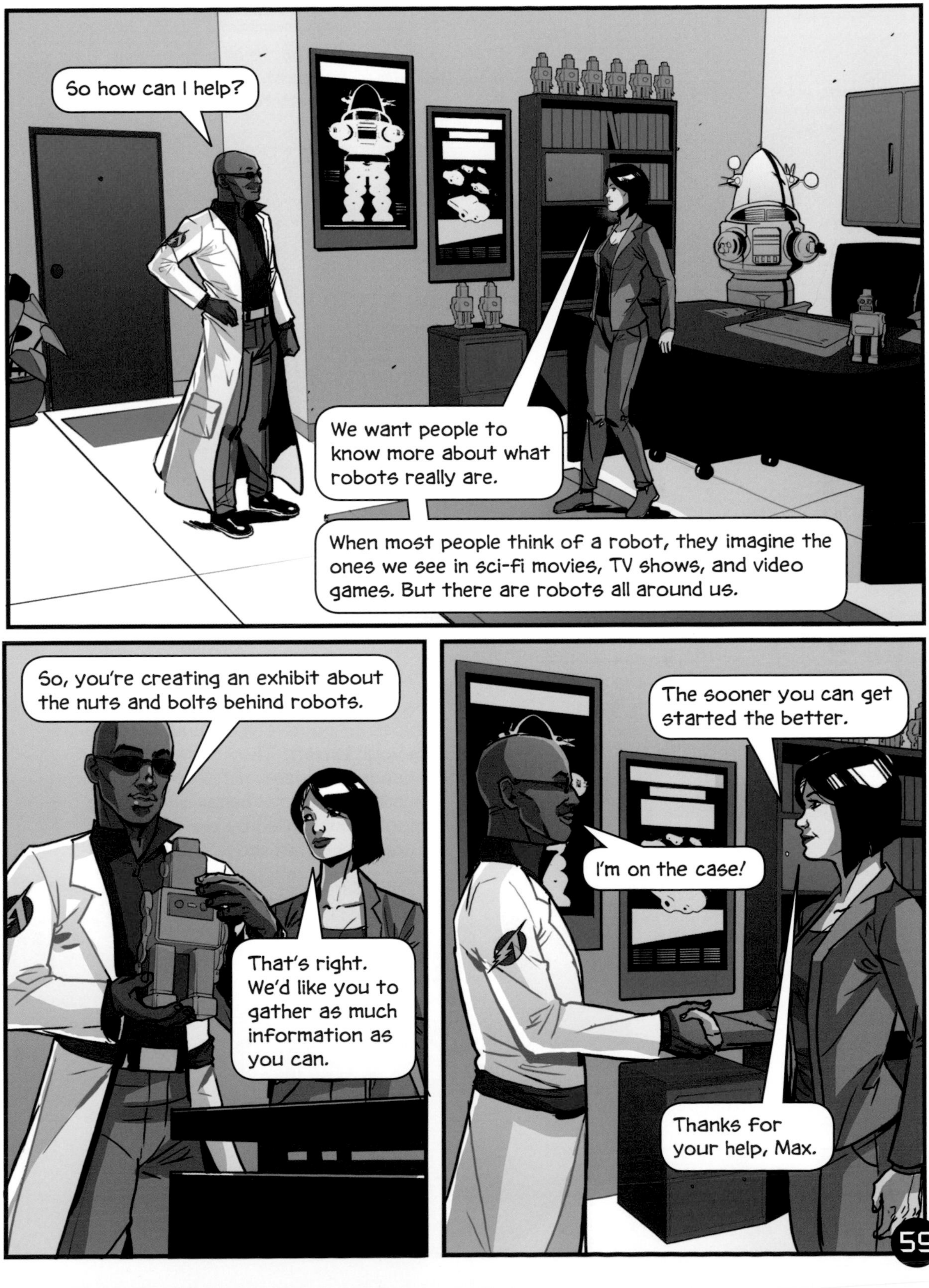

So how can I help?
We want people to know more about what robots really are.
When most people think of a robot, they imagine the ones we see in sci-fi movies, TV shows, and video games. But there are robots all around us.
So, you're creating an exhibit about the nuts and bolts behind robots.
That's right. We'd like you to gather as much information as you can.
The sooner you can get started the better.
I'm on the case!
Thanks for your help, Max.

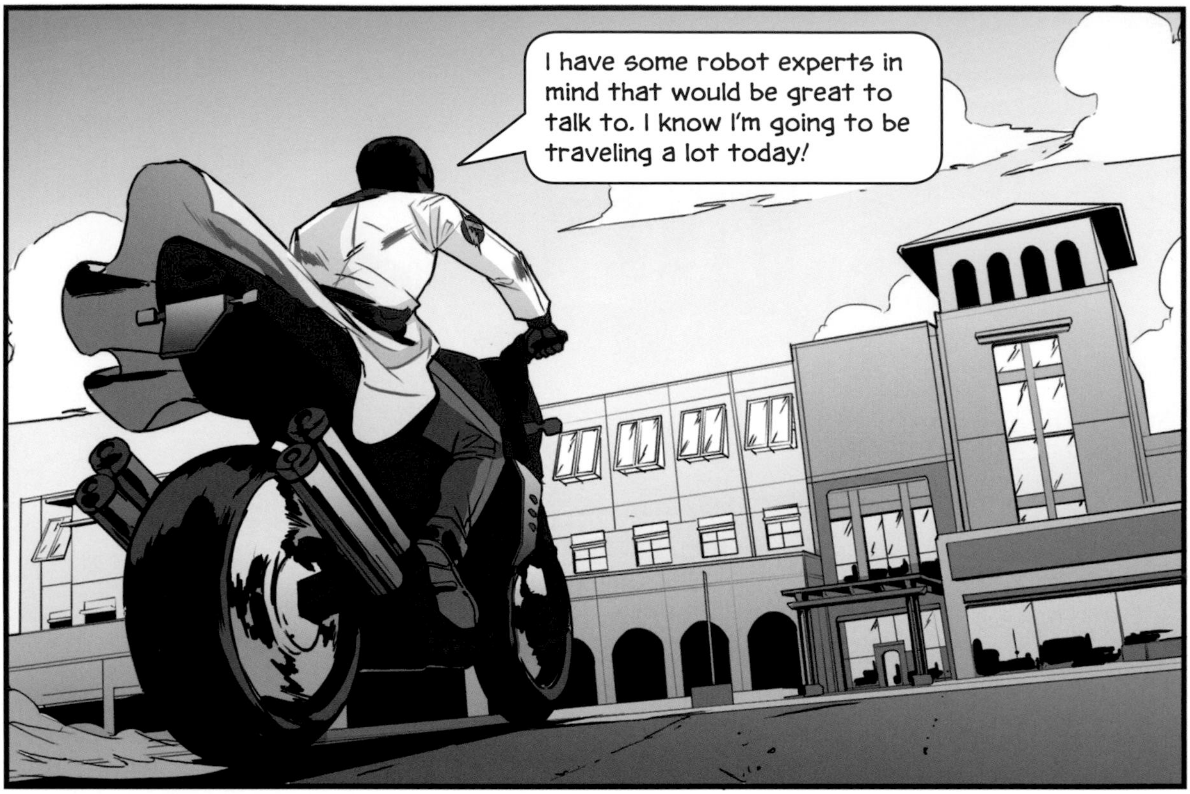
I have some robot experts in mind that would be great to talk to. I know I'm going to be traveling a lot today!

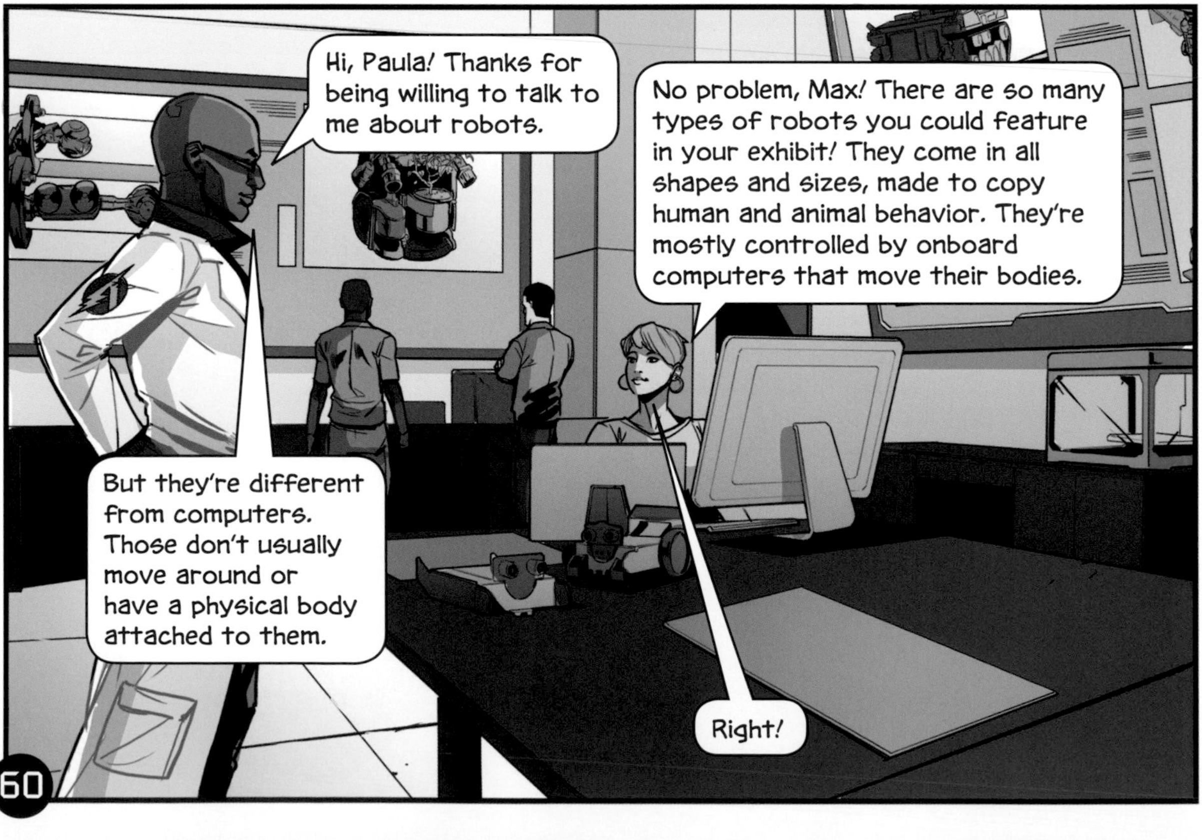
Hi, Paula! Thanks for being willing to talk to me about robots.
No problem, Max! There are so many types of robots you could feature in your exhibit! They come in all shapes and sizes, made to copy human and animal behavior. They're mostly controlled by onboard computers that move their bodies.
But they're different from computers. Those don't usually move around or have a physical body attached to them.
Right!

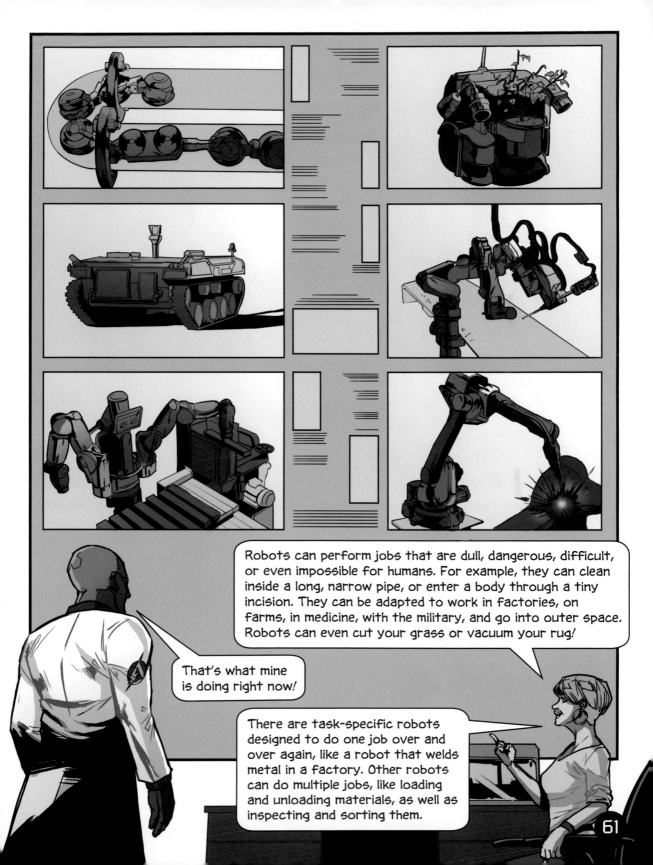

Robots can perform jobs that are dull, dangerous, difficult, or even impossible for humans. For example, they can clean inside a long, narrow pipe, or enter a body through a tiny incision. They can be adapted to work in factories, on farms, in medicine, with the military, and go into outer space. Robots can even cut your grass or vacuum your rug!

That's what mine is doing right now!

There are task-specific robots designed to do one job over and over again, like a robot that welds metal in a factory. Other robots can do multiple jobs, like loading and unloading materials, as well as inspecting and sorting them.

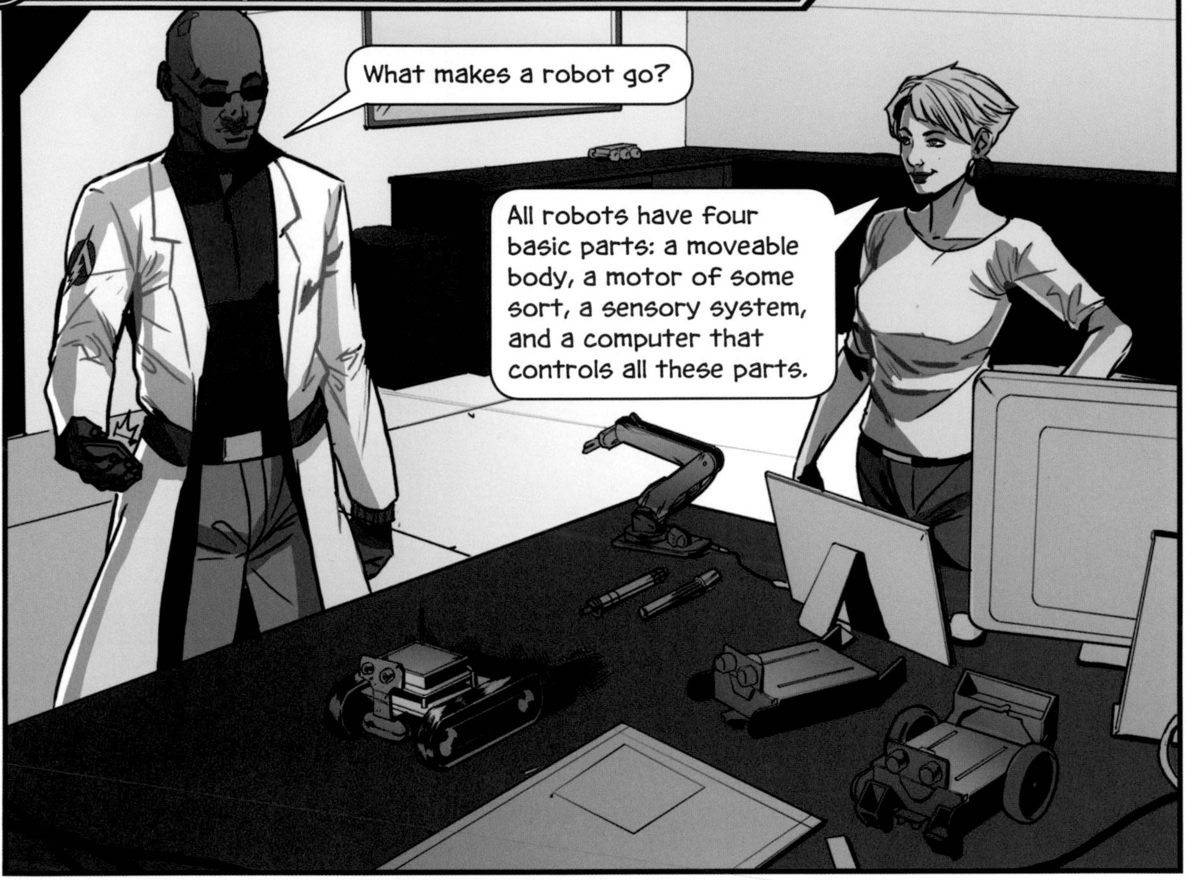
What makes a robot go?
All robots have four basic parts: a moveable body, a motor of some sort, a sensory system, and a computer that controls all these parts.

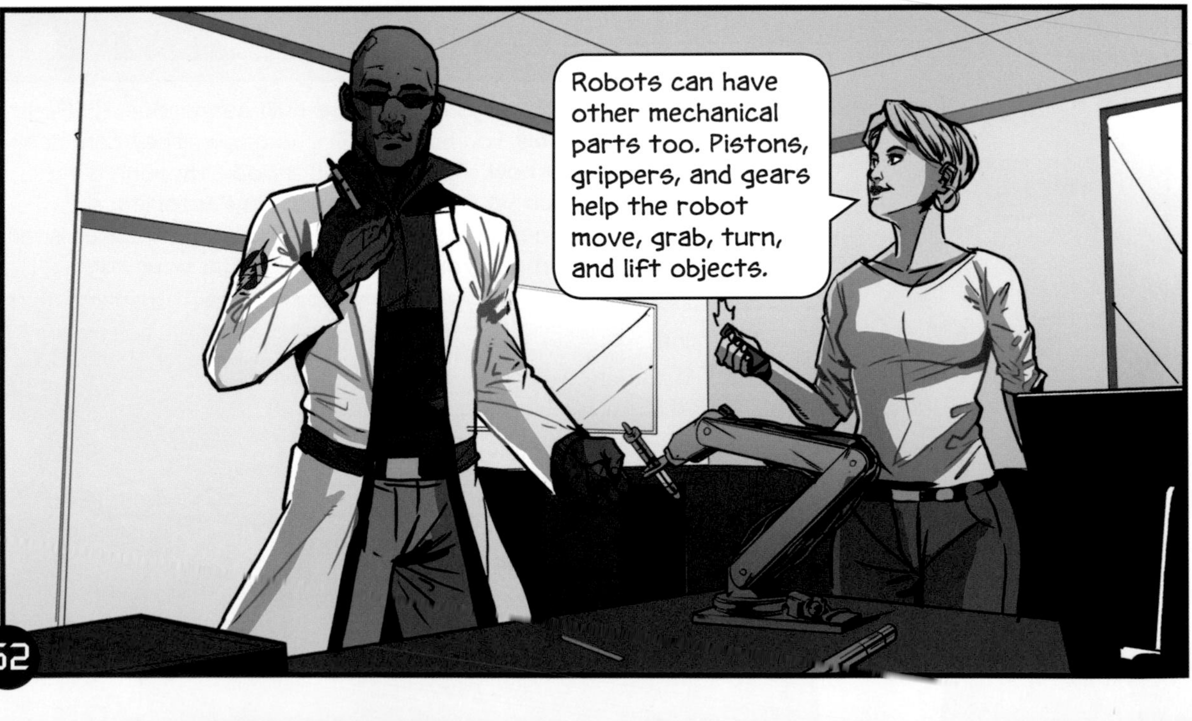
Robots can have other mechanical parts too. Pistons, grippers, and gears help the robot move, grab, turn, and lift objects.

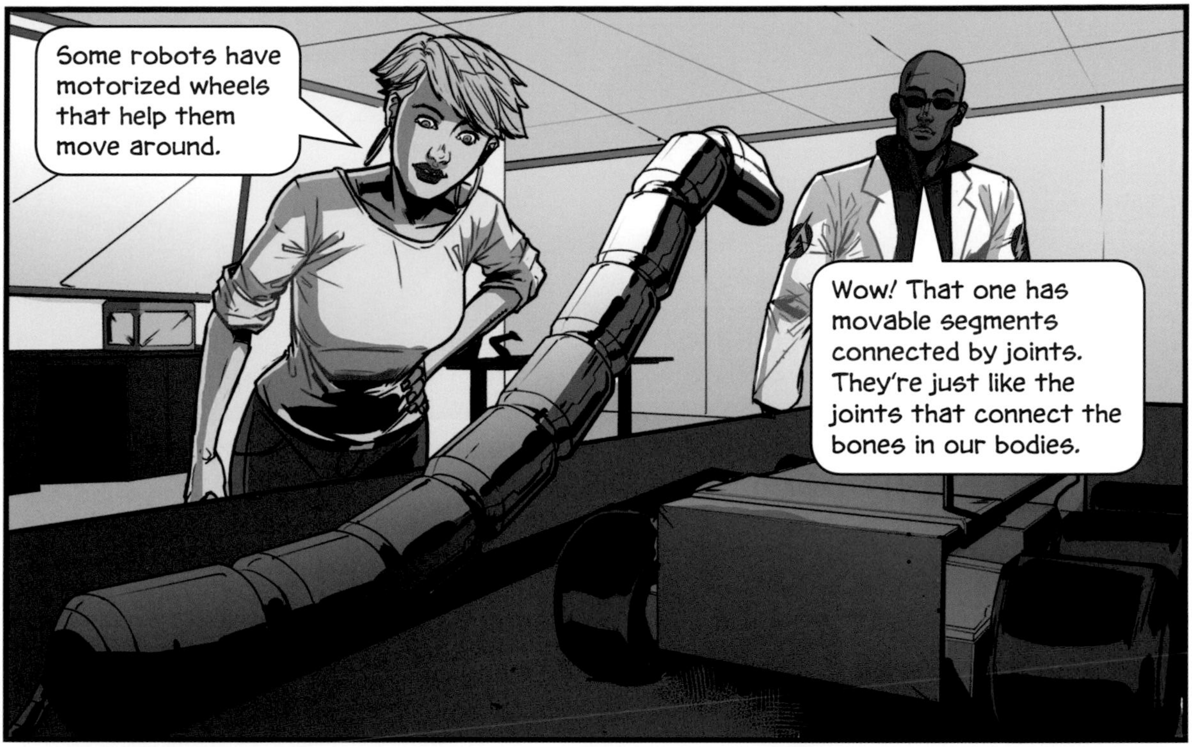
Some robots have motorized wheels that help them move around.
Wow! That one has movable segments connected by joints. They're just like the joints that connect the bones in our bodies.

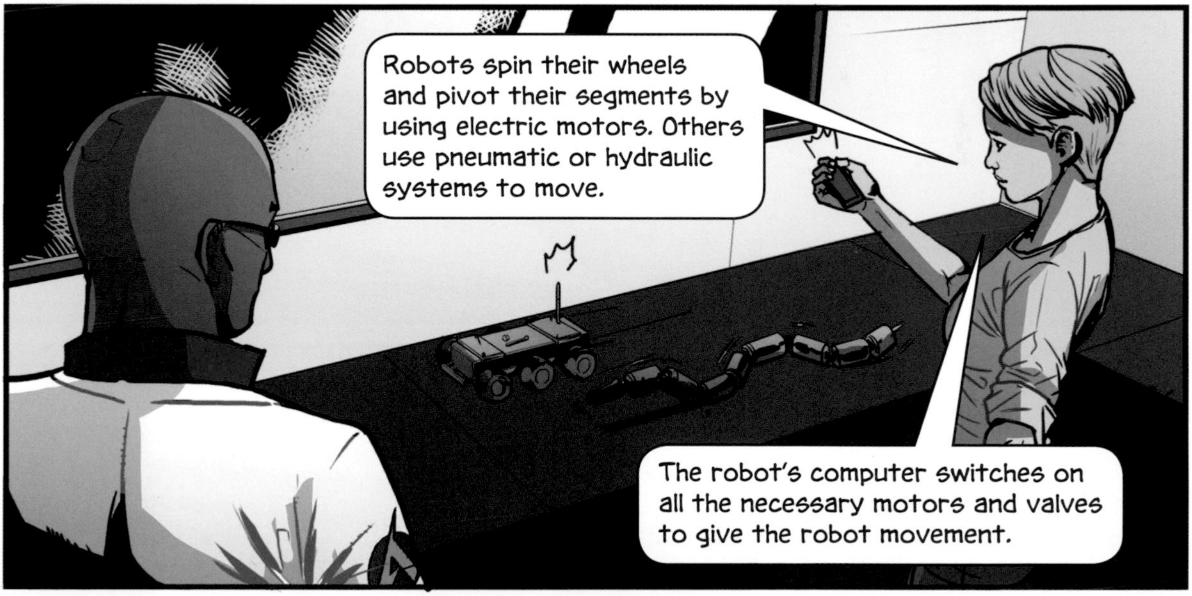
Robots spin their wheels and pivot their segments by using electric motors. Others use pneumatic or hydraulic systems to move.
The robot's computer switches on all the necessary motors and valves to give the robot movement.

HYDRAULIC AND PNEUMATIC SYSTEMS

Some robots use hydraulic or pneumatic systems to move. In pneumatic systems, pressurized air is used to produce movement. In hydraulic systems, trapped, pressurized water forces movement instead.

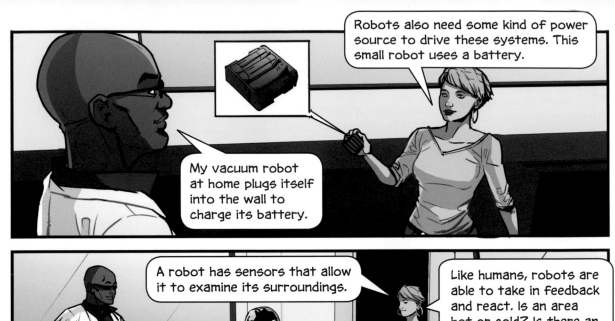

Robots also need some kind of power source to drive these systems. This small robot uses a battery.

My vacuum robot at home plugs itself into the wall to charge its battery.

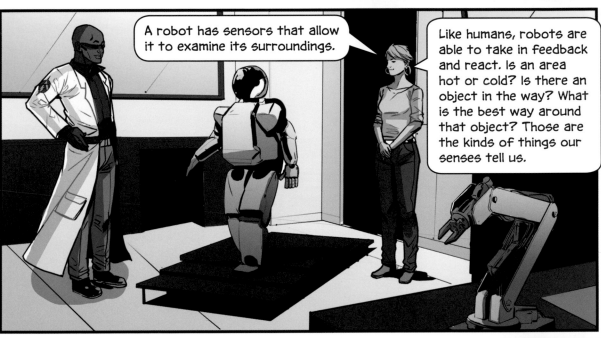

A robot has sensors that allow it to examine its surroundings.

Like humans, robots are able to take in feedback and react. Is an area hot or cold? Is there an object in the way? What is the best way around that object? Those are the kinds of things our senses tell us.

The most common robotic sense is the robot's ability to monitor how it moves. This robot can identify the right amount of pressure so it won't crush my hand.

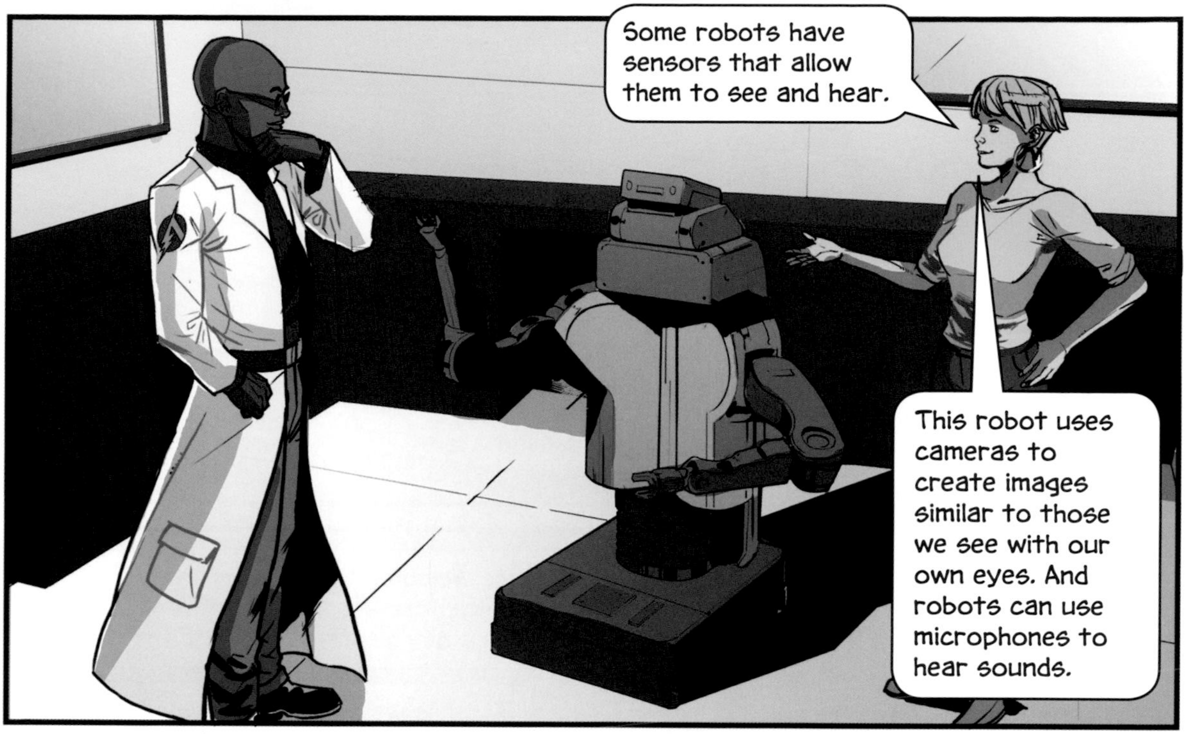
Some robots have sensors that allow them to see and hear.
This robot uses cameras to create images similar to those we see with our own eyes. And robots can use microphones to hear sounds.

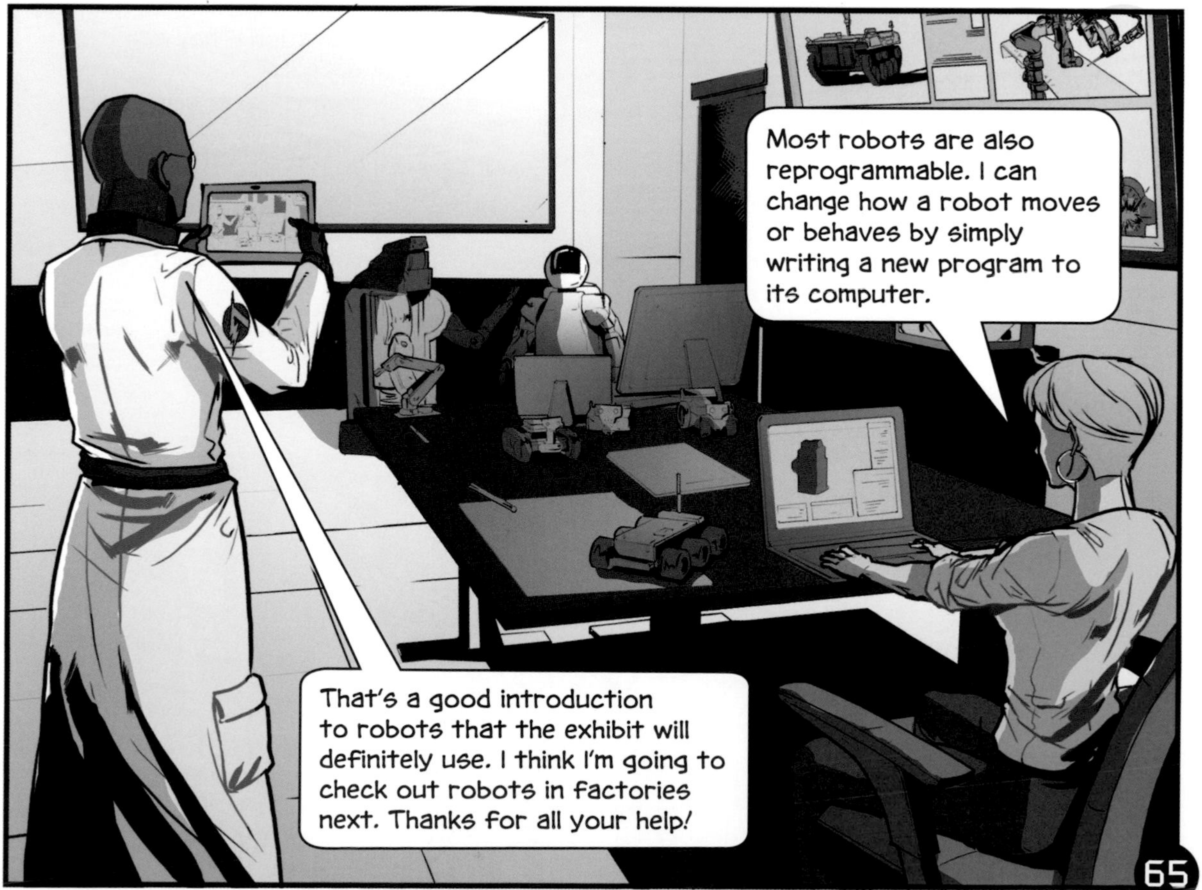
Most robots are also reprogrammable. I can change how a robot moves or behaves by simply writing a new program to its computer.
That's a good introduction to robots that the exhibit will definitely use. I think I'm going to check out robots in factories next. Thanks for all your help!

INDUSTRIAL, MOBILE, AND MILITARY ROBOTS

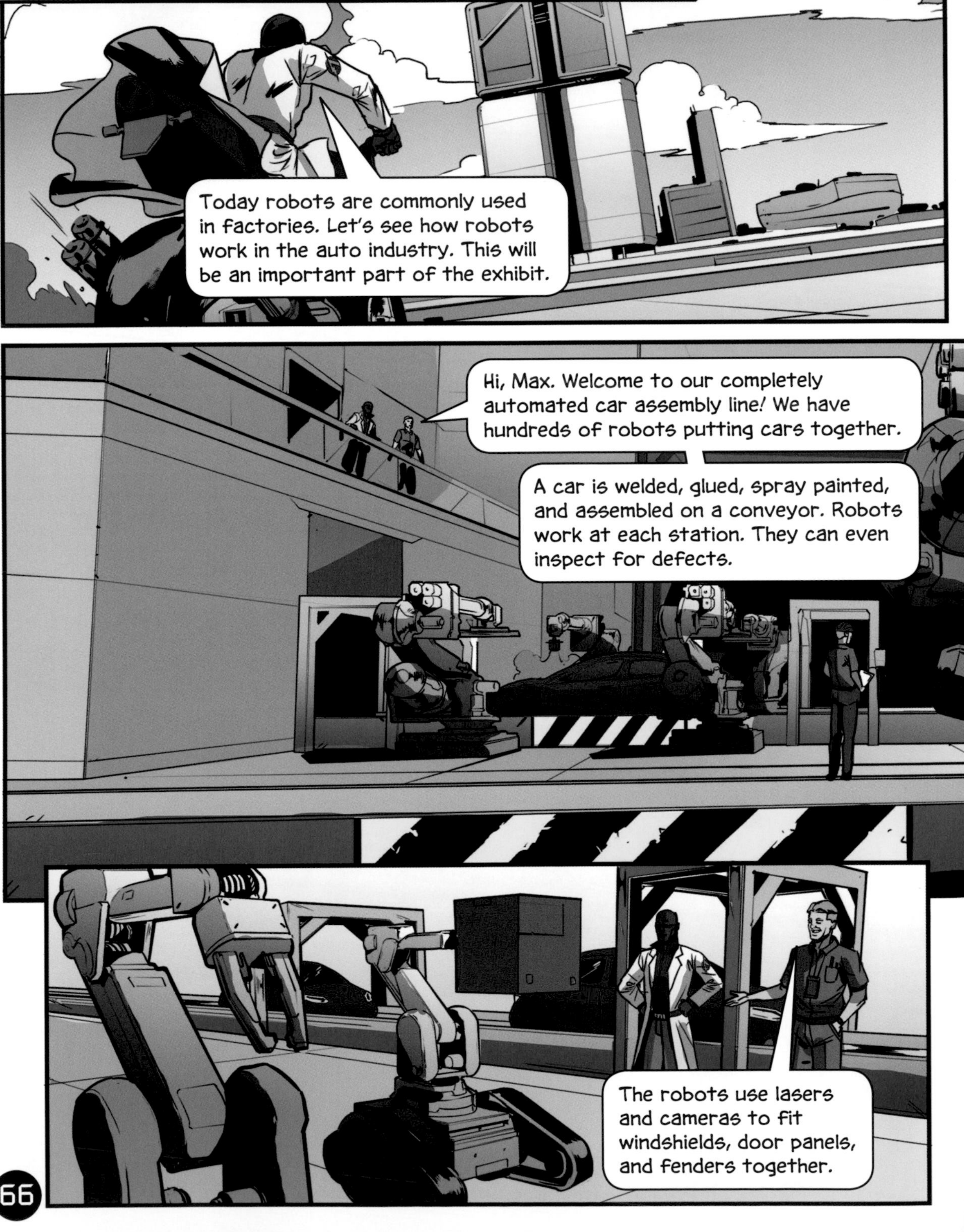
Today robots are commonly used in factories. Let's see how robots work in the auto industry. This will be an important part of the exhibit.
Hi, Max. Welcome to our completely automated car assembly line! We have hundreds of robots putting cars together.
A car is welded, glued, spray painted, and assembled on a conveyor. Robots work at each station. They can even inspect for defects.
The robots use lasers and cameras to fit windshields, door panels, and fenders together.

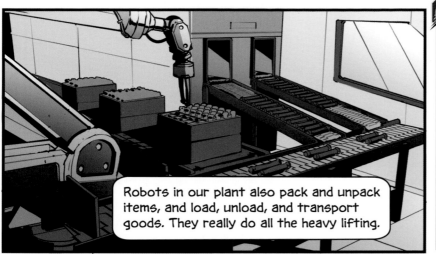

Robots in our plant also pack and unpack items, and load, unload, and transport goods. They really do all the heavy lifting.

The first industrial robot, Unimate, was a 4,000-pound programmable robotic arm. General Motors used Unimate in 1961 in its auto assembly line. It took die castings from machines and welded auto bodies.

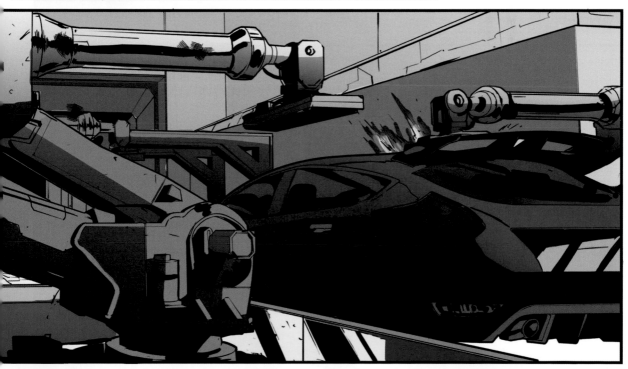

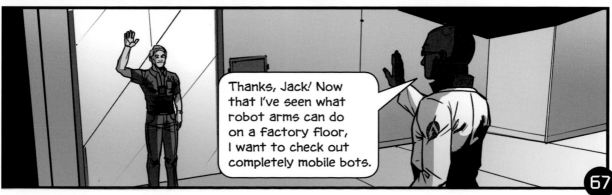

Thanks, Jack! Now that I've seen what robot arms can do on a factory floor, I want to check out completely mobile bots.

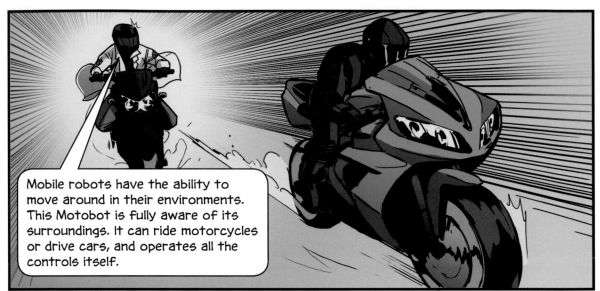

Mobile robots have the ability to move around in their environments. This Motobot is fully aware of its surroundings. It can ride motorcycles or drive cars, and operates all the controls itself.

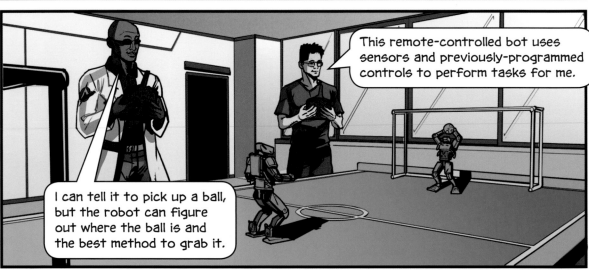

This remote-controlled bot uses sensors and previously-programmed controls to perform tasks for me.

I can tell it to pick up a ball, but the robot can figure out where the ball is and the best method to grab it.

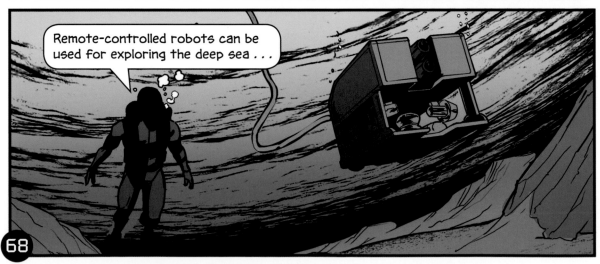

Remote-controlled robots can be used for exploring the deep sea . . .

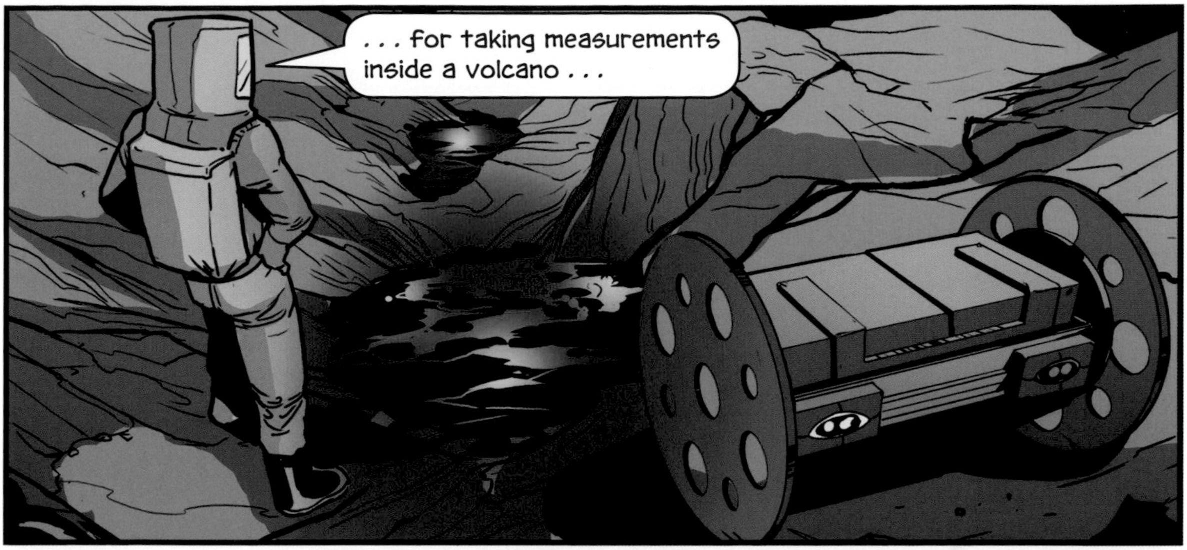
. . . for taking measurements inside a volcano . . .

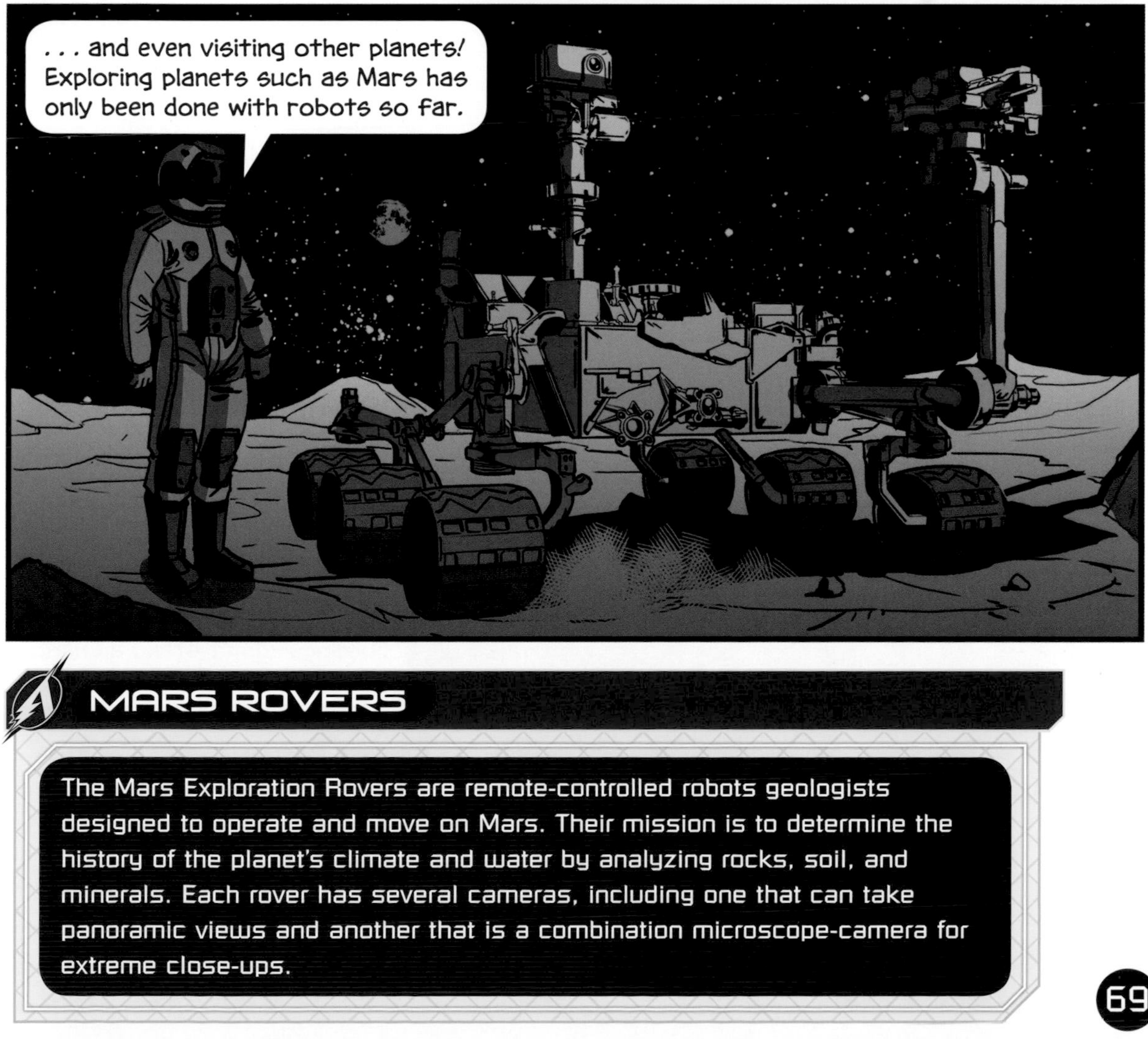
. . . and even visiting other planets! Exploring planets such as Mars has only been done with robots so far.

MARS ROVERS

The Mars Exploration Rovers are remote-controlled robots geologists designed to operate and move on Mars. Their mission is to determine the history of the planet's climate and water by analyzing rocks, soil, and minerals. Each rover has several cameras, including one that can take panoramic views and another that is a combination microscope-camera for extreme close-ups.

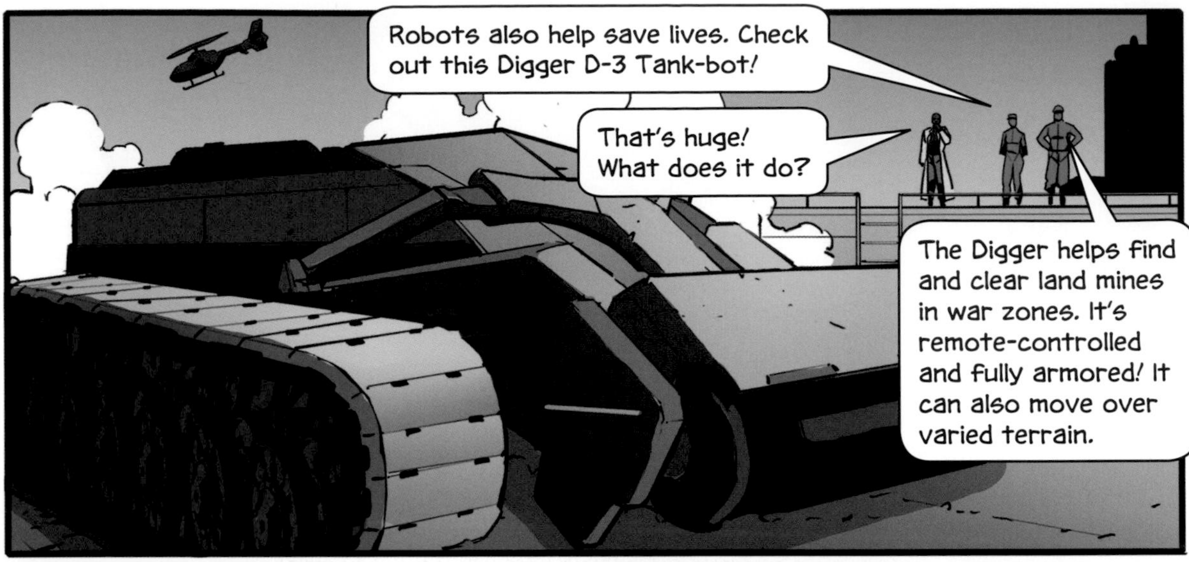
Robots also help save lives. Check out this Digger D-3 Tank-bot!
That's huge! What does it do?
The Digger helps find and clear land mines in war zones. It's remote-controlled and fully armored! It can also move over varied terrain.

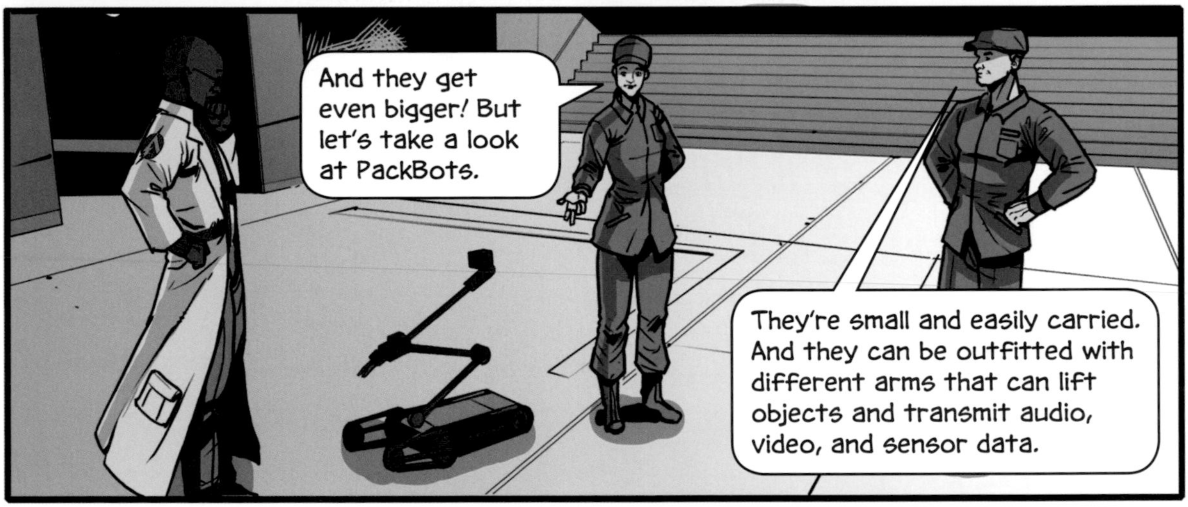
And they get even bigger! But let's take a look at PackBots.
They're small and easily carried. And they can be outfitted with different arms that can lift objects and transmit audio, video, and sensor data.

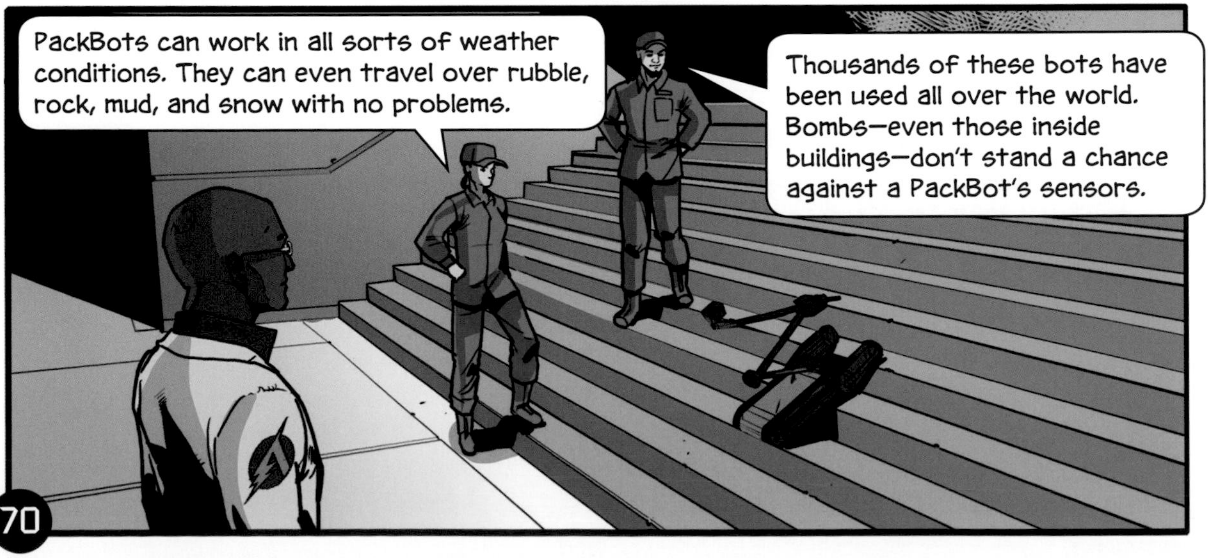
PackBots can work in all sorts of weather conditions. They can even travel over rubble, rock, mud, and snow with no problems.
Thousands of these bots have been used all over the world. Bombs—even those inside buildings—don't stand a chance against a PackBot's sensors.

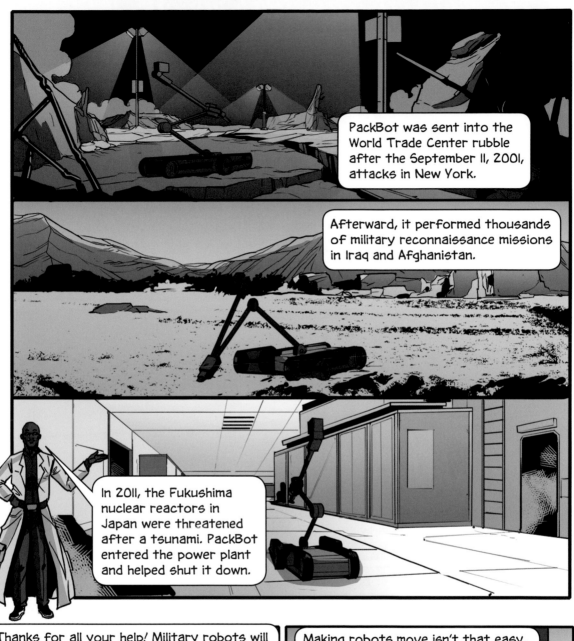

PackBot was sent into the World Trade Center rubble after the September 11, 2001, attacks in New York.

Afterward, it performed thousands of military reconnaissance missions in Iraq and Afghanistan.

In 2011, the Fukushima nuclear reactors in Japan were threatened after a tsunami. PackBot entered the power plant and helped shut it down.

Thanks for all your help! Military robots will be another important part of the exhibit.

Making robots move isn't that easy. I know a lab that specializes in robot movement. I'm going to check it out!

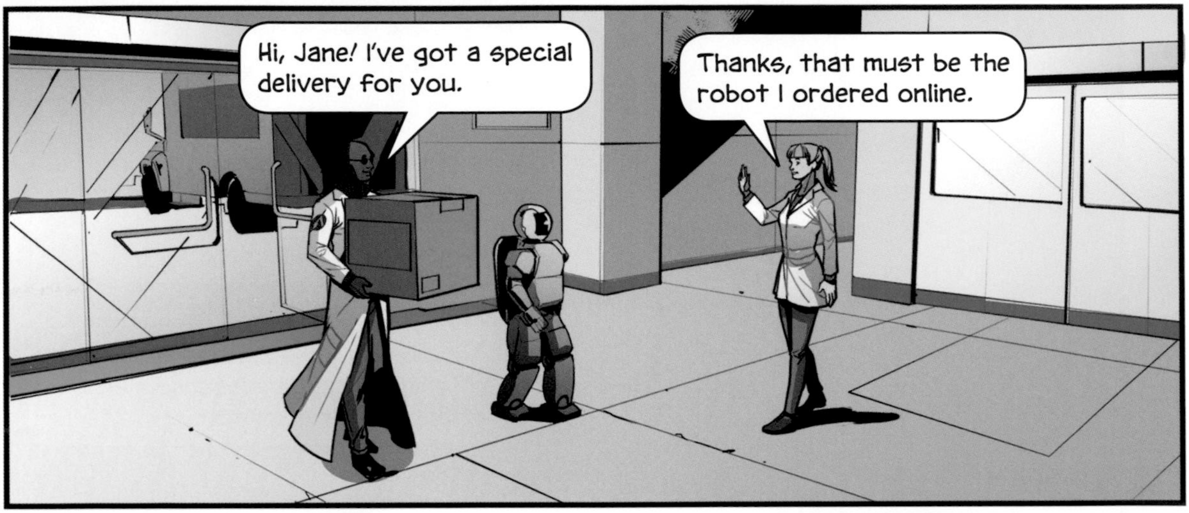
Hi, Jane! I've got a special delivery for you.
Thanks, that must be the robot I ordered online.

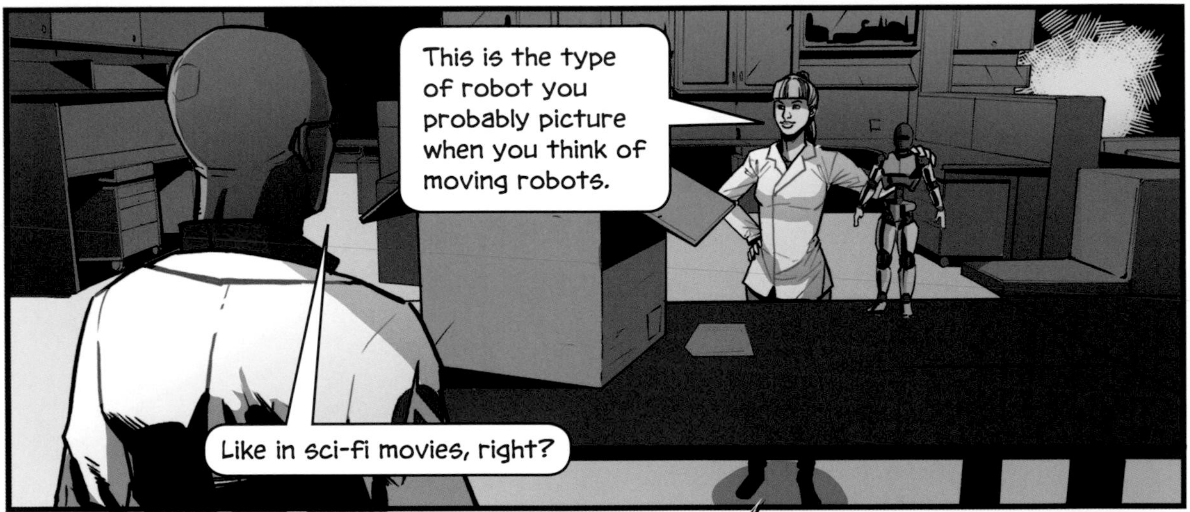
This is the type of robot you probably picture when you think of moving robots.
Like in sci-fi movies, right?

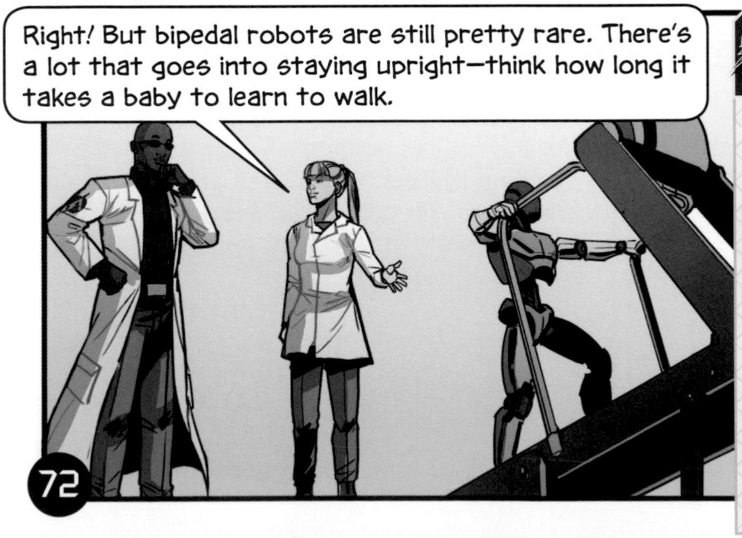
Right! But bipedal robots are still pretty rare. There's a lot that goes into staying upright—think how long it takes a baby to learn to walk.

FINDING THE RIGHT BALANCE

Robot designers have to figure out the right combination of movements involved in walking to program a robot's computer. Many robots have built-in balance systems that tell the computer when to correct its movements so it won't fall.

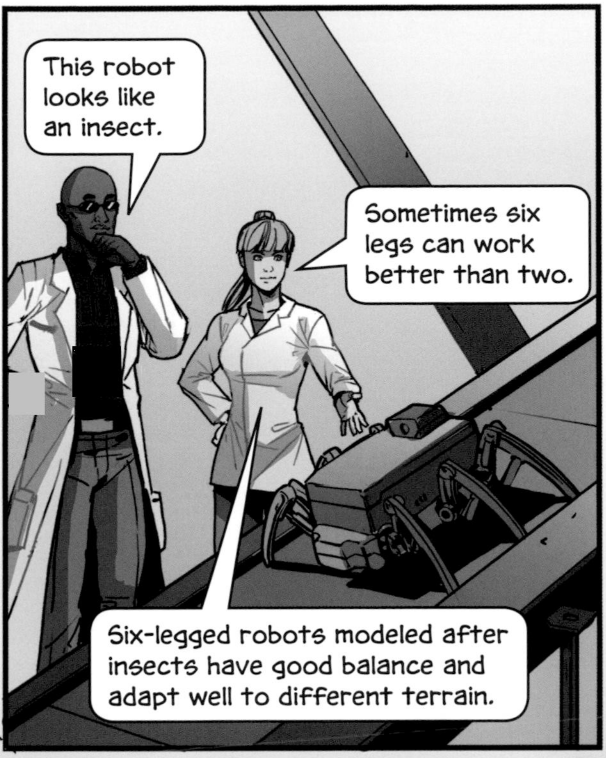
This robot looks like an insect.
Sometimes six legs can work better than two.
Six-legged robots modeled after insects have good balance and adapt well to different terrain.

FAKE BAIT

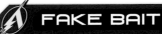

Wildlife officers are using robotic taxidermied animals as bait to catch poachers. The robo-animal is placed in an area where illegal hunting might be happening. The officers hide nearby and use a remote control to operate the robot. When a poacher takes the bait, the officers act.

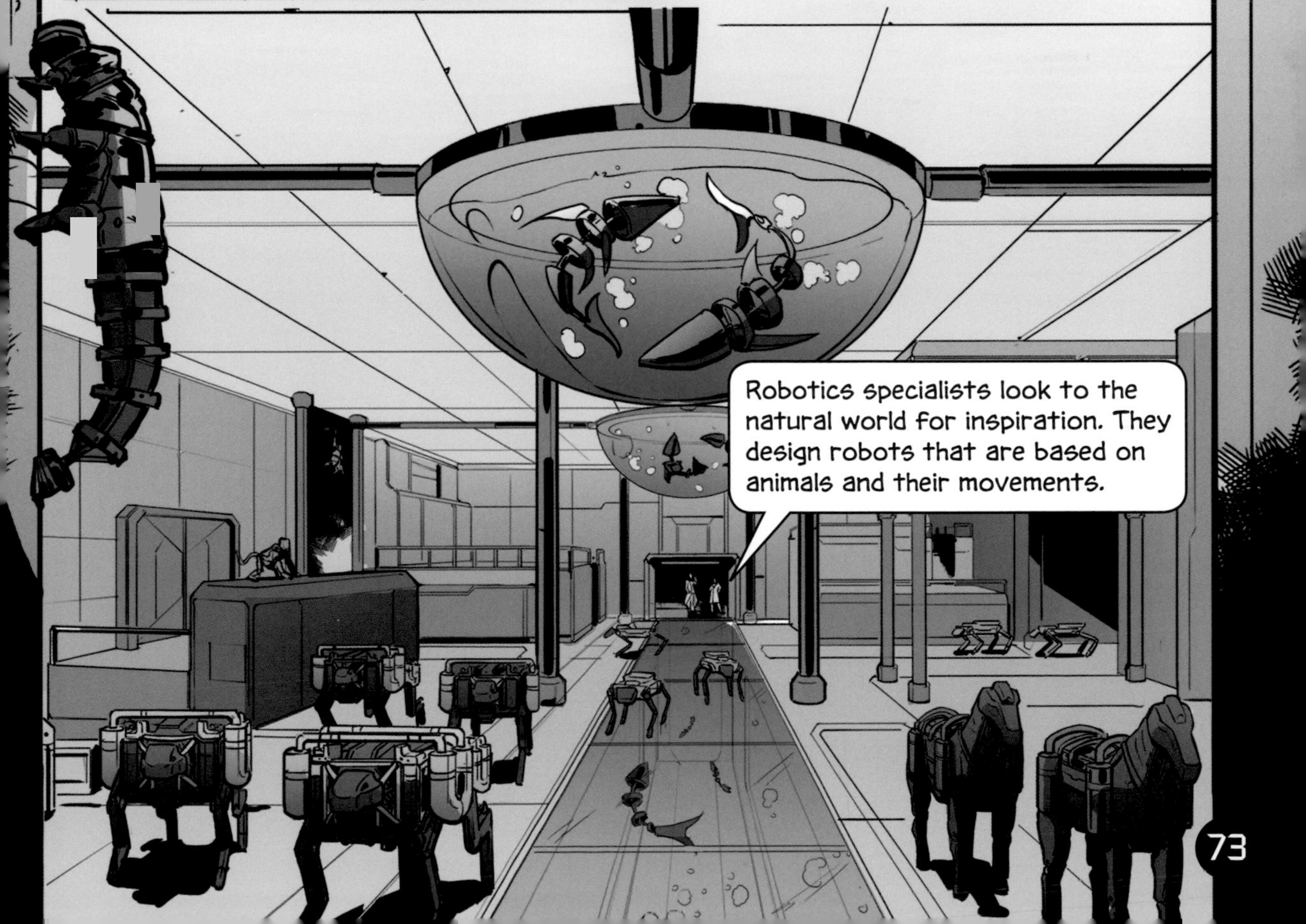
Robotics specialists look to the natural world for inspiration. They design robots that are based on animals and their movements.

Deployable Air-Land Exploration Robot (DALER)

The DALER is inspired by the vampire bat. Designed for search and rescue, it surveys the ground from above and then crawls into hard-to-reach or dangerous areas.

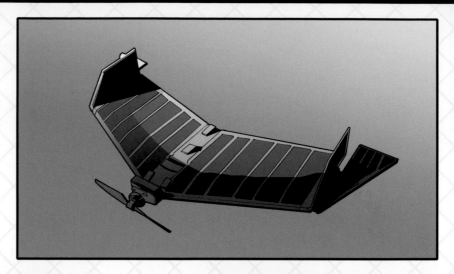

The Nano Air Vehicle

This hummingbirdlike robot can hover in the air. The fully controllable surveillace robot is used to patrol battlefields and sends video data back to its operator.

The Ghost Swimmer

The U.S. Navy's underwater drone is the size of an albacore tuna and swims like a shark. It is designed for intelligence, reconaissance, and surveillance missions.

These animal-based robots are awesome!

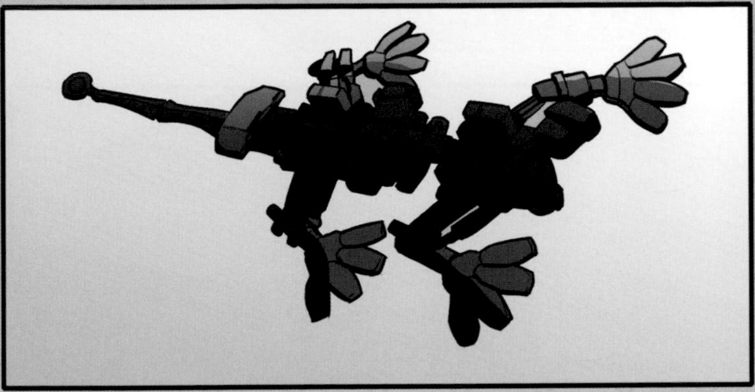

The Stickybot

This gecko-inspired robot was developed at Stanford University. It can walk on any smooth surface using special adhesives on its feet.

The Cheetah

The cheetah-inspired robot at Boston Dynamics is fast! It can run at speeds approaching 30 miles per hour—the fastest recorded land-speed times for a robot. The Masssachusetts Institute of Technology (MIT) also has a cheetah. Moving at 5 miles per hour, it can estimate the height, size, and distance of objects in its path, and jump over them.

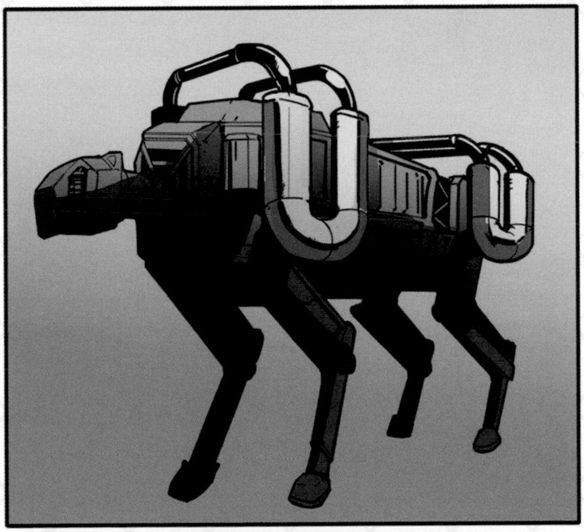

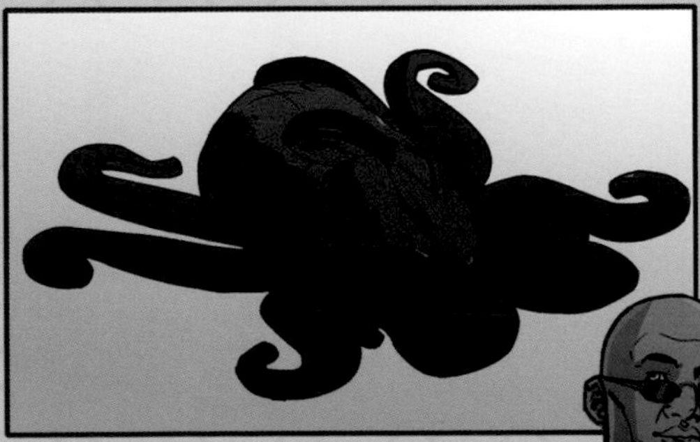

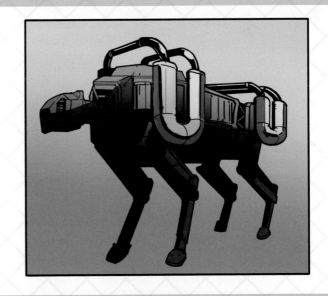

The Octobot

Harvard's Octobot is the world's first entirely soft robot. Made from squishy gel, it has no power cord and uses no electronics or batteries to move. Instead, it uses gas released from chemical reactions within its "veins" to power its body.

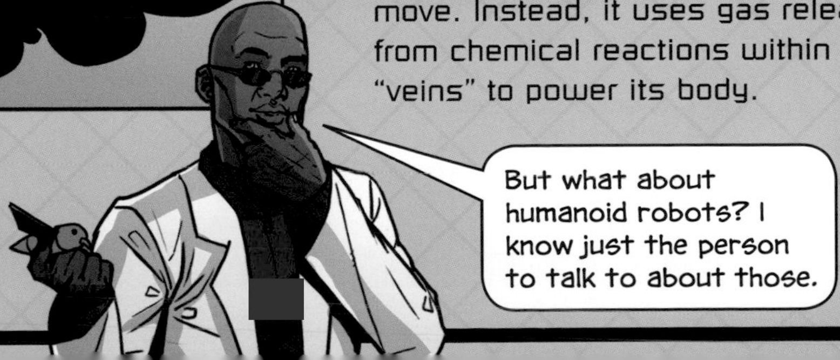
But what about humanoid robots? I know just the person to talk to about those.

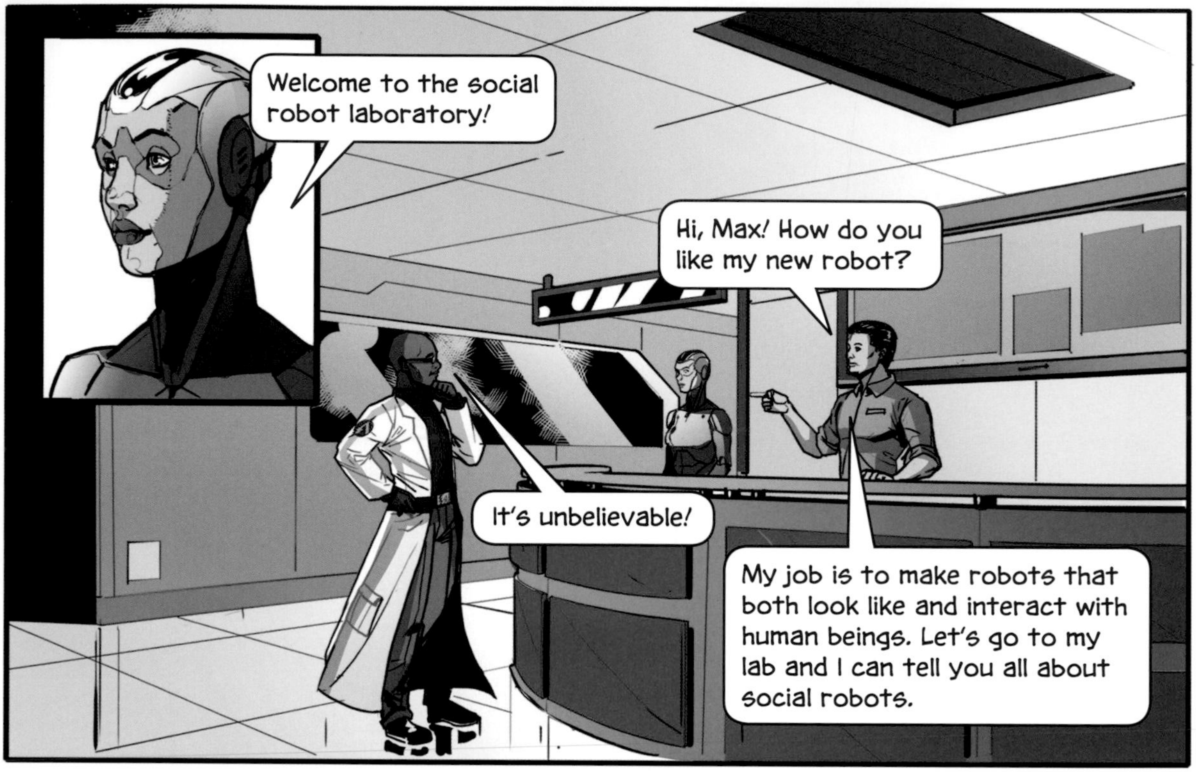
Welcome to the social robot laboratory!
Hi, Max! How do you like my new robot?
It's unbelievable!
My job is to make robots that both look like and interact with human beings. Let's go to my lab and I can tell you all about social robots.

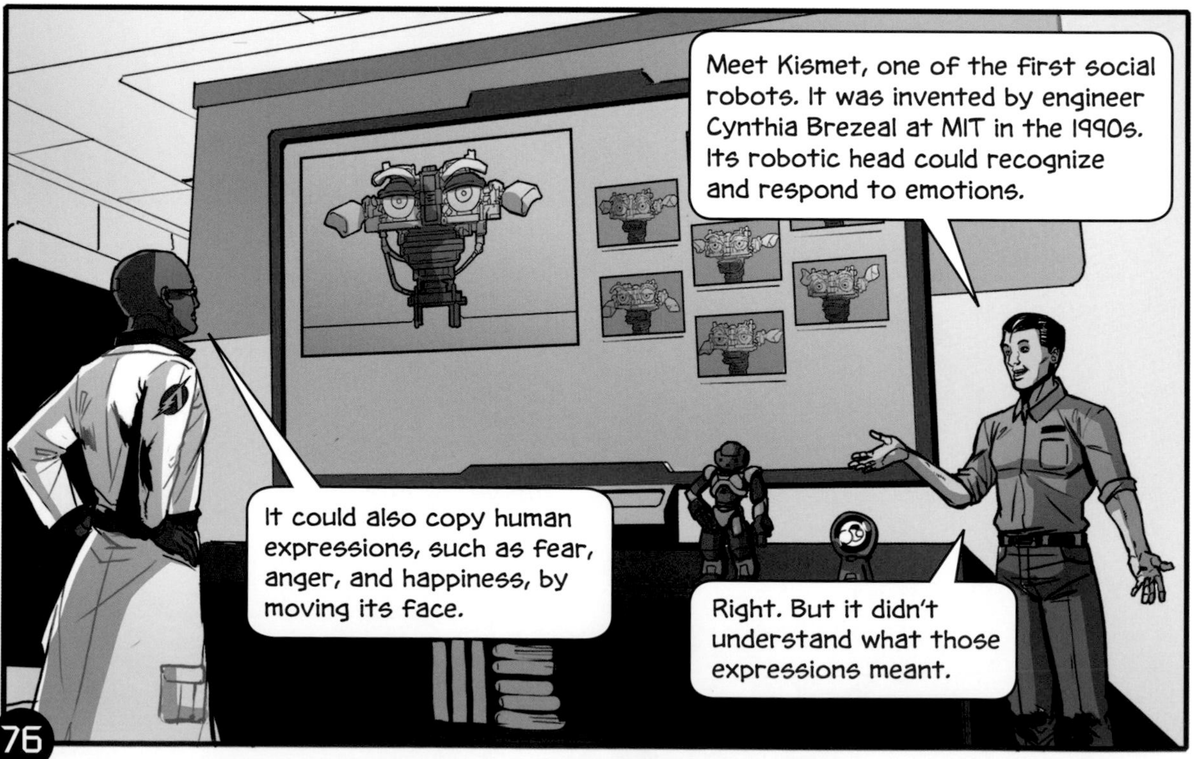
Meet Kismet, one of the first social robots. It was invented by engineer Cynthia Brezeal at MIT in the 1990s. Its robotic head could recognize and respond to emotions.
It could also copy human expressions, such as fear, anger, and happiness, by moving its face.
Right. But it didn't understand what those expressions meant.

This robot is called Jibo. It is meant to be a friendly assistant to families. Alexa or Siri can answer your questions, but Jibo can react to them and have a conversation with you.

But there are robots today that look a lot more human than Kismet or Jibo.

Humanoid robots are built to resemble people. NAO robots can walk, talk, listen, and even recognize your face. One version of this robot is being used to help teach kids in school.

Androids are humanoid robots with skin, hair, and realistic eyes. This one is used to welcome customers to a store in Japan. She can give directions and make conversation using a preprogrammed script.

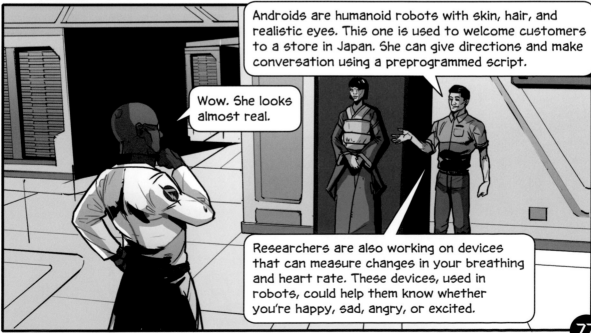

Wow. She looks almost real.

Researchers are also working on devices that can measure changes in your breathing and heart rate. These devices, used in robots, could help them know whether you're happy, sad, angry, or excited.

Do you think robots will be even more humanlike in the future?

Maybe! But they could also be completely different. These bacteria-sized nanobots are already being researched and developed for work in the medical field.

They are so small that they can squeeze through the tiniest spaces—even in our bodies.

They could act as artificial white blood cells and destroy germs in our blood. They could target and destroy cancer cells. And, if controlled by a doctor, they could even perform surgery on individual cells.

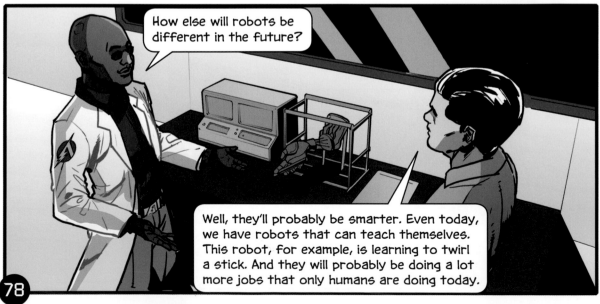

How else will robots be different in the future?

Well, they'll probably be smarter. Even today, we have robots that can teach themselves. This robot, for example, is learning to twirl a stick. And they will probably be doing a lot more jobs that only humans are doing today.

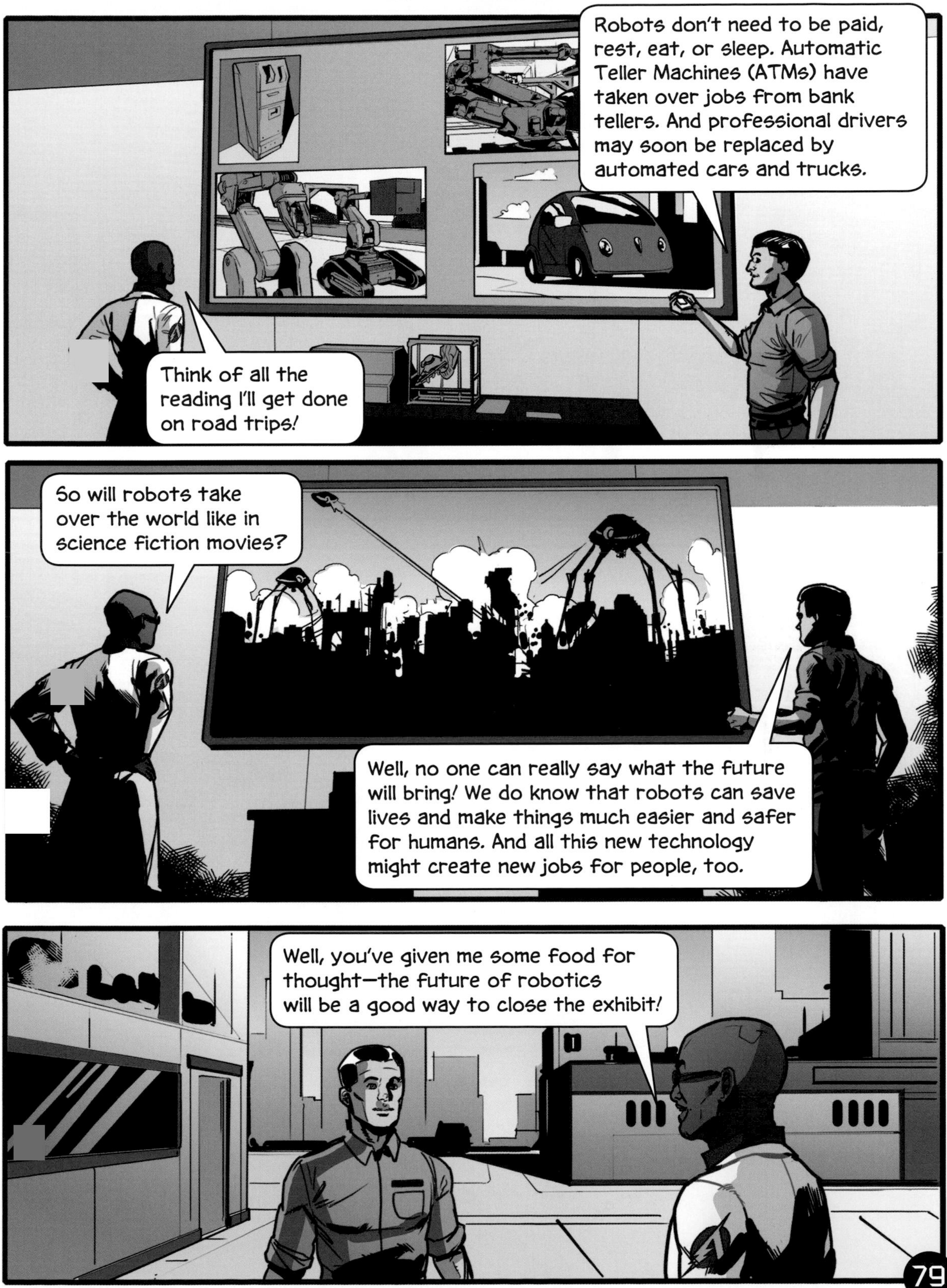
Robots don't need to be paid, rest, eat, or sleep. Automatic Teller Machines (ATMs) have taken over jobs from bank tellers. And professional drivers may soon be replaced by automated cars and trucks.
Think of all the reading I'll get done on road trips!
So will robots take over the world like in science fiction movies?
Well, no one can really say what the future will bring! We do know that robots can save lives and make things much easier and safer for humans. And all this new technology might create new jobs for people, too.
Well, you've given me some food for thought—the future of robotics will be a good way to close the exhibit!

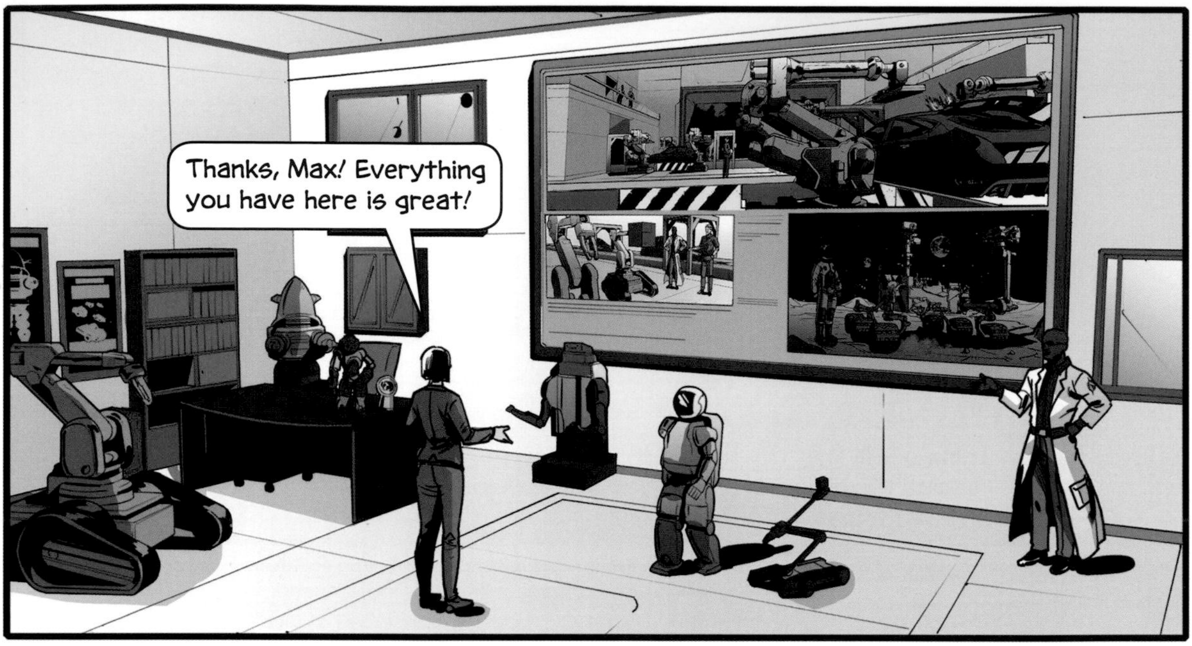
Thanks, Max! Everything you have here is great!

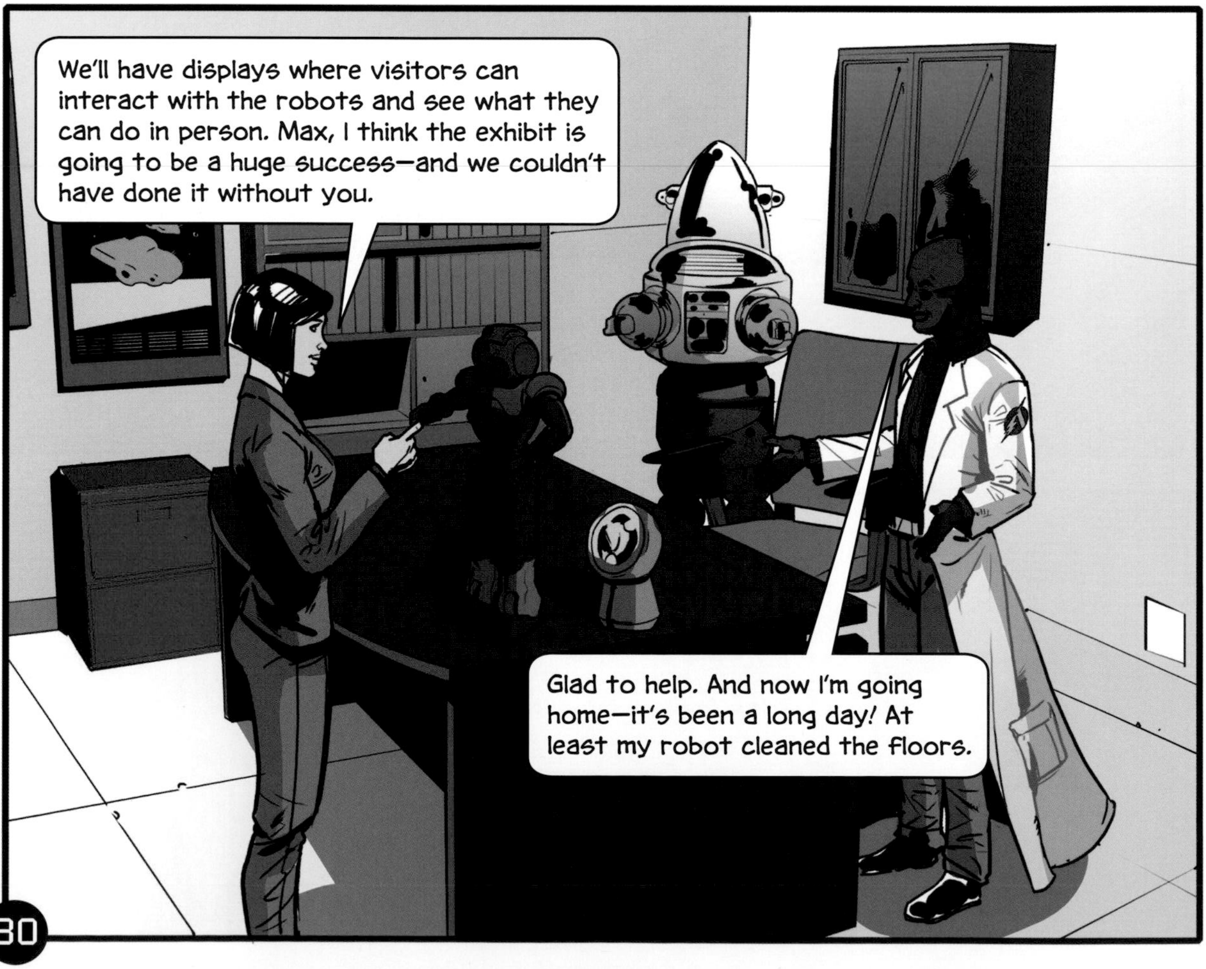
We'll have displays where visitors can interact with the robots and see what they can do in person. Max, I think the exhibit is going to be a huge success—and we couldn't have done it without you.
Glad to help. And now I'm going home—it's been a long day! At least my robot cleaned the floors.

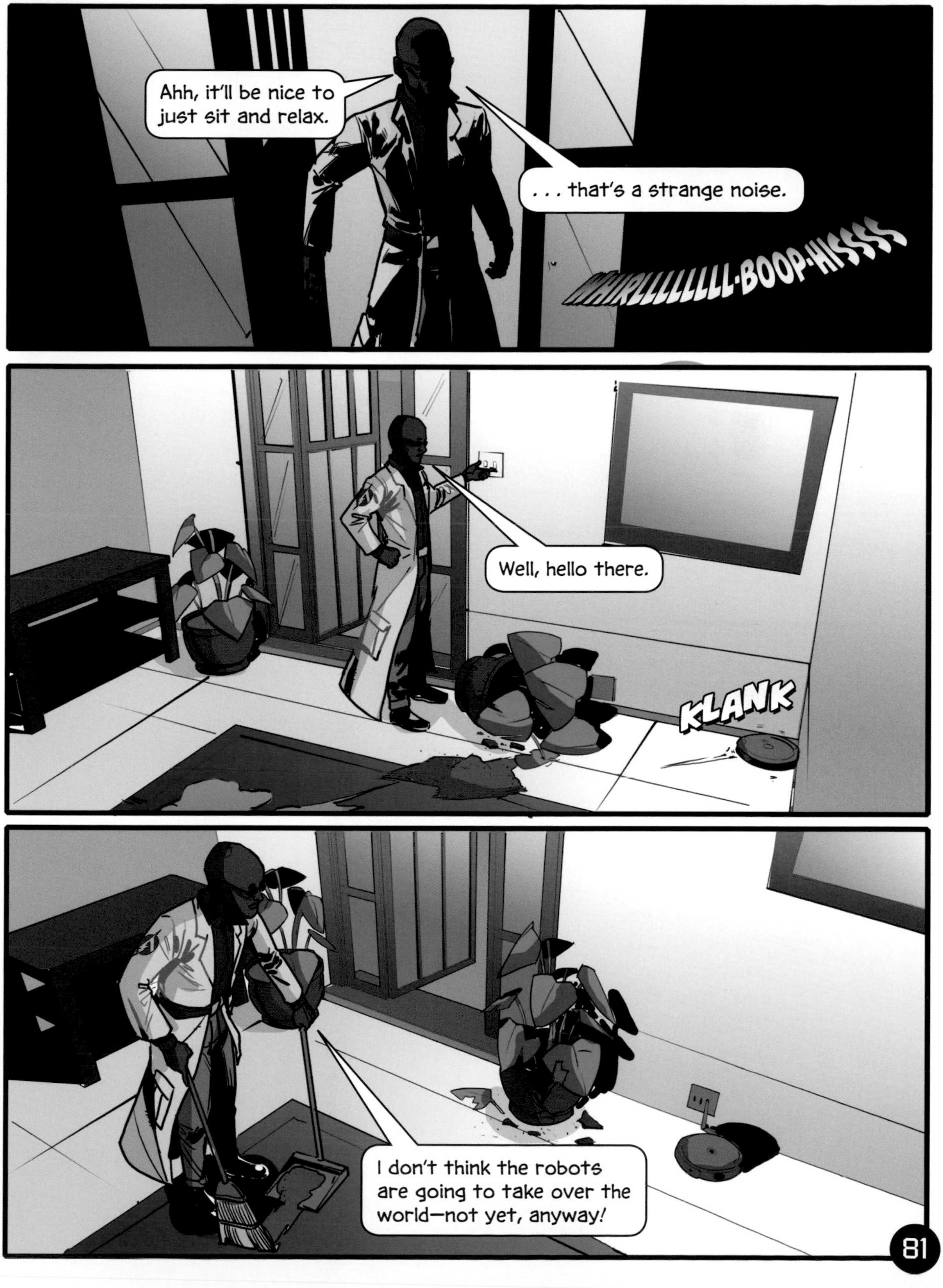
Ahh, it'll be nice to just sit and relax.
. . . that's a strange noise.
WHIRLLLLLLLLL-BOOP-HISSSS
Well, hello there.
KLANK
I don't think the robots are going to take over the world—not yet, anyway!

Some robots have sensors that allow them to smell and taste. They have been use to judge contests and even verify the authenticity of Thai food. Robots that can smell, known as "electronic noses," can be programmed to recognize the smell of alcohol, blood, urine, and sweat. These robots could be used in search-and-rescue missions, as well as to sense and warn of dangerous gas leaks.

Tiny flying robots are being developed to help pollinate crops in the future. Harvard University's RoboBee has a wingspan of 1.2 inches (3 centimeters). It can both fly and swim.

Robot cops are already patrolling our streets. Police in Cleveland, Ohio, enlist the help of a robot called Griffin, a small, six-wheeled rover that can look for explosives. In Los Angeles, a robot called BatCat can pick up car bombs with a 50-foot- (15.2-meter-) long arm. It can also rip through houses to end standoffs.

Lifelike robotic pets are bringing companionship and comfort to people who might not be able to care for real ones. Robotic cats that purr when stroked and robotic dogs that bark and cock their heads when spoken to are already on the market. Paro, a baby harp seal robot developed in Japan, has been used as a soothing tool in hospitals and nursing homes since 2003. Similar to a live animal, Paro is said to help reduce a patient's stress and helps patients and caregivers talk to each other.

CHAPTER 4

The Amazing Story of Space Travel

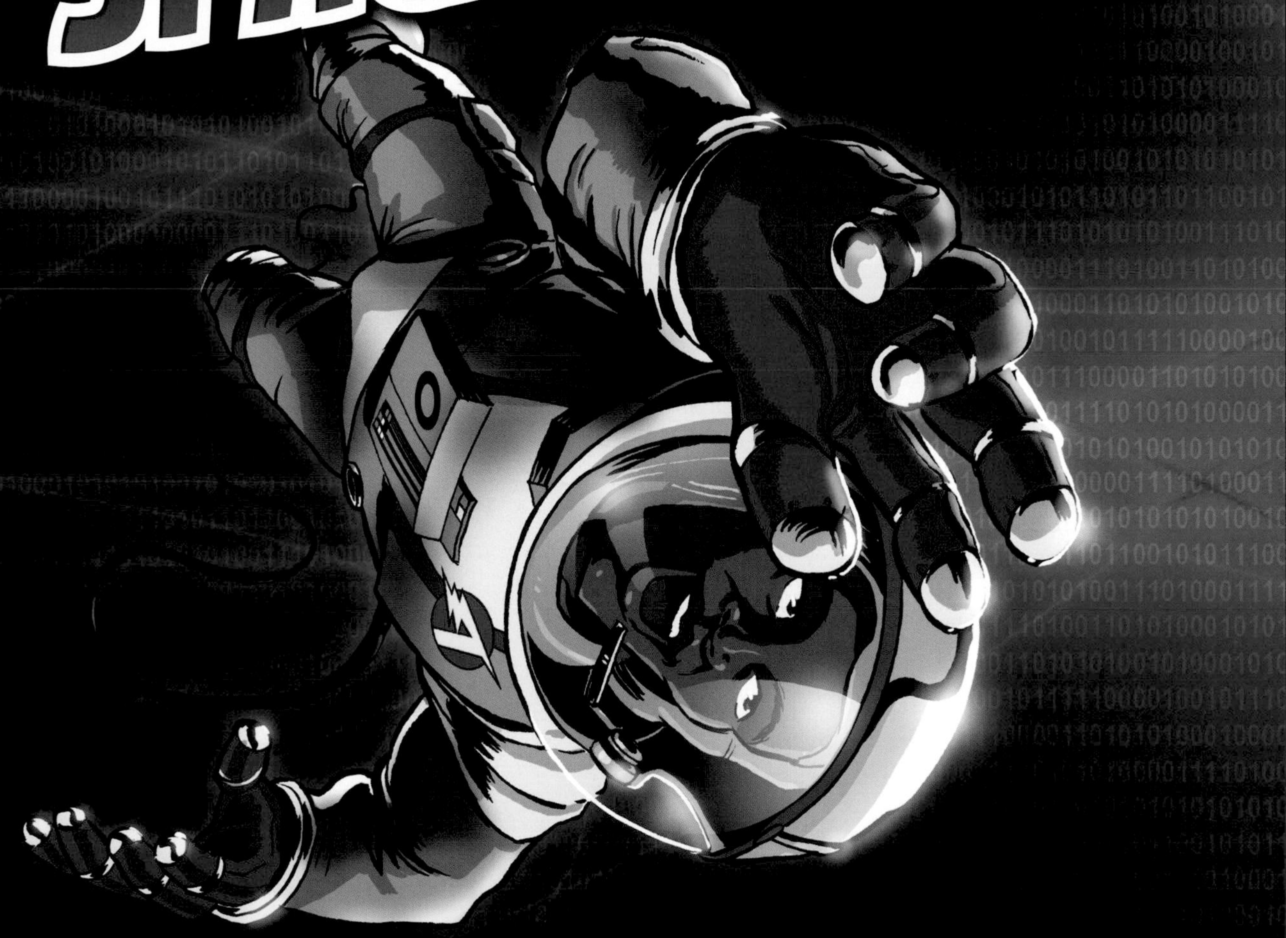

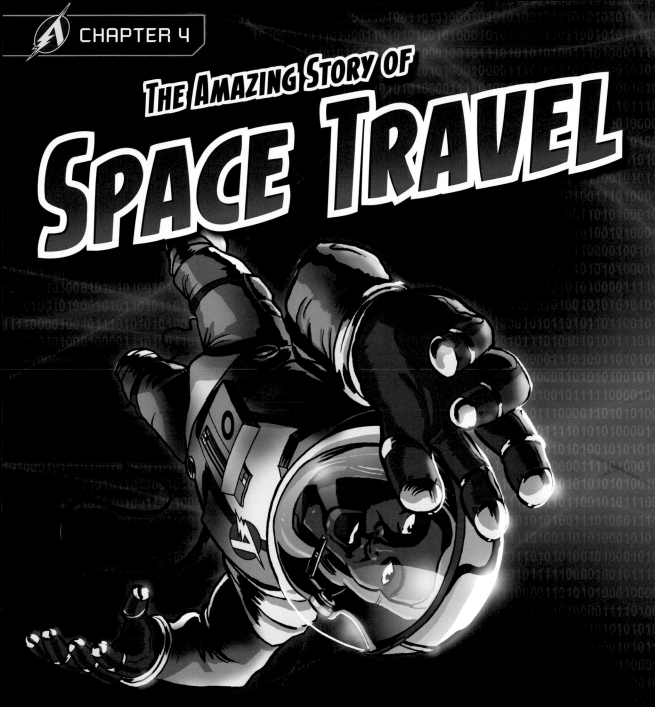

by Agnieszka Biskup

illustrated by Pop Art Properties

Consultant: Jeffrey A. Hoffman, PhD | Former NASA Astronaut
Professor of the Practice of Aerospace Engineering
Massachusetts Institute of Technology (MIT) | Cambridge, Massachusetts

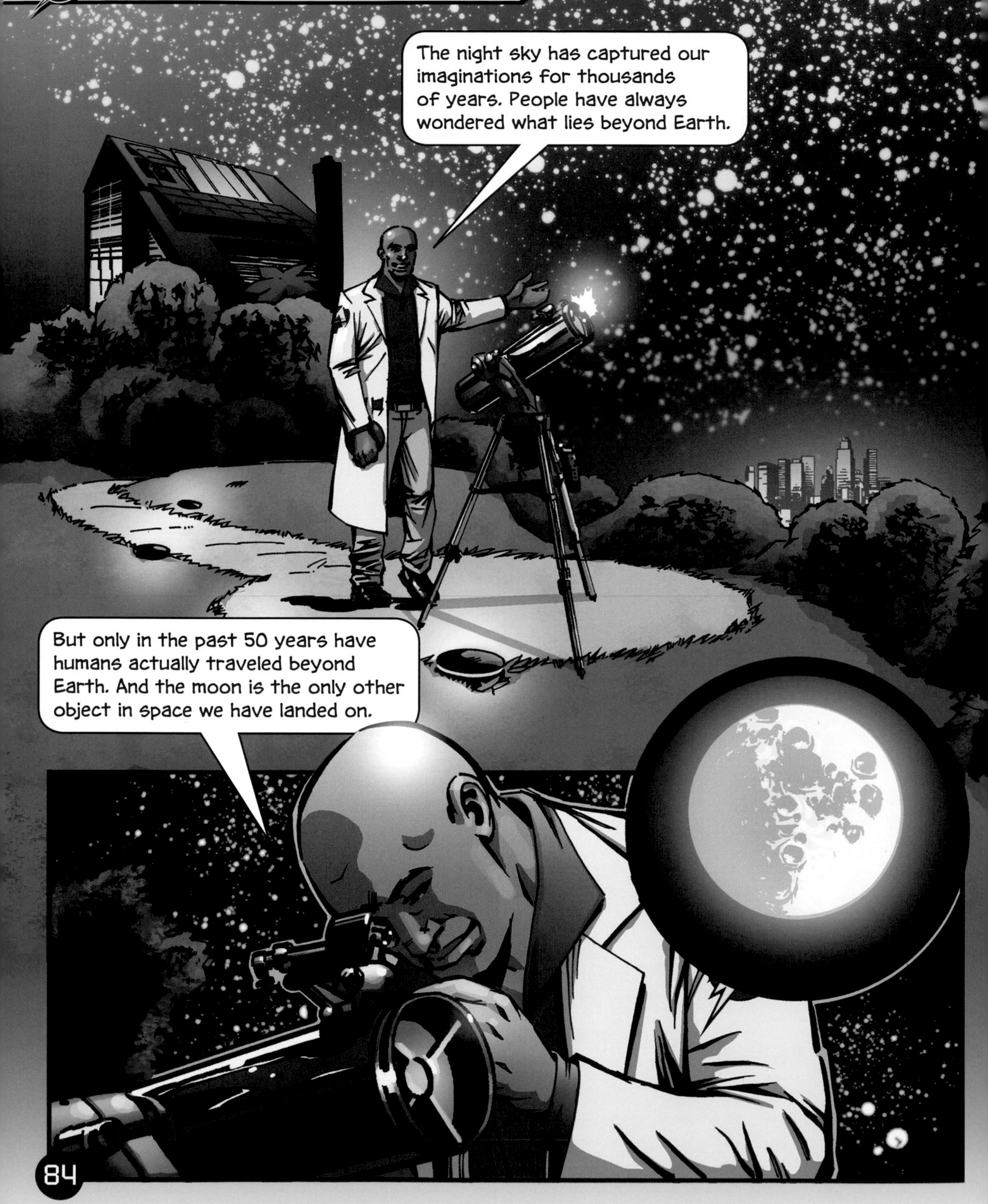
The night sky has captured our imaginations for thousands of years. People have always wondered what lies beyond Earth.
But only in the past 50 years have humans actually traveled beyond Earth. And the moon is the only other object in space we have landed on.

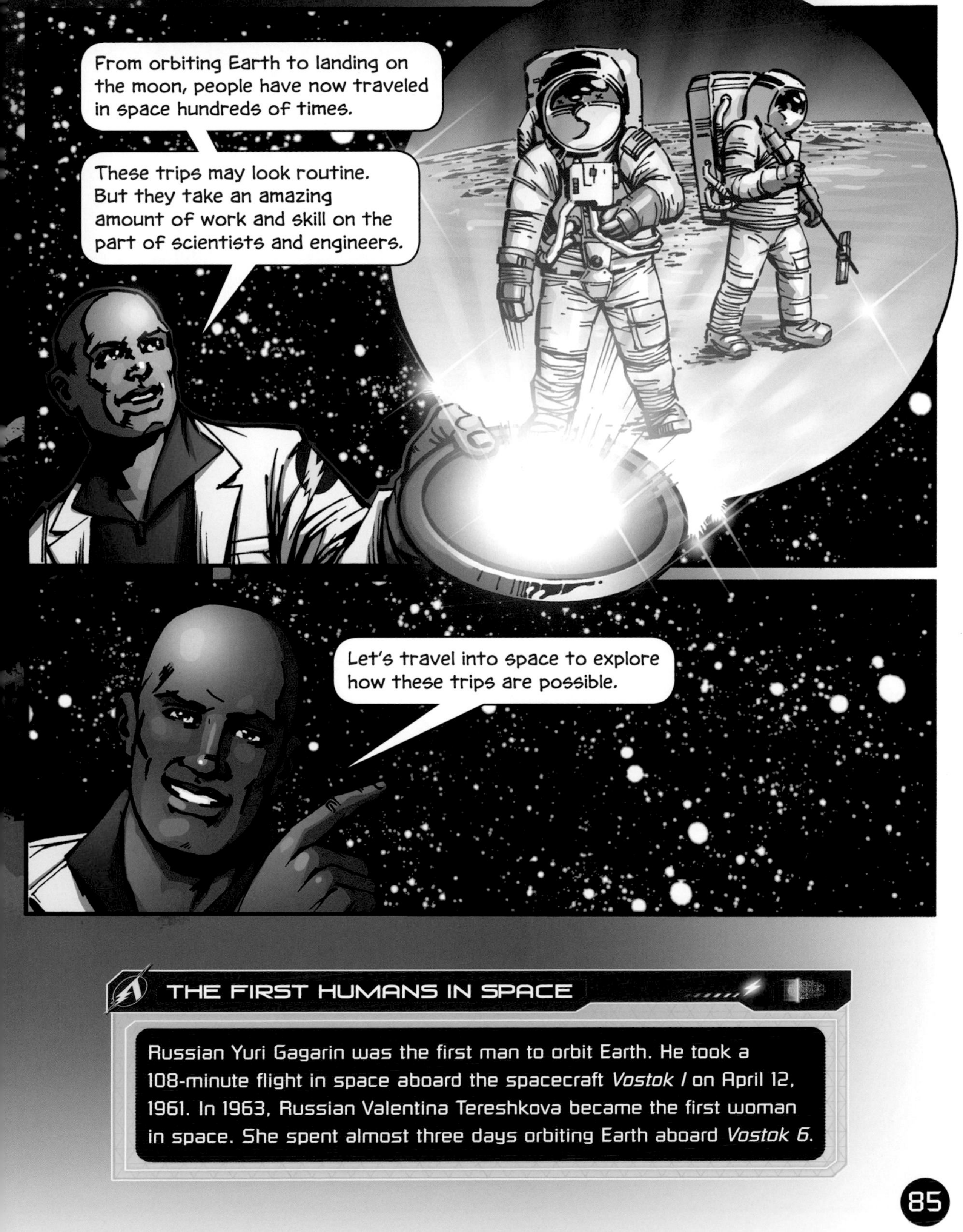
From orbiting Earth to landing on the moon, people have now traveled in space hundreds of times.
These trips may look routine. But they take an amazing amount of work and skill on the part of scientists and engineers.
Let's travel into space to explore how these trips are possible.

THE FIRST HUMANS IN SPACE

Russian Yuri Gagarin was the first man to orbit Earth. He took a 108-minute flight in space aboard the spacecraft *Vostok I* on April 12, 1961. In 1963, Russian Valentina Tereshkova became the first woman in space. She spent almost three days orbiting Earth aboard *Vostok 6*.

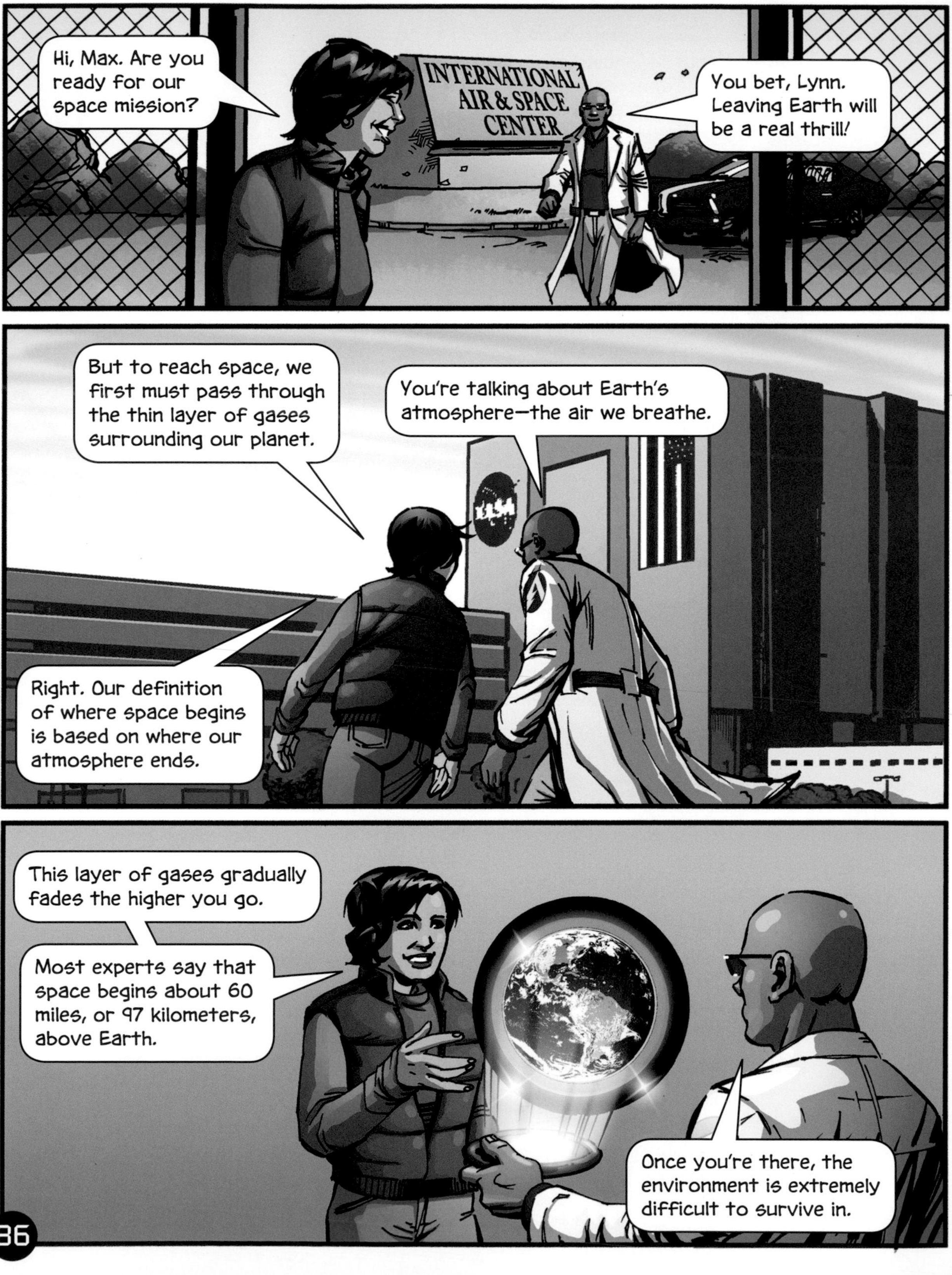
Hi, Max. Are you ready for our space mission?
INTERNATIONAL AIR & SPACE CENTER
You bet, Lynn. Leaving Earth will be a real thrill!
But to reach space, we first must pass through the thin layer of gases surrounding our planet.
You're talking about Earth's atmosphere—the air we breathe.
Right. Our definition of where space begins is based on where our atmosphere ends.
This layer of gases gradually fades the higher you go.
Most experts say that space begins about 60 miles, or 97 kilometers, above Earth.
Once you're there, the environment is extremely difficult to survive in.

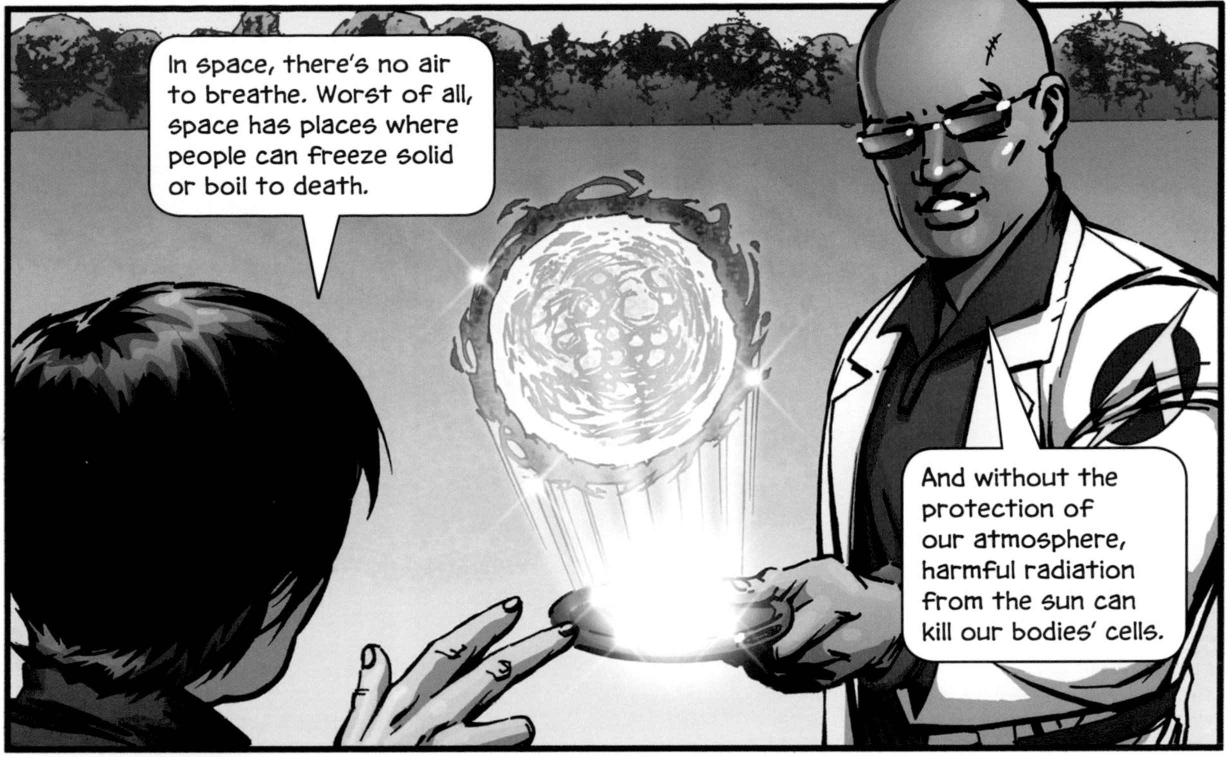
In space, there's no air to breathe. Worst of all, space has places where people can freeze solid or boil to death.
And without the protection of our atmosphere, harmful radiation from the sun can kill our bodies' cells.

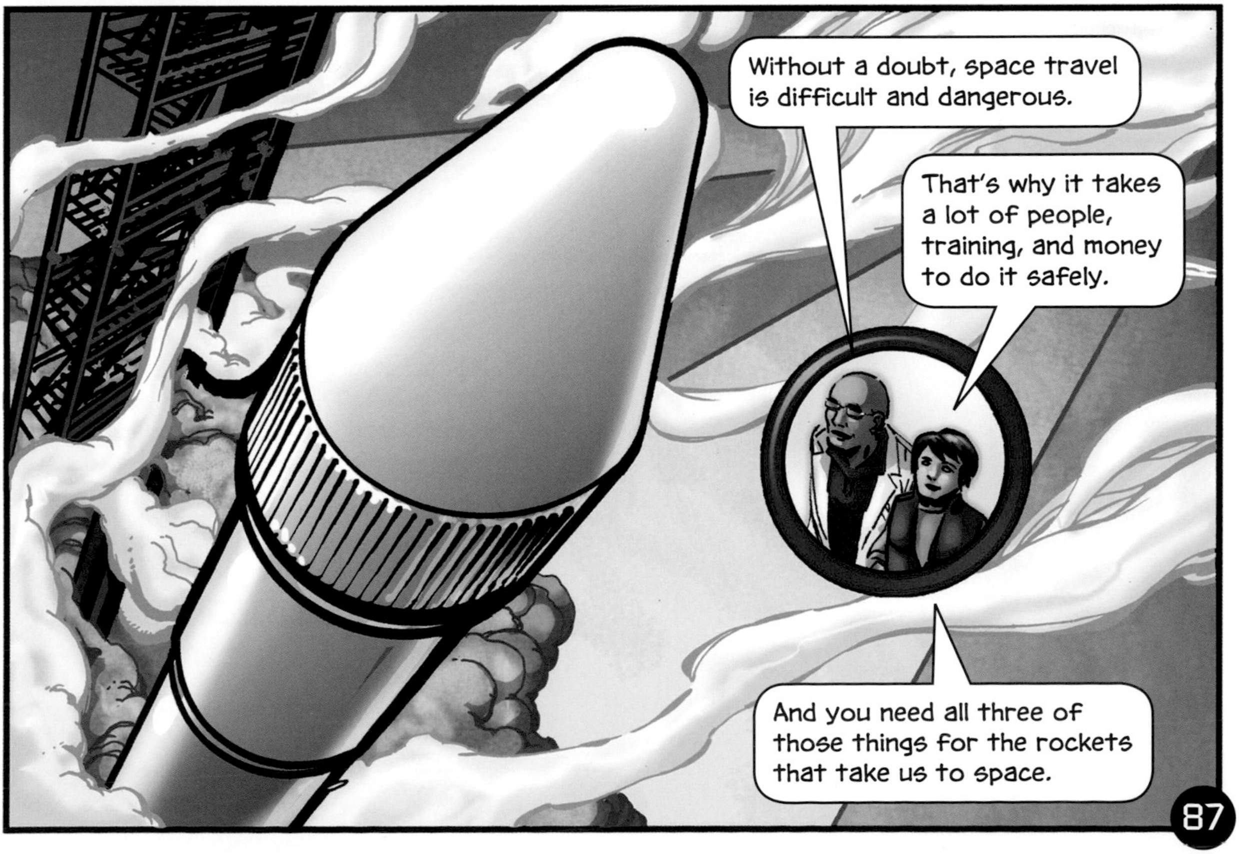
Without a doubt, space travel is difficult and dangerous.
That's why it takes a lot of people, training, and money to do it safely.
And you need all three of those things for the rockets that take us to space.

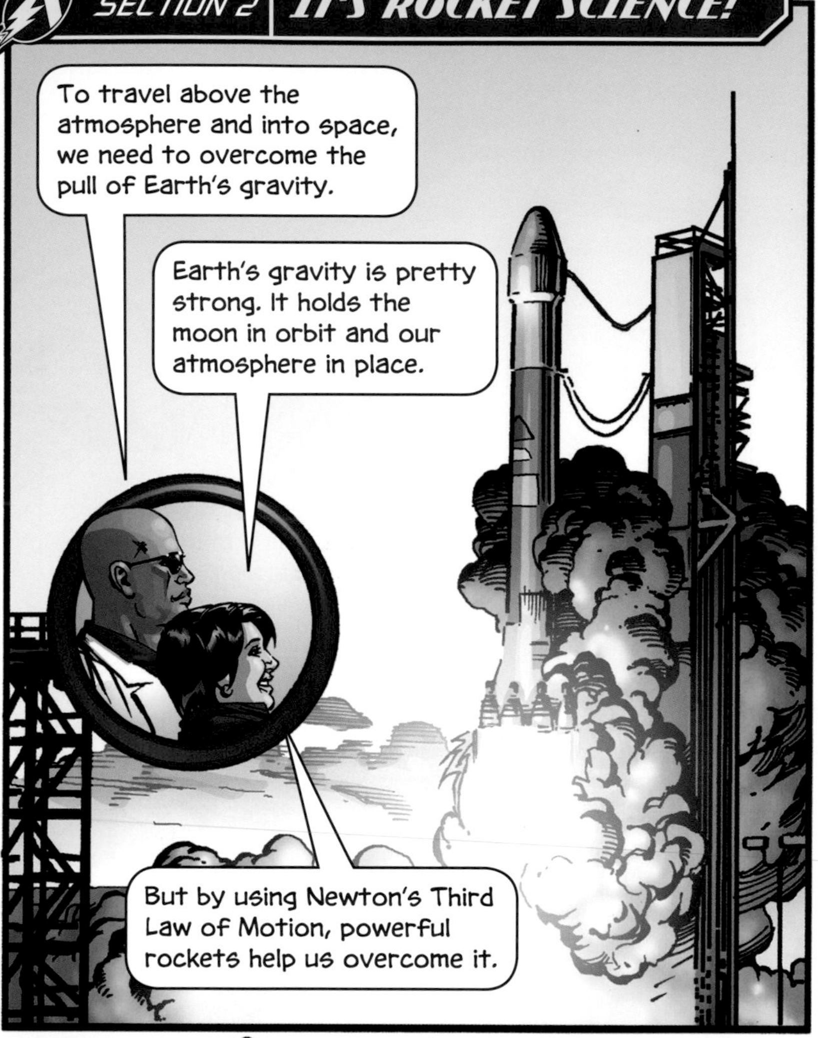
To travel above the atmosphere and into space, we need to overcome the pull of Earth's gravity.
Earth's gravity is pretty strong. It holds the moon in orbit and our atmosphere in place.
But by using Newton's Third Law of Motion, powerful rockets help us overcome it.

It's the Law

More than 300 years ago, English scientist Isaac Newton came up with three simple laws that describe how forces make things move. His third law is probably the most famous. It says that for every action there is an equal and opposite reaction. By actions, Newton meant forces. Rockets aren't the only things that use this law. You can see it in action by blowing up a balloon and then letting it go. The force of the air coming out of the balloon is equal to the force of the balloon whizzing around you.

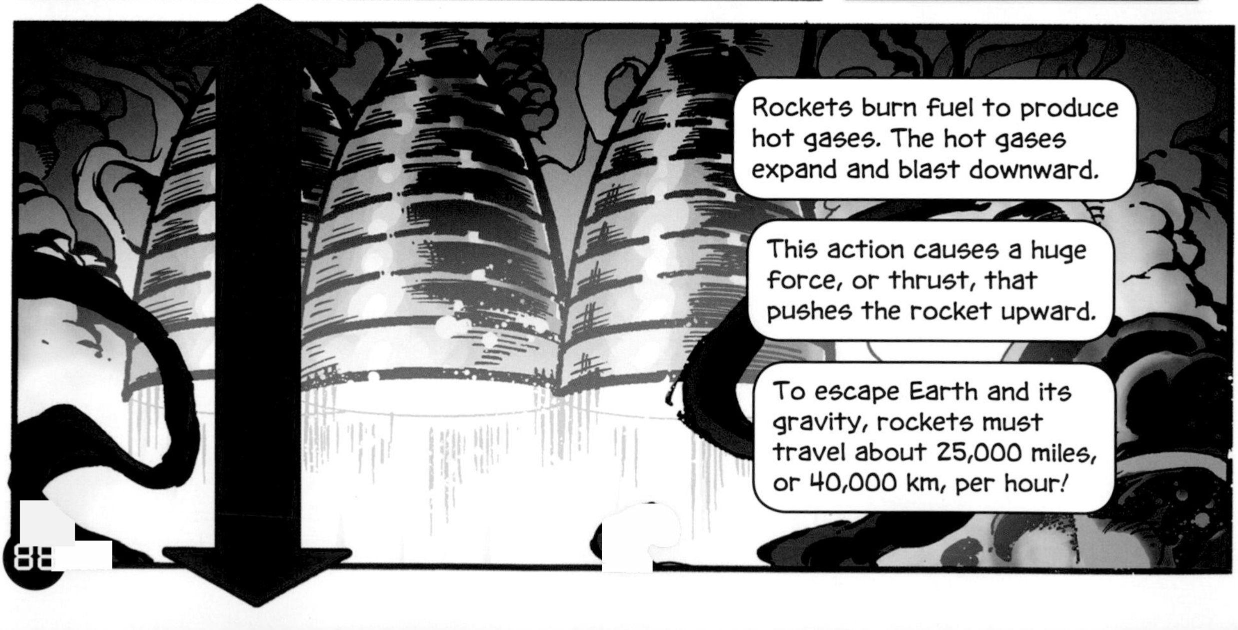
Rockets burn fuel to produce hot gases. The hot gases expand and blast downward.
This action causes a huge force, or thrust, that pushes the rocket upward.
To escape Earth and its gravity, rockets must travel about 25,000 miles, or 40,000 km, per hour!

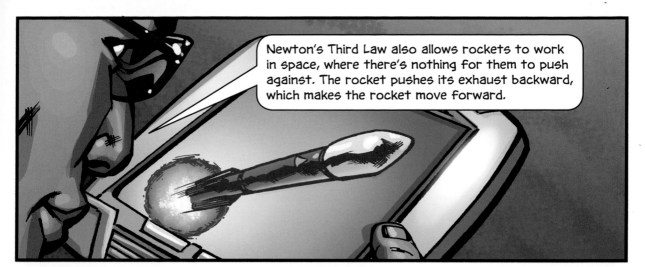

Newton's Third Law also allows rockets to work in space, where there's nothing for them to push against. The rocket pushes its exhaust backward, which makes the rocket move forward.

Rockets come in many sizes, and some are more powerful than others. Heavy lift rockets are among the most powerful. They can send people to the moon and beyond.

Our rocket to the International Space Station is going to launch from this spaceport too. It's so huge that we can get a better look at it from the air.

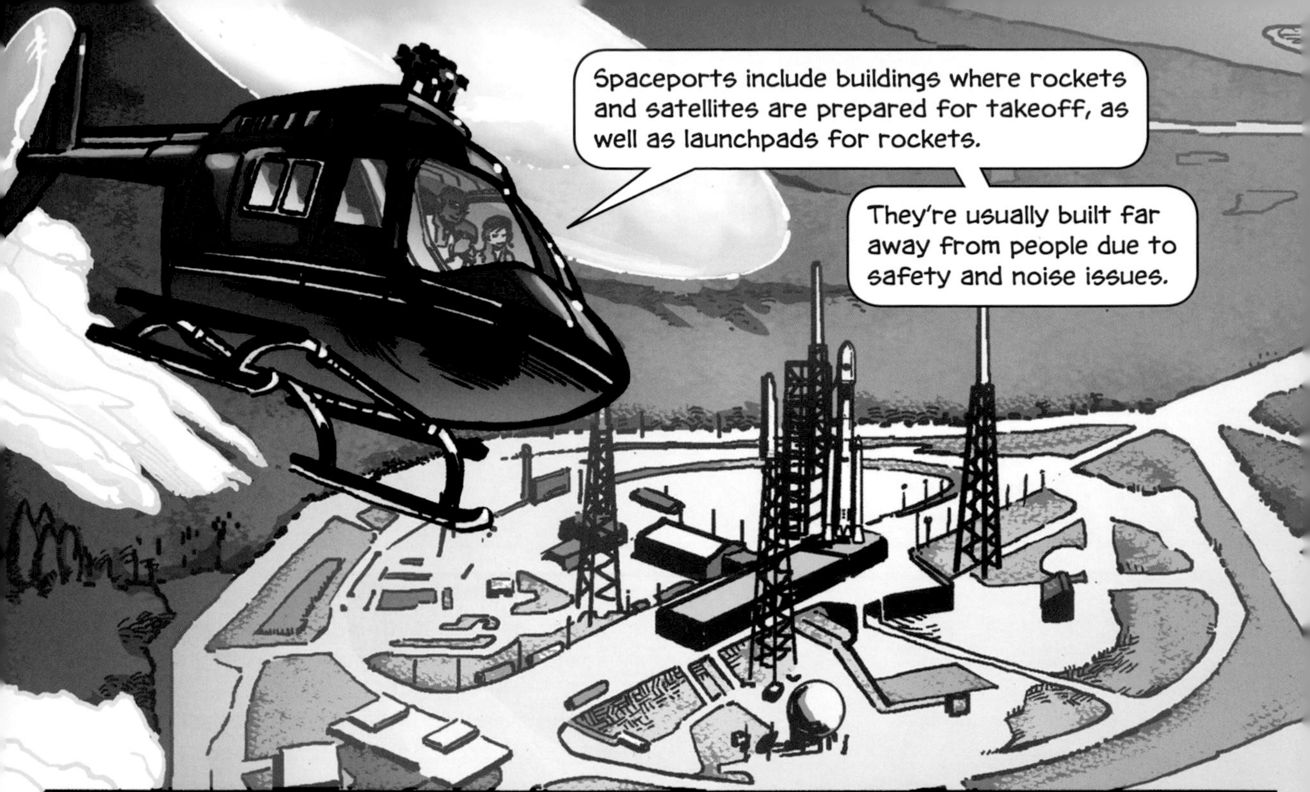
Spaceports include buildings where rockets and satellites are prepared for takeoff, as well as launchpads for rockets.
They're usually built far away from people due to safety and noise issues.

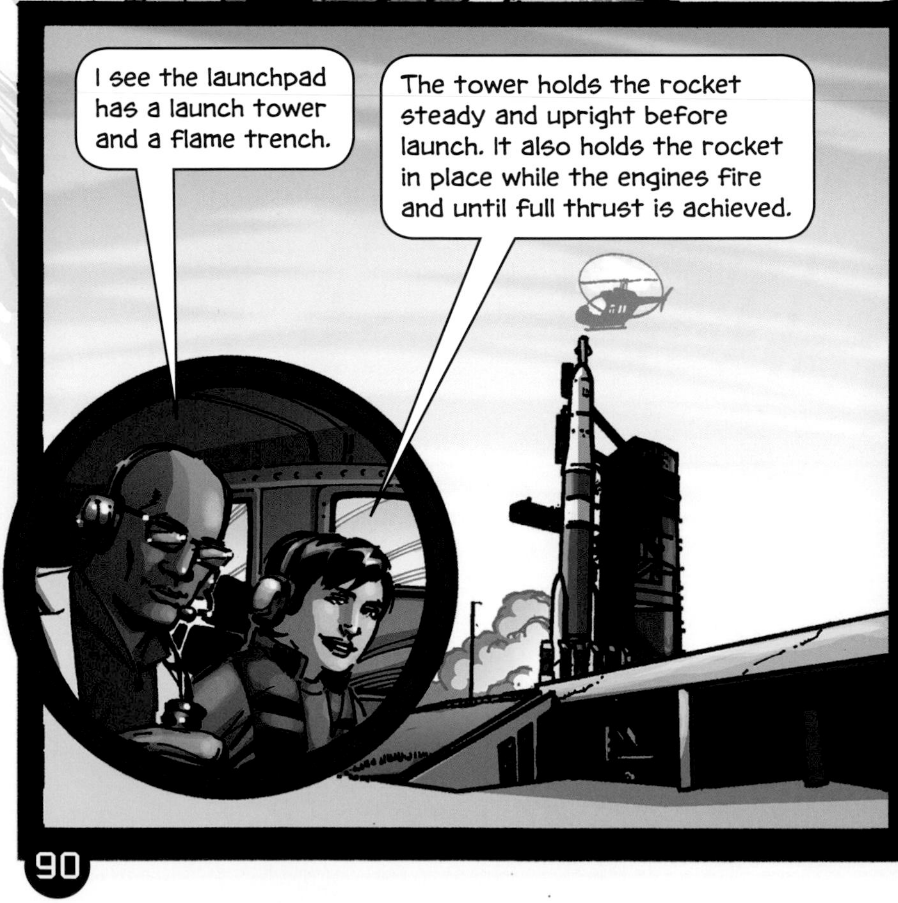
I see the launchpad has a launch tower and a flame trench.
The tower holds the rocket steady and upright before launch. It also holds the rocket in place while the engines fire and until full thrust is achieved.

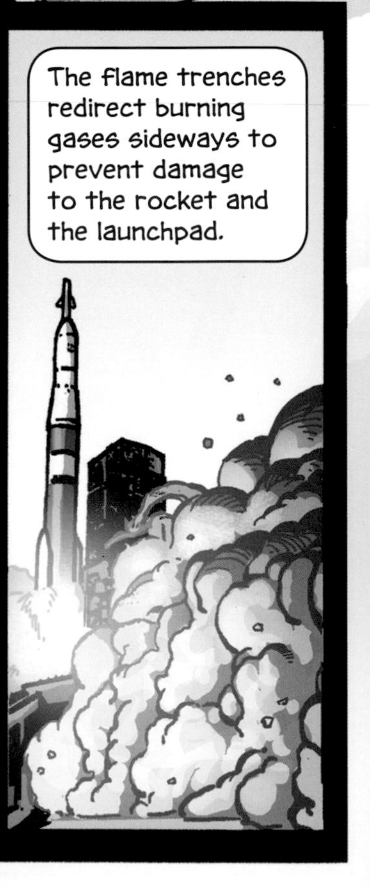
The flame trenches redirect burning gases sideways to prevent damage to the rocket and the launchpad.

It must take a huge team of engineers to prepare the rocket.

Let's check it out.

You're just in time. We're moving the launch vehicle to the launchpad.

This vehicle is the rocket that launches the spacecraft the astronauts sit in.

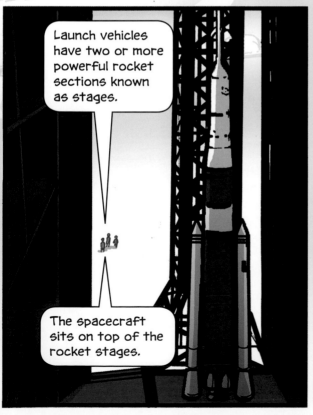

Launch vehicles have two or more powerful rocket sections known as stages.

The spacecraft sits on top of the rocket stages.

Now that the rocket is on the launchpad, we'll begin filling its fuel tanks.

In the meantime, we'll check out mission control before suiting up for our flight.

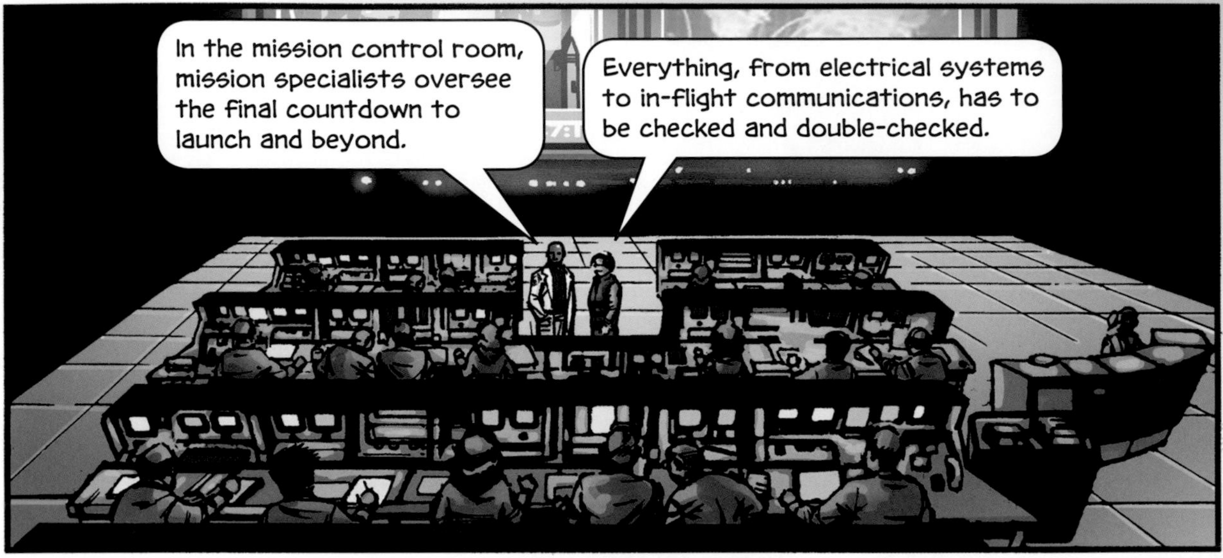
In the mission control room, mission specialists oversee the final countdown to launch and beyond.
Everything, from electrical systems to in-flight communications, has to be checked and double-checked.

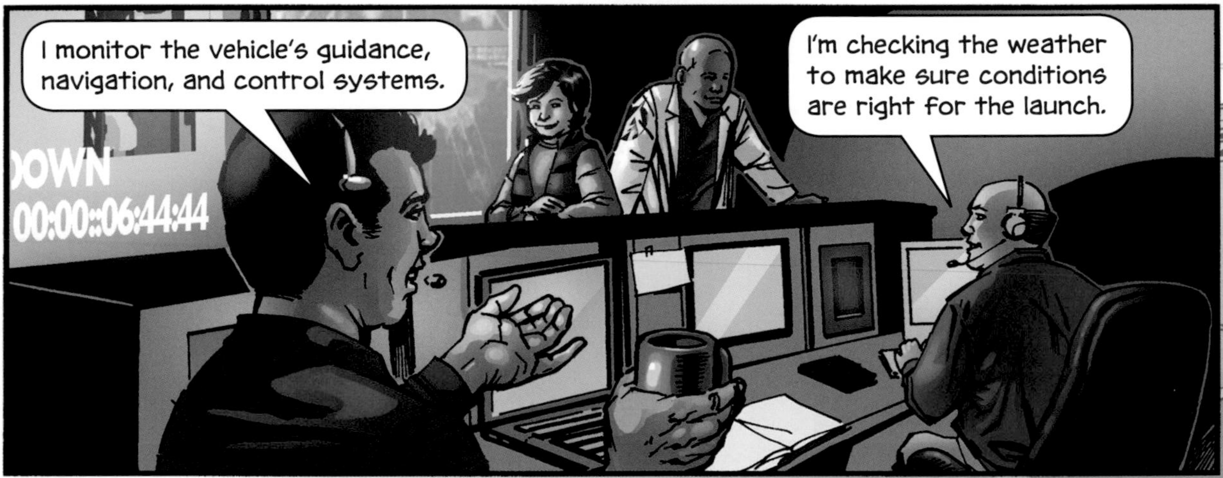
I monitor the vehicle's guidance, navigation, and control systems.
OWN
00:00::06:44:44
I'm checking the weather to make sure conditions are right for the launch.

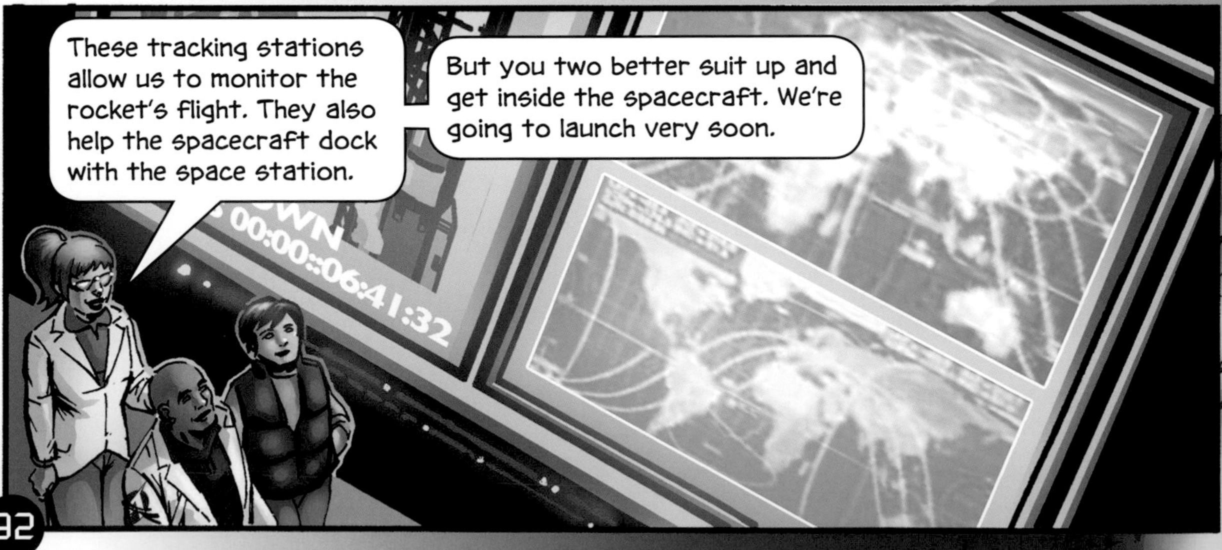
These tracking stations allow us to monitor the rocket's flight. They also help the spacecraft dock with the space station.
But you two better suit up and get inside the spacecraft. We're going to launch very soon.
00:00::06:41:32

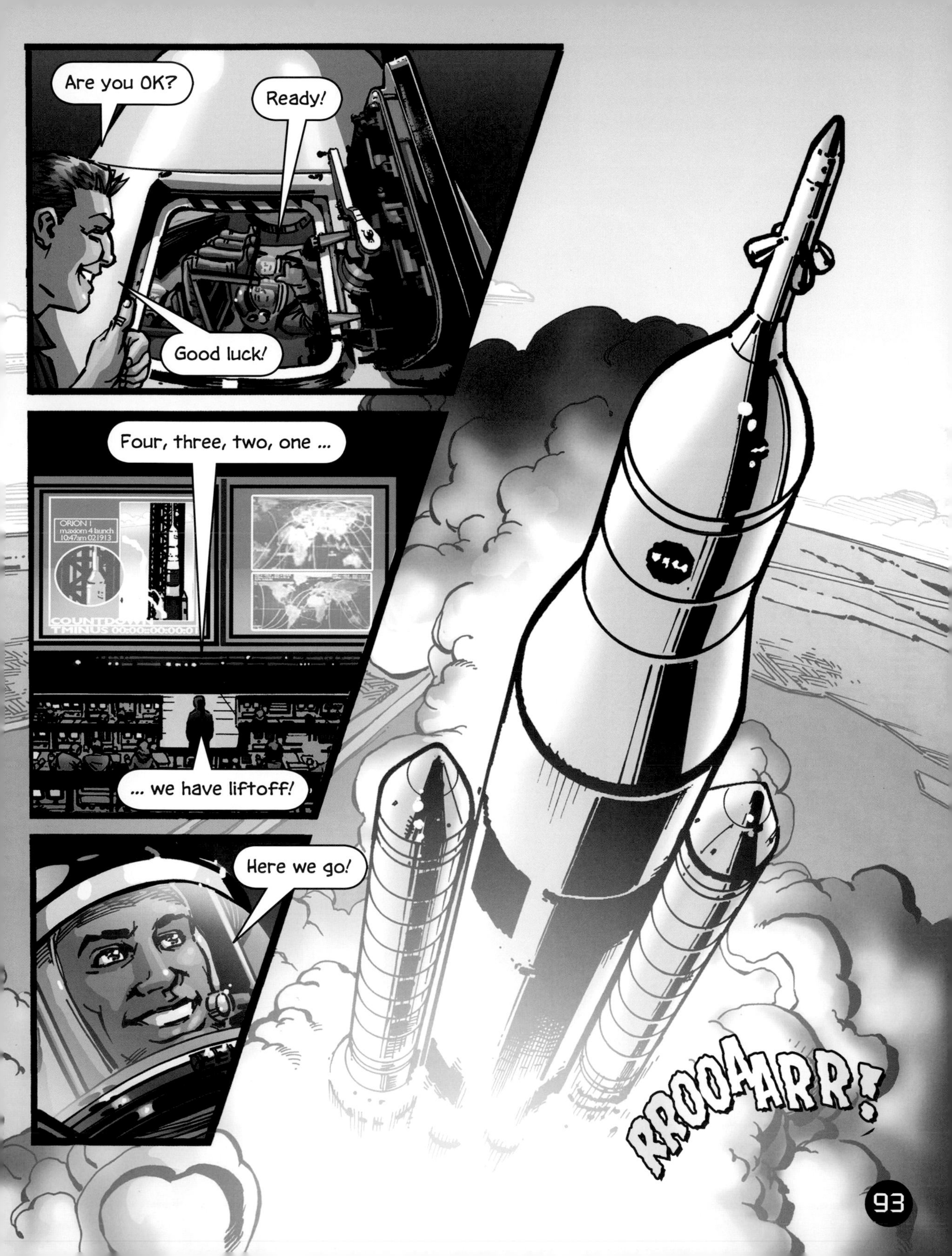
Are you OK?
Ready!
Good luck!
Four, three, two, one ...
... we have liftoff!
Here we go!
RROOAARR!

Launching a craft into space is a multi-stage process. First, thrust causes the launch vehicle to rise above the launchpad.

A few minutes later, the rocket's first stage falls away when its fuel has been used up.

Then the rocket's second stage fires.

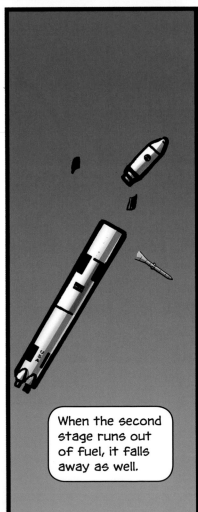

When the second stage runs out of fuel, it falls away as well.

Then the spacecraft reaches orbit.

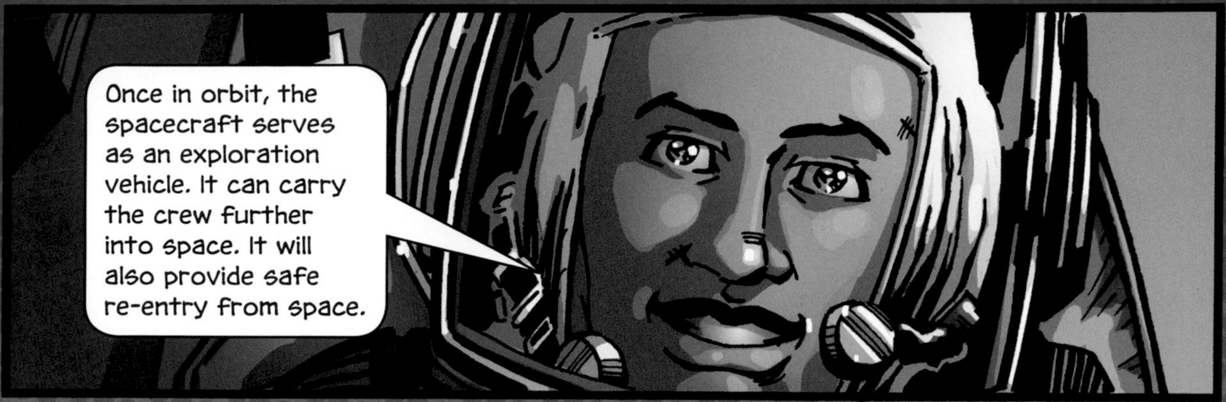
Once in orbit, the spacecraft serves as an exploration vehicle. It can carry the crew further into space. It will also provide safe re-entry from space.

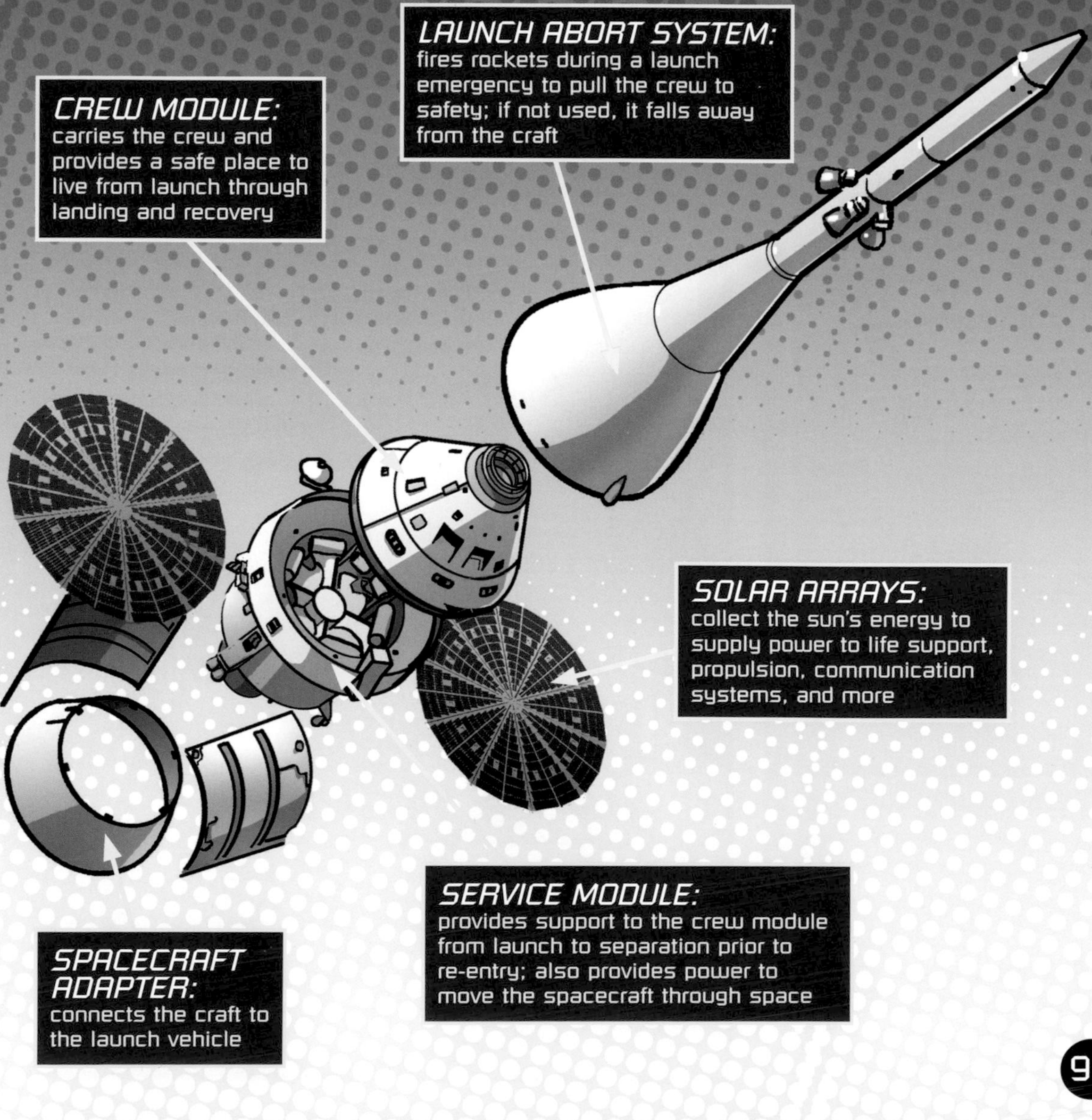
LAUNCH ABORT SYSTEM:
fires rockets during a launch emergency to pull the crew to safety; if not used, it falls away from the craft
CREW MODULE:
carries the crew and provides a safe place to live from launch through landing and recovery
SOLAR ARRAYS:
collect the sun's energy to supply power to life support, propulsion, communication systems, and more
SERVICE MODULE:
provides support to the crew module from launch to separation prior to re-entry; also provides power to move the spacecraft through space
SPACECRAFT ADAPTER:
connects the craft to the launch vehicle

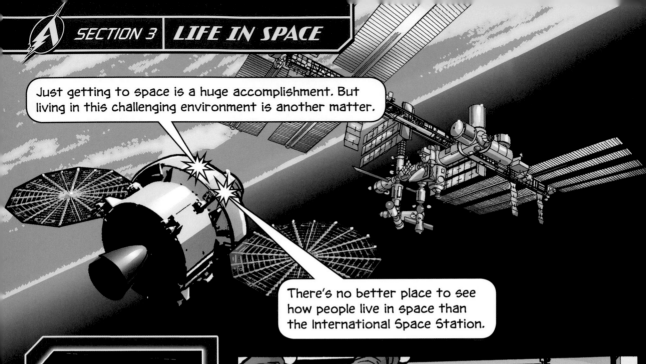

Just getting to space is a huge accomplishment. But living in this challenging environment is another matter.

There's no better place to see how people live in space than the International Space Station.

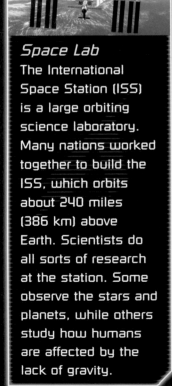

Space Lab
The International Space Station (ISS) is a large orbiting science laboratory. Many nations worked together to build the ISS, which orbits about 240 miles (386 km) above Earth. Scientists do all sorts of research at the station. Some observe the stars and planets, while others study how humans are affected by the lack of gravity.

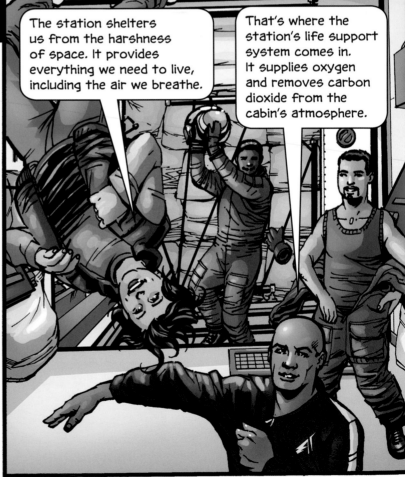

The station shelters us from the harshness of space. It provides everything we need to live, including the air we breathe.

That's where the station's life support system comes in. It supplies oxygen and removes carbon dioxide from the cabin's atmosphere.

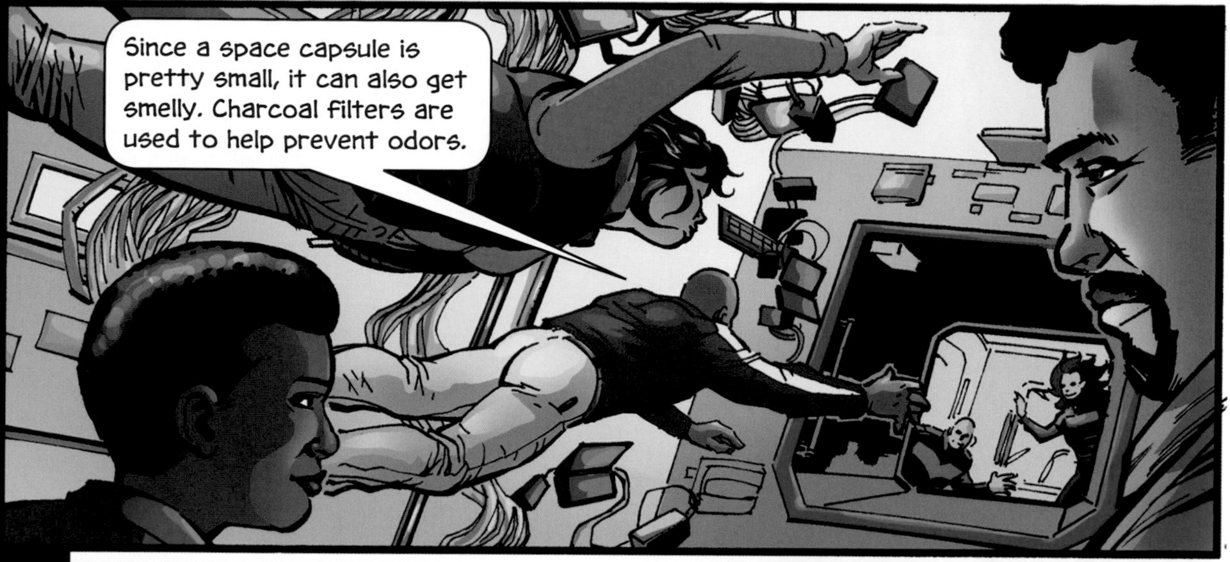
Since a space capsule is pretty small, it can also get smelly. Charcoal filters are used to help prevent odors.

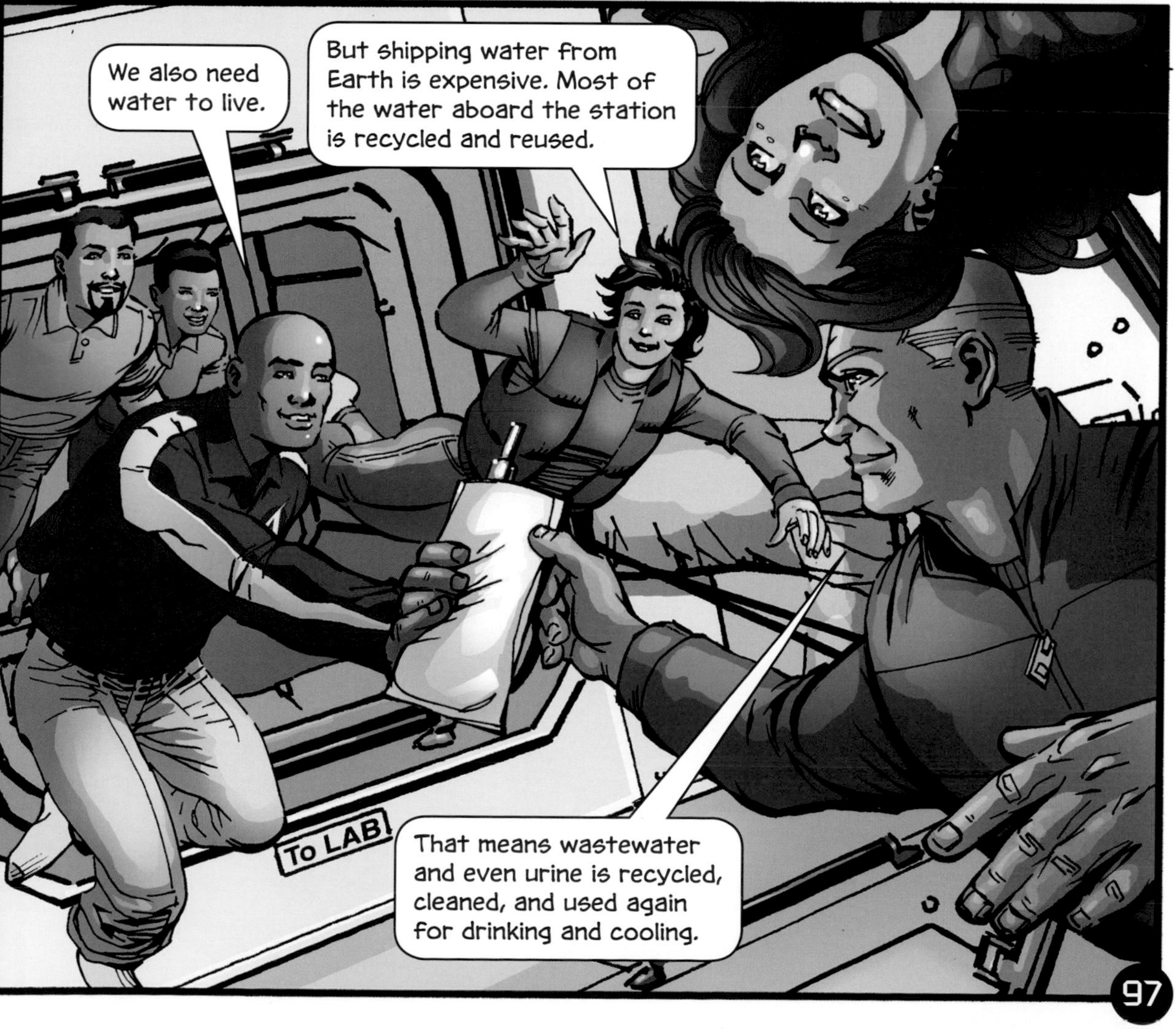
We also need water to live.
But shipping water from Earth is expensive. Most of the water aboard the station is recycled and reused.
To LAB
That means wastewater and even urine is recycled, cleaned, and used again for drinking and cooling.

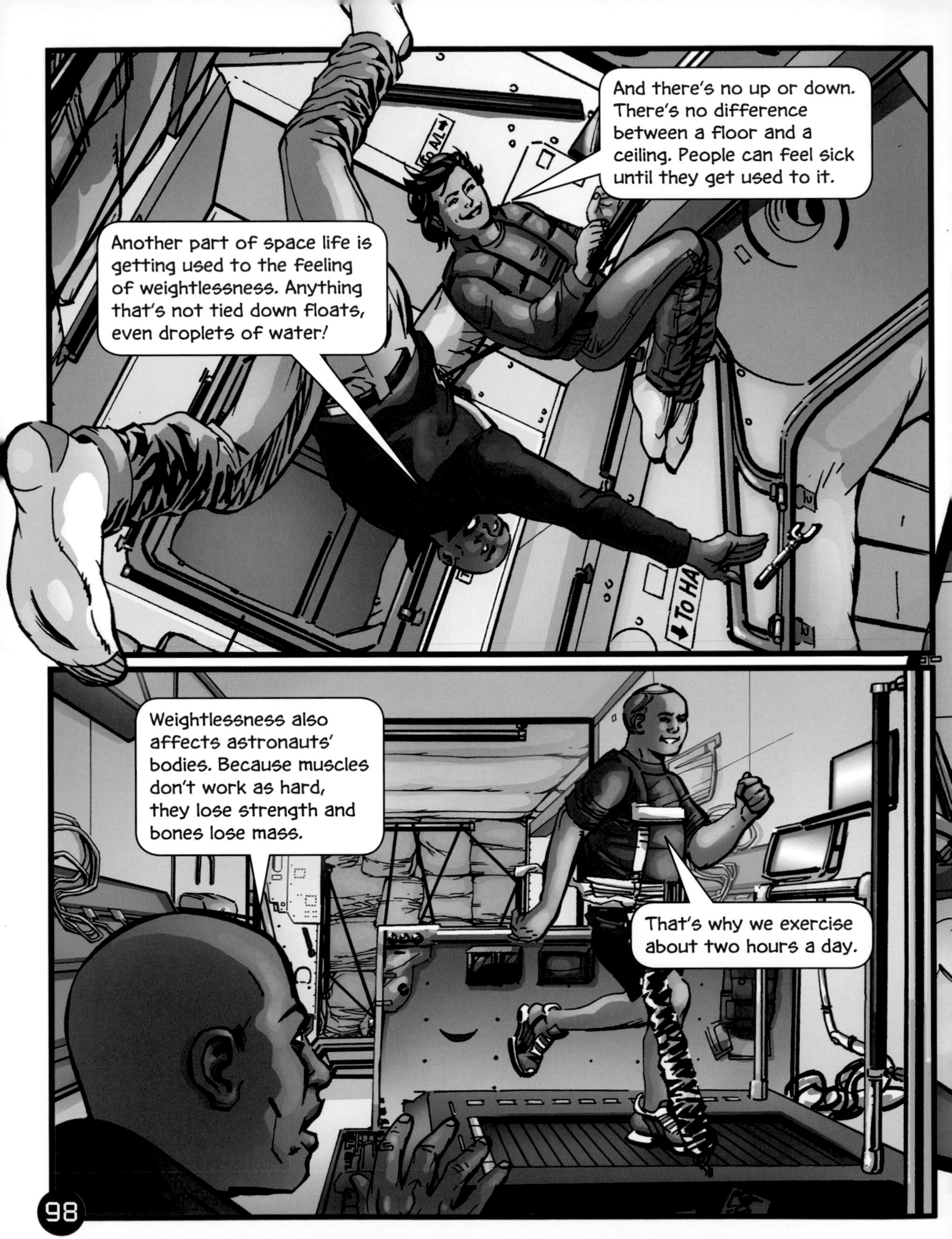
Another part of space life is getting used to the feeling of weightlessness. Anything that's not tied down floats, even droplets of water!
And there's no up or down. There's no difference between a floor and a ceiling. People can feel sick until they get used to it.
Weightlessness also affects astronauts' bodies. Because muscles don't work as hard, they lose strength and bones lose mass.
That's why we exercise about two hours a day.

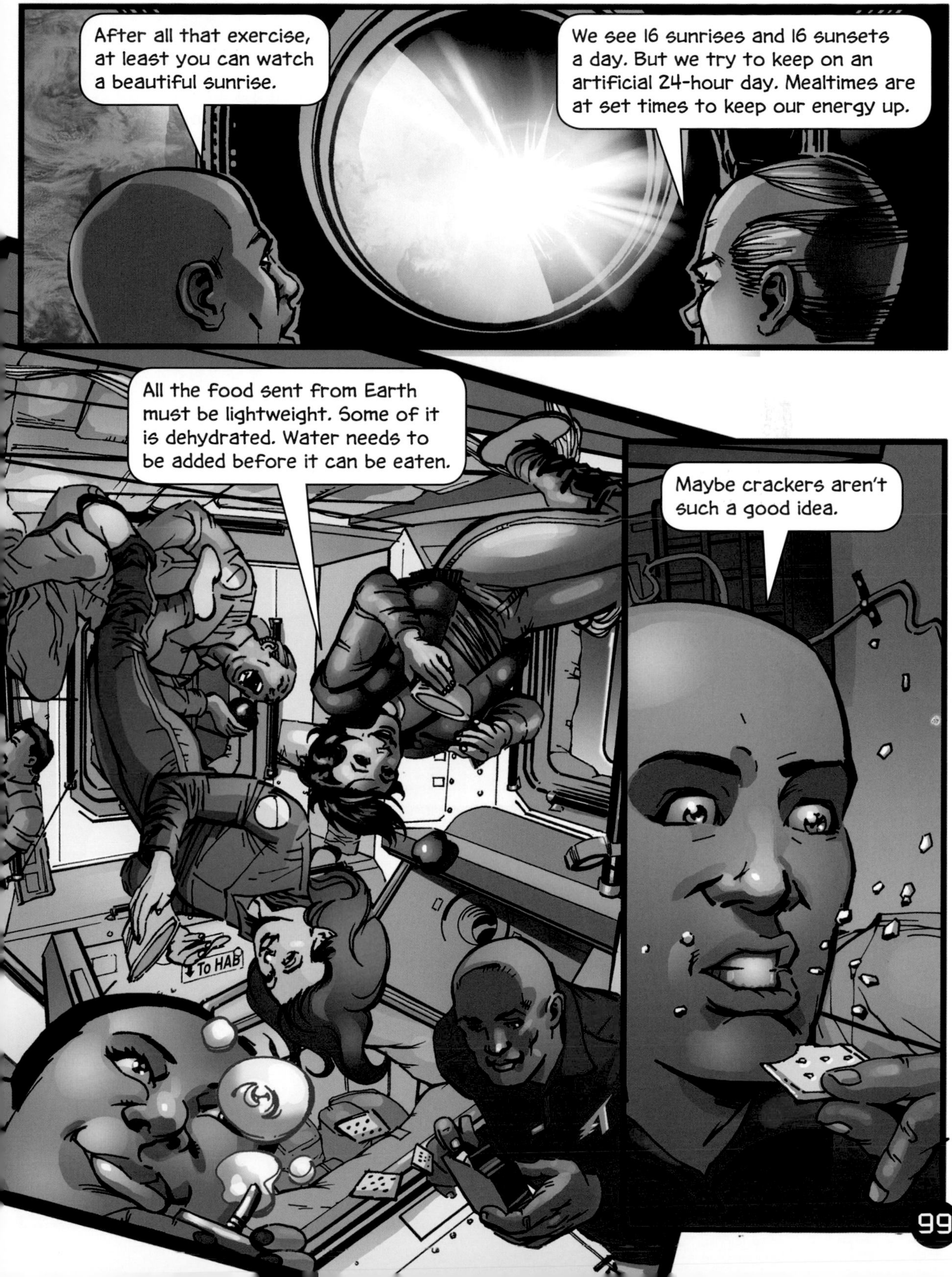
After all that exercise, at least you can watch a beautiful sunrise.
We see 16 sunrises and 16 sunsets a day. But we try to keep on an artificial 24-hour day. Mealtimes are at set times to keep our energy up.
All the food sent from Earth must be lightweight. Some of it is dehydrated. Water needs to be added before it can be eaten.
Maybe crackers aren't such a good idea.
TO HAB

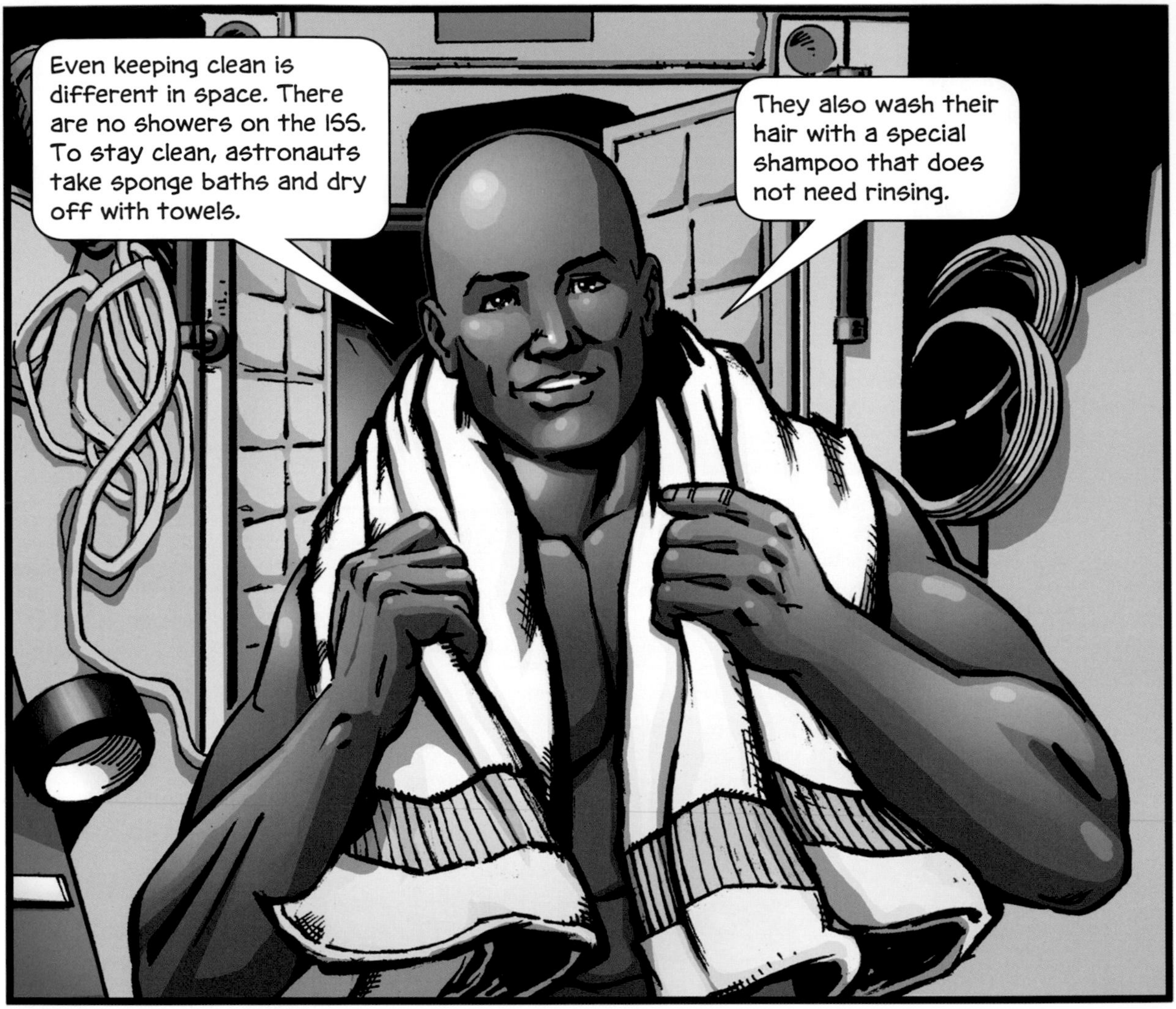
Even keeping clean is different in space. There are no showers on the ISS. To stay clean, astronauts take sponge baths and dry off with towels.
They also wash their hair with a special shampoo that does not need rinsing.

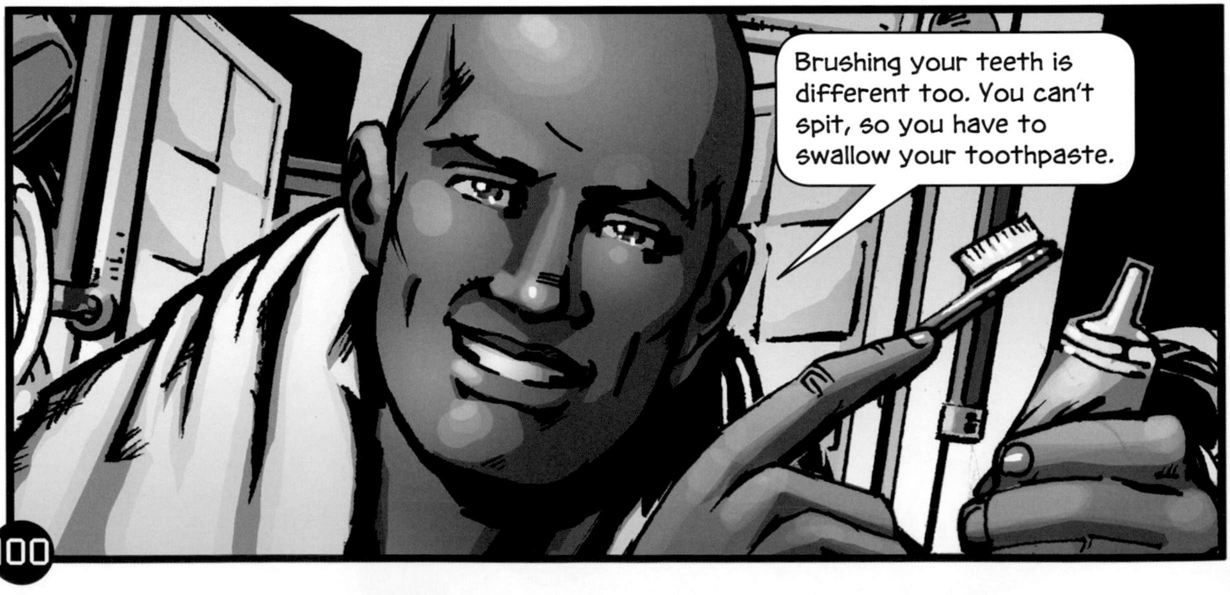
Brushing your teeth is different too. You can't spit, so you have to swallow your toothpaste.

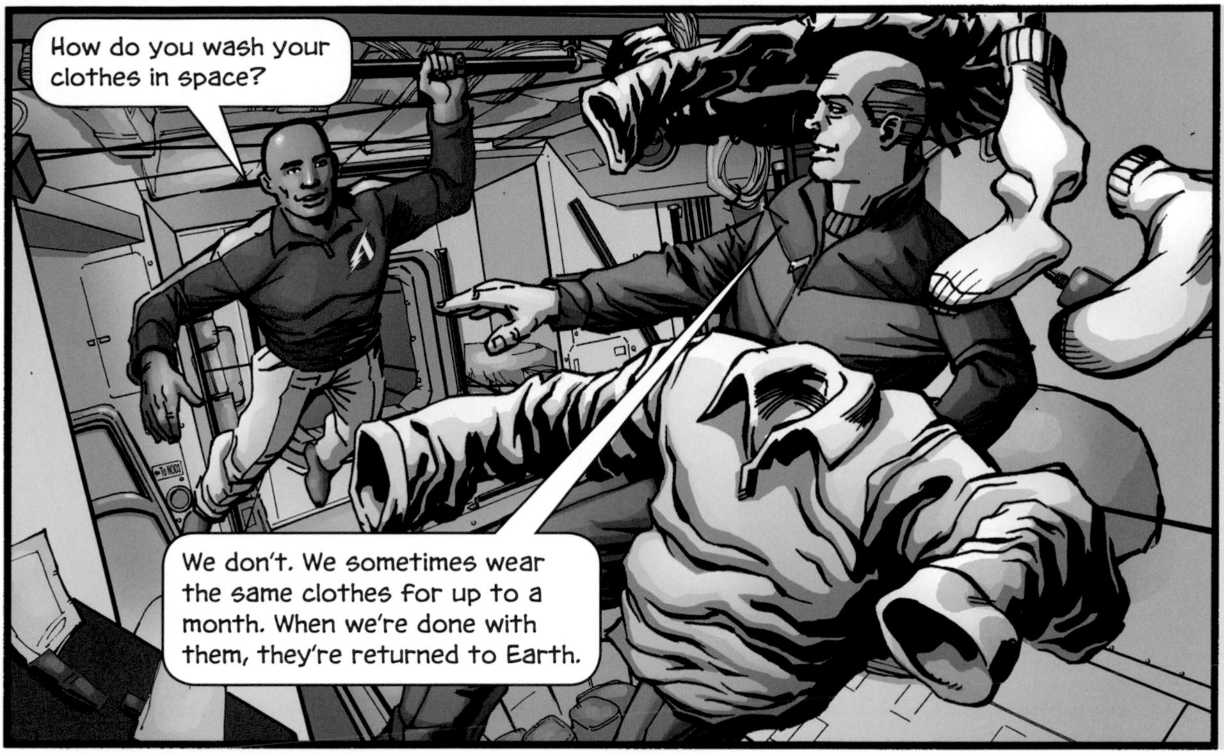
How do you wash your clothes in space?
We don't. We sometimes wear the same clothes for up to a month. When we're done with them, they're returned to Earth.

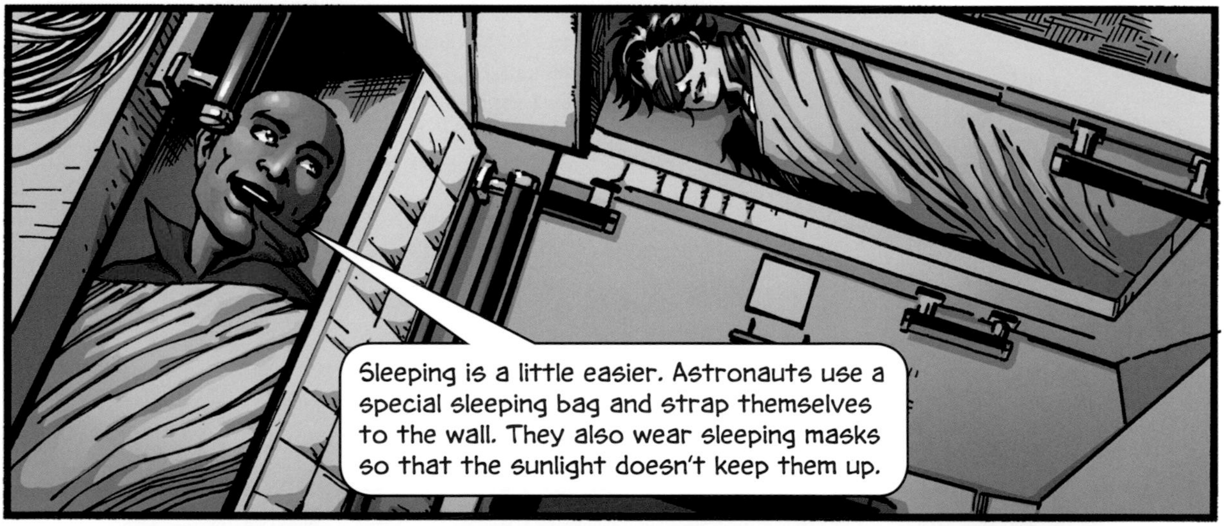
Sleeping is a little easier. Astronauts use a special sleeping bag and strap themselves to the wall. They also wear sleeping masks so that the sunlight doesn't keep them up.

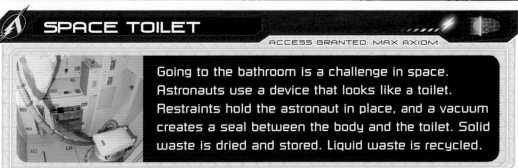

SPACE TOILET

ACCESS GRANTED: MAX AXIOM

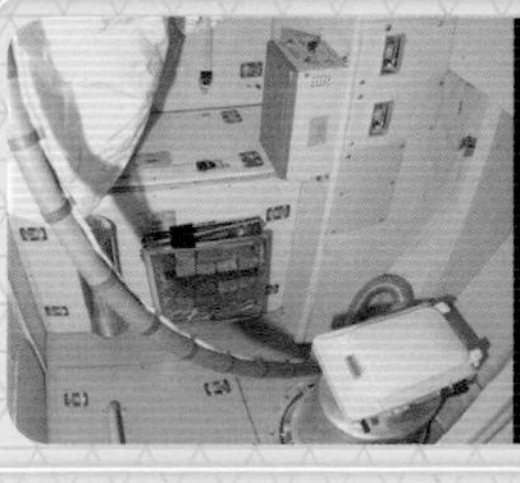

Going to the bathroom is a challenge in space. Astronauts use a device that looks like a toilet. Restraints hold the astronaut in place, and a vacuum creates a seal between the body and the toilet. Solid waste is dried and stored. Liquid waste is recycled.

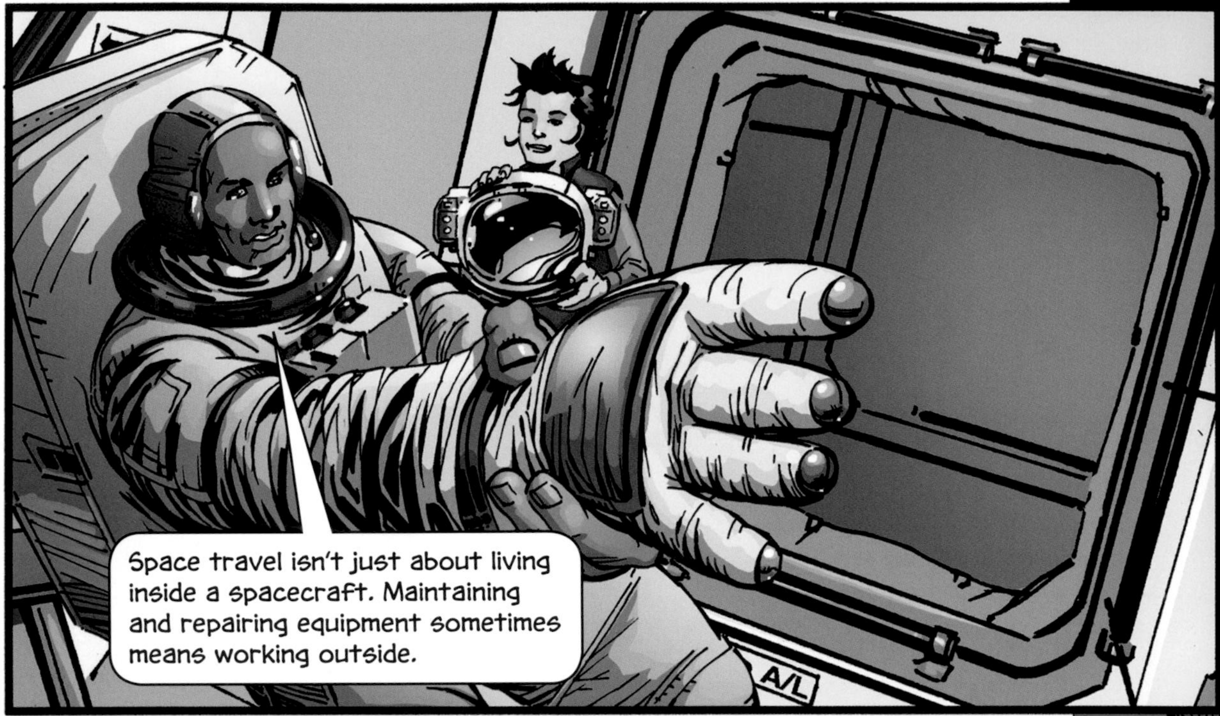
Space travel isn't just about living inside a spacecraft. Maintaining and repairing equipment sometimes means working outside.
A/L

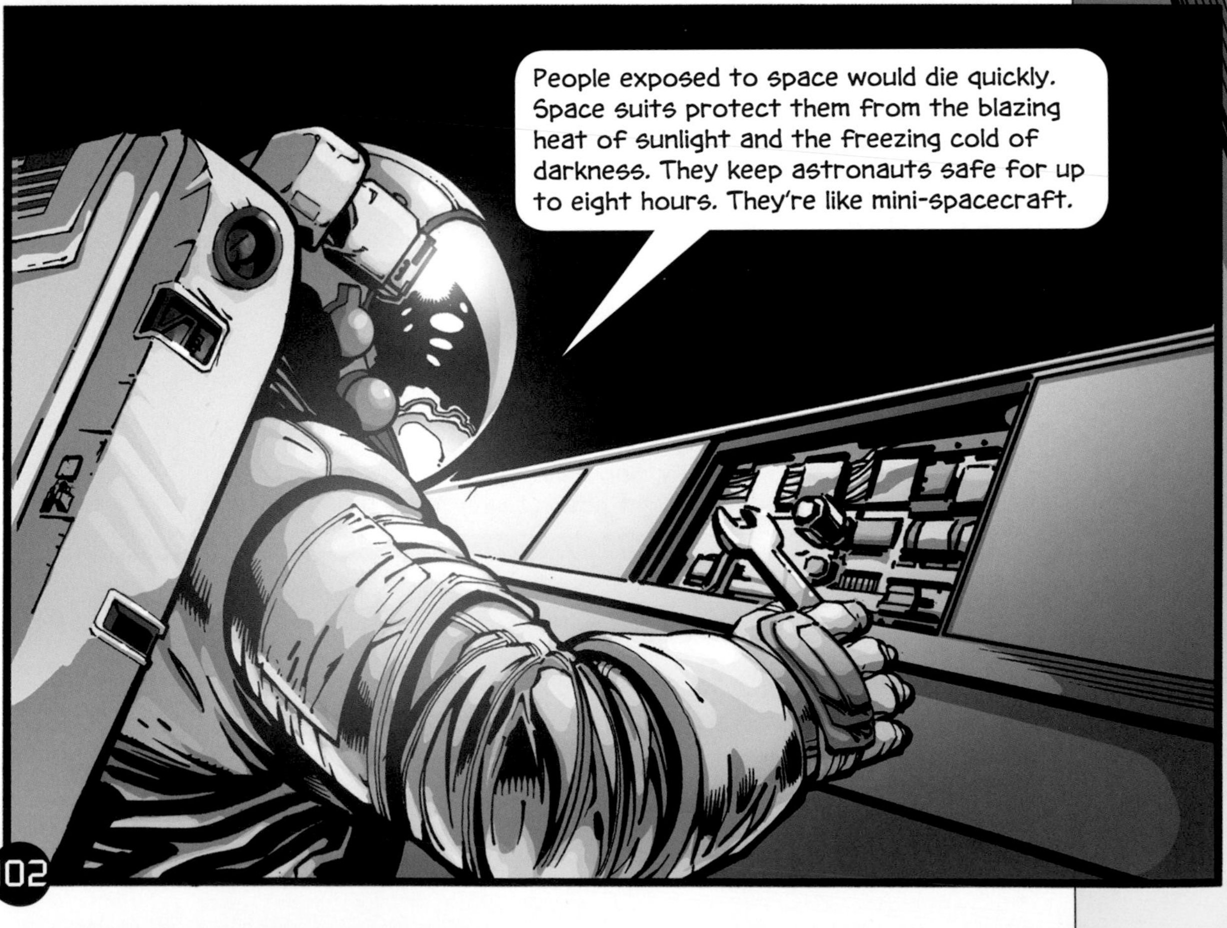
People exposed to space would die quickly. Space suits protect them from the blazing heat of sunlight and the freezing cold of darkness. They keep astronauts safe for up to eight hours. They're like mini-spacecraft.

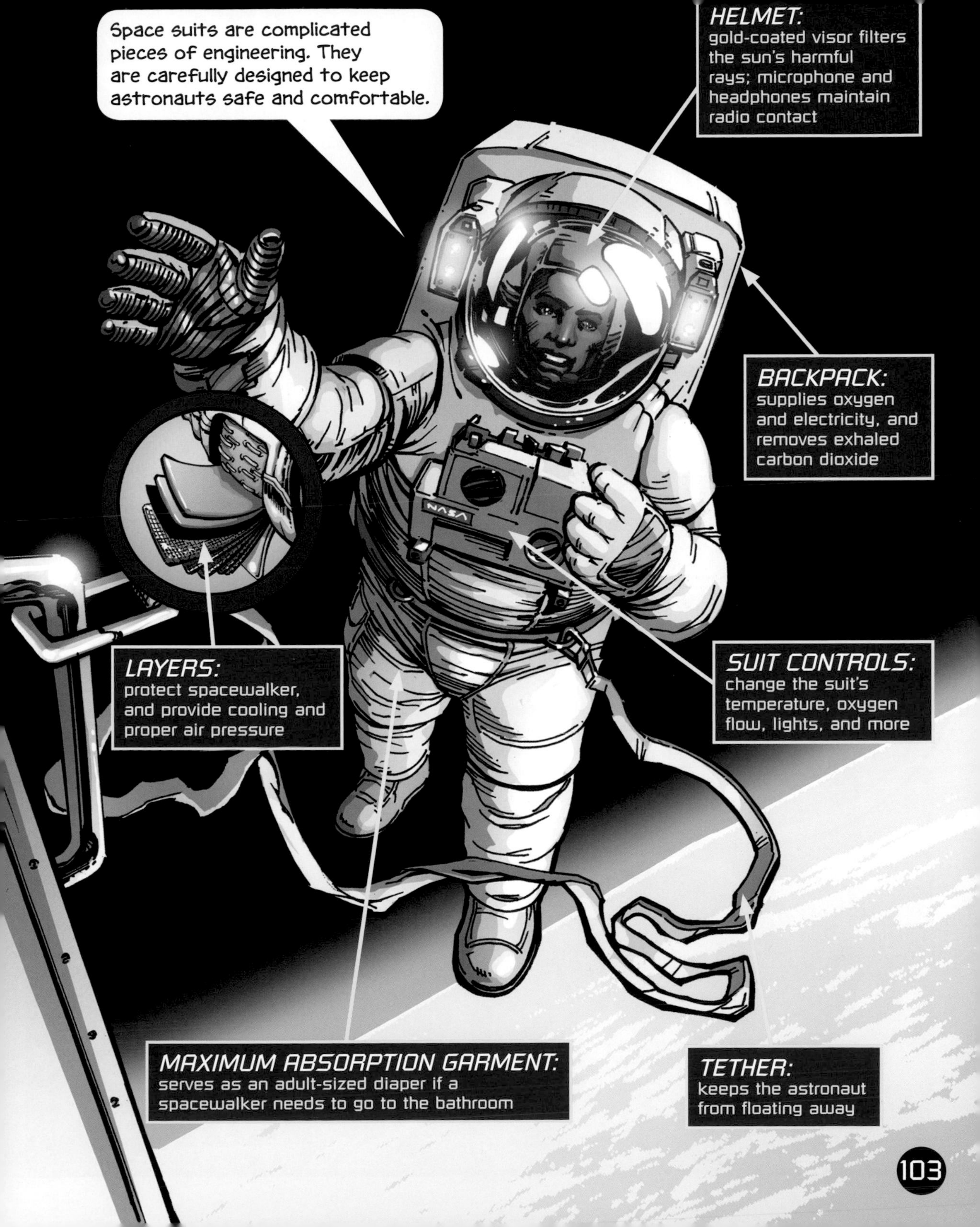
Space suits are complicated pieces of engineering. They are carefully designed to keep astronauts safe and comfortable.
HELMET: gold-coated visor filters the sun's harmful rays; microphone and headphones maintain radio contact
BACKPACK: supplies oxygen and electricity, and removes exhaled carbon dioxide
NASA
LAYERS: protect spacewalker, and provide cooling and proper air pressure
SUIT CONTROLS: change the suit's temperature, oxygen flow, lights, and more
MAXIMUM ABSORPTION GARMENT: serves as an adult-sized diaper if a spacewalker needs to go to the bathroom
TETHER: keeps the astronaut from floating away

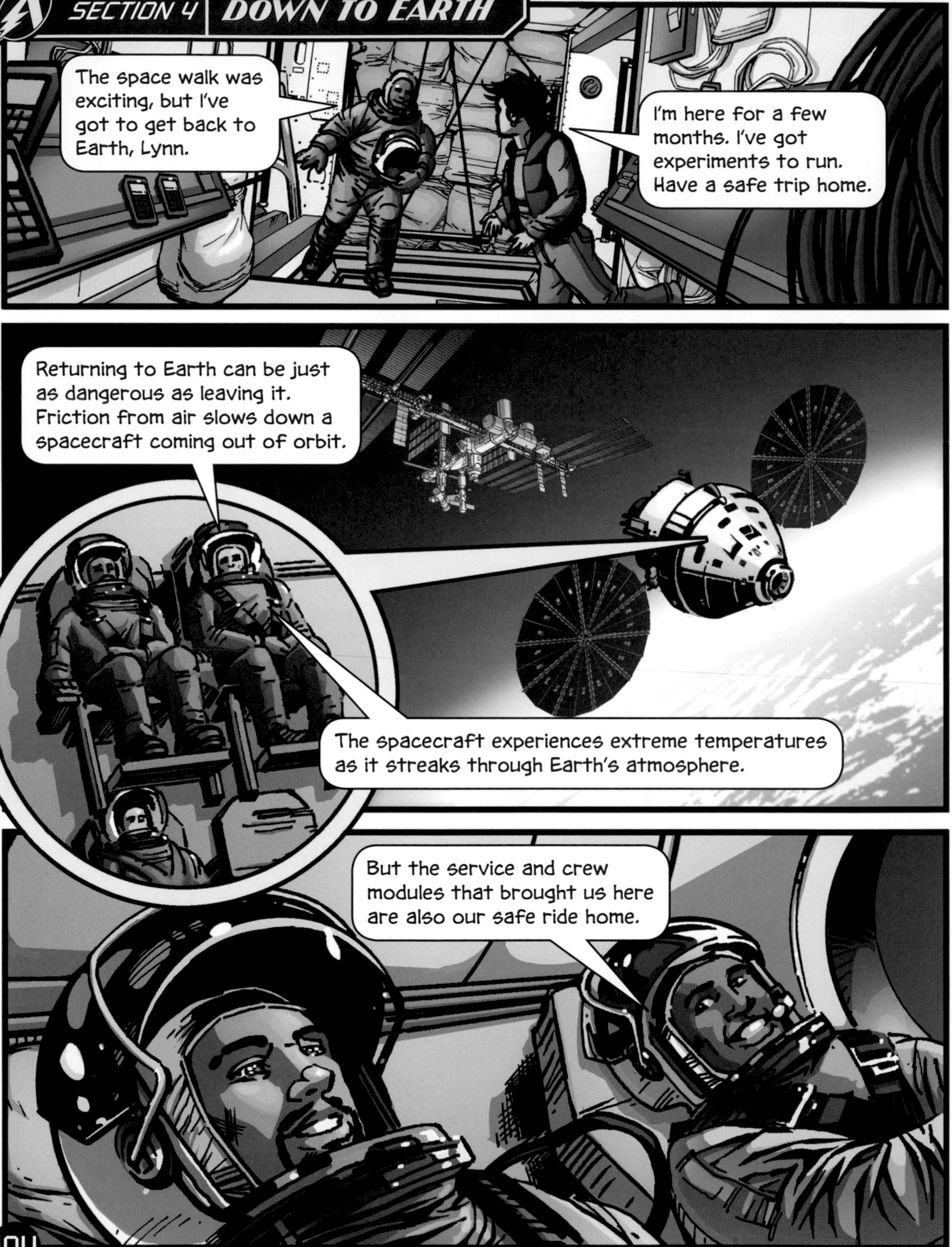
The space walk was exciting, but I've got to get back to Earth, Lynn.
I'm here for a few months. I've got experiments to run. Have a safe trip home.
Returning to Earth can be just as dangerous as leaving it. Friction from air slows down a spacecraft coming out of orbit.
The spacecraft experiences extreme temperatures as it streaks through Earth's atmosphere.
But the service and crew modules that brought us here are also our safe ride home.

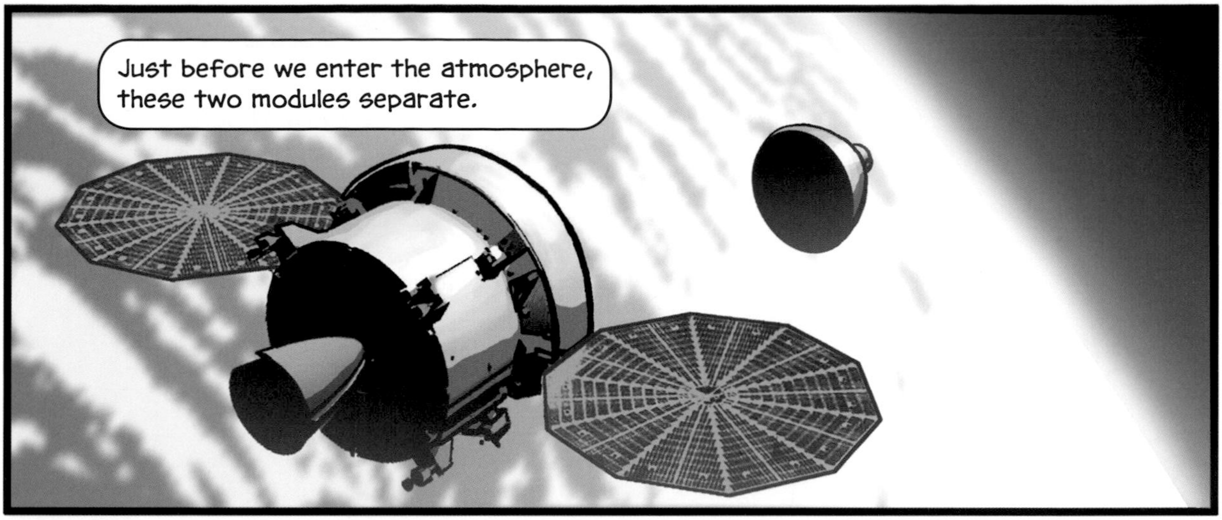
Just before we enter the atmosphere, these two modules separate.

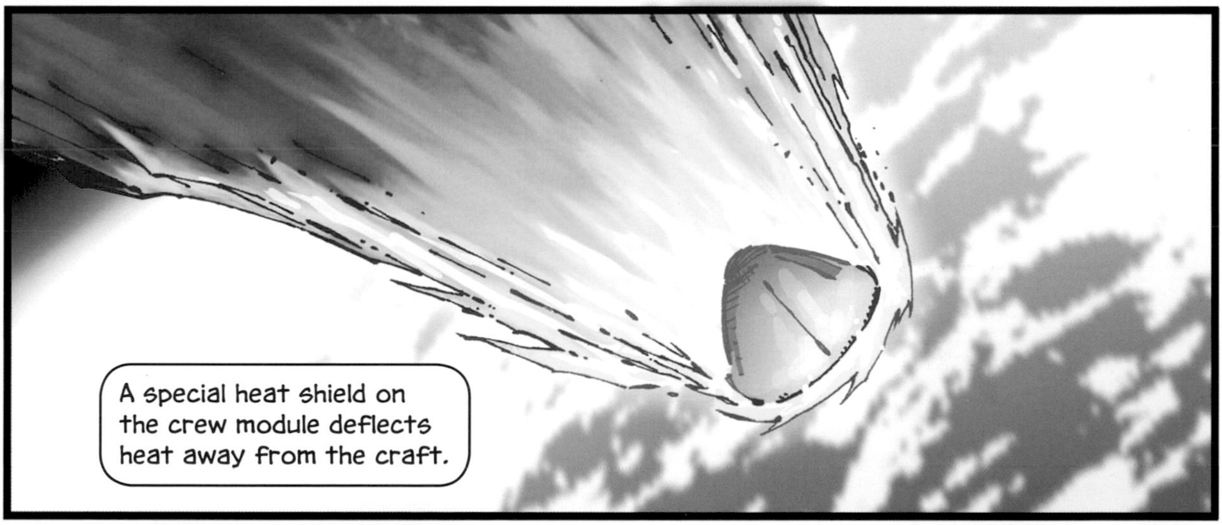
A special heat shield on the crew module deflects heat away from the craft.

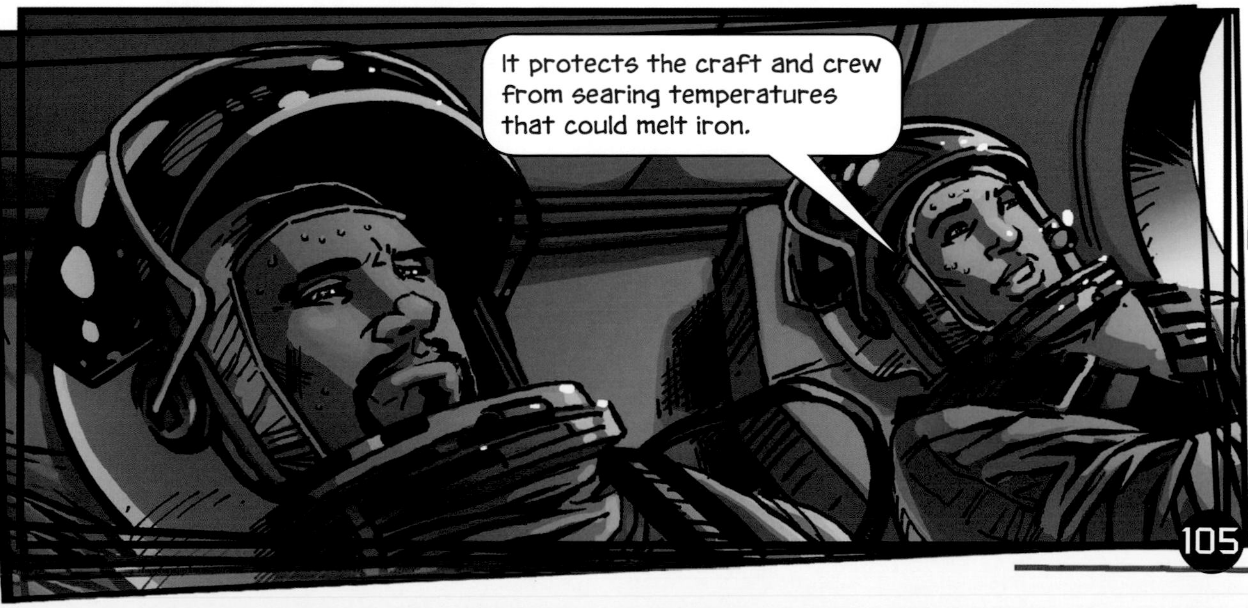
It protects the craft and crew from searing temperatures that could melt iron.

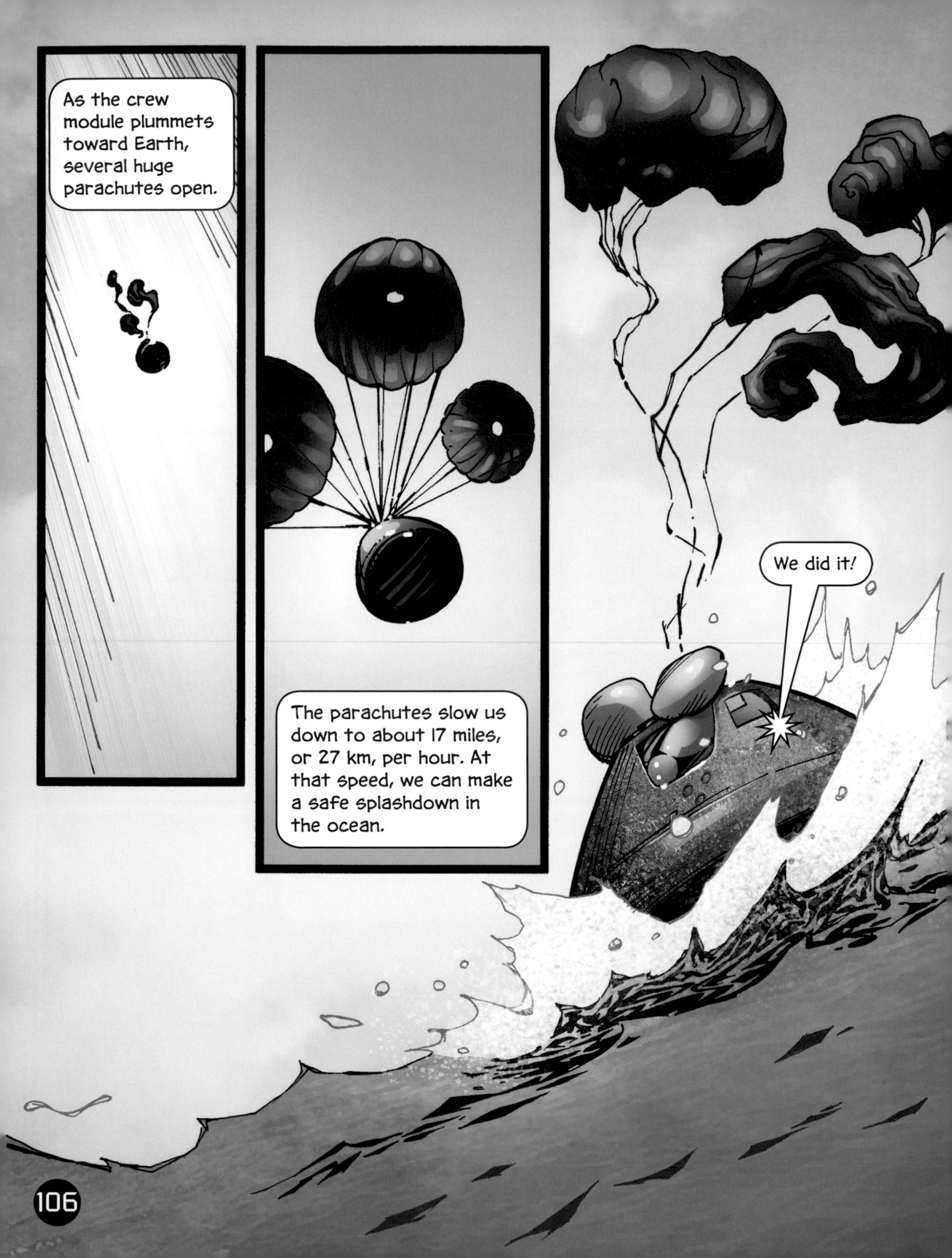
As the crew module plummets toward Earth, several huge parachutes open.
The parachutes slow us down to about 17 miles, or 27 km, per hour. At that speed, we can make a safe splashdown in the ocean.
We did it!

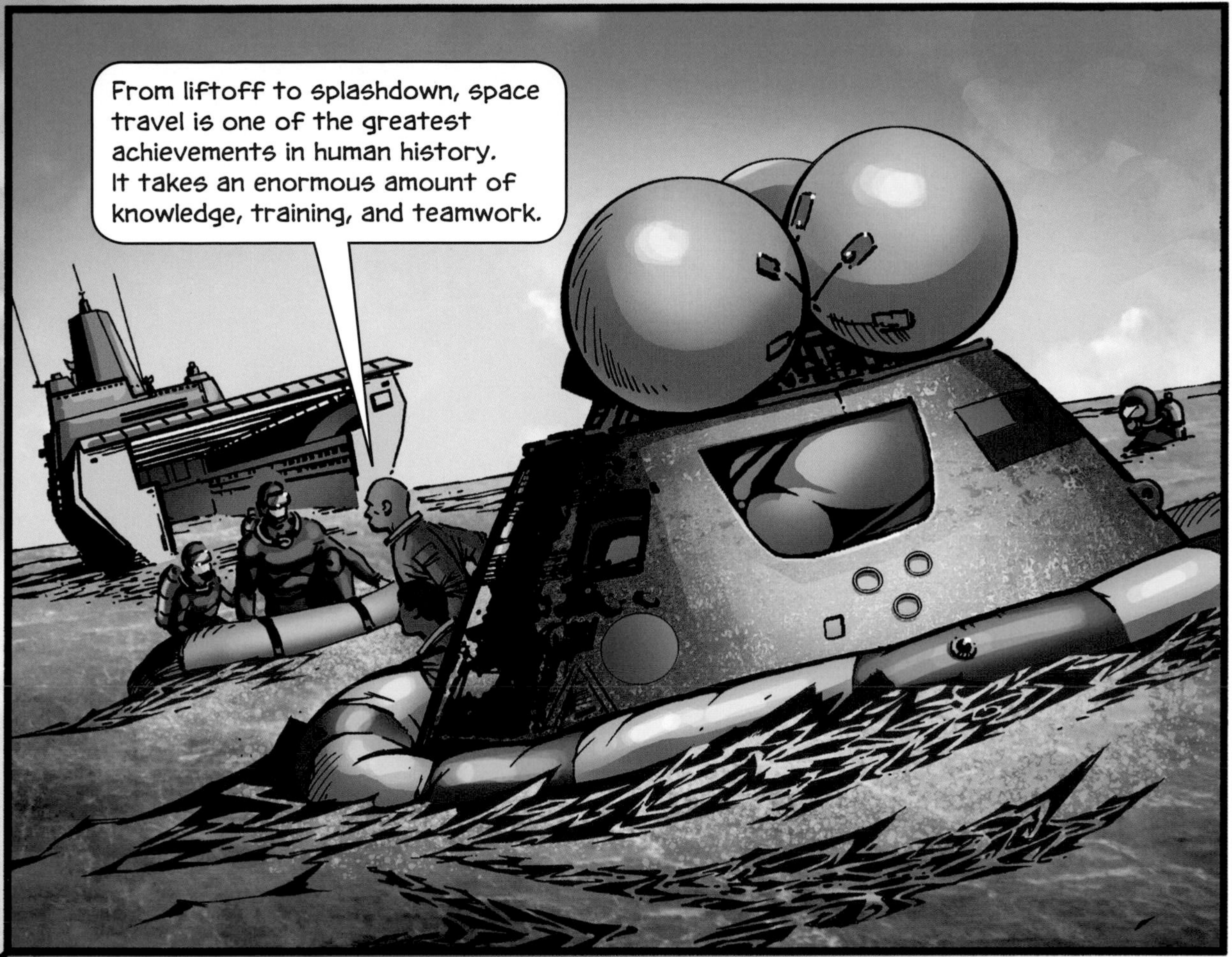
From liftoff to splashdown, space travel is one of the greatest achievements in human history. It takes an enormous amount of knowledge, training, and teamwork.

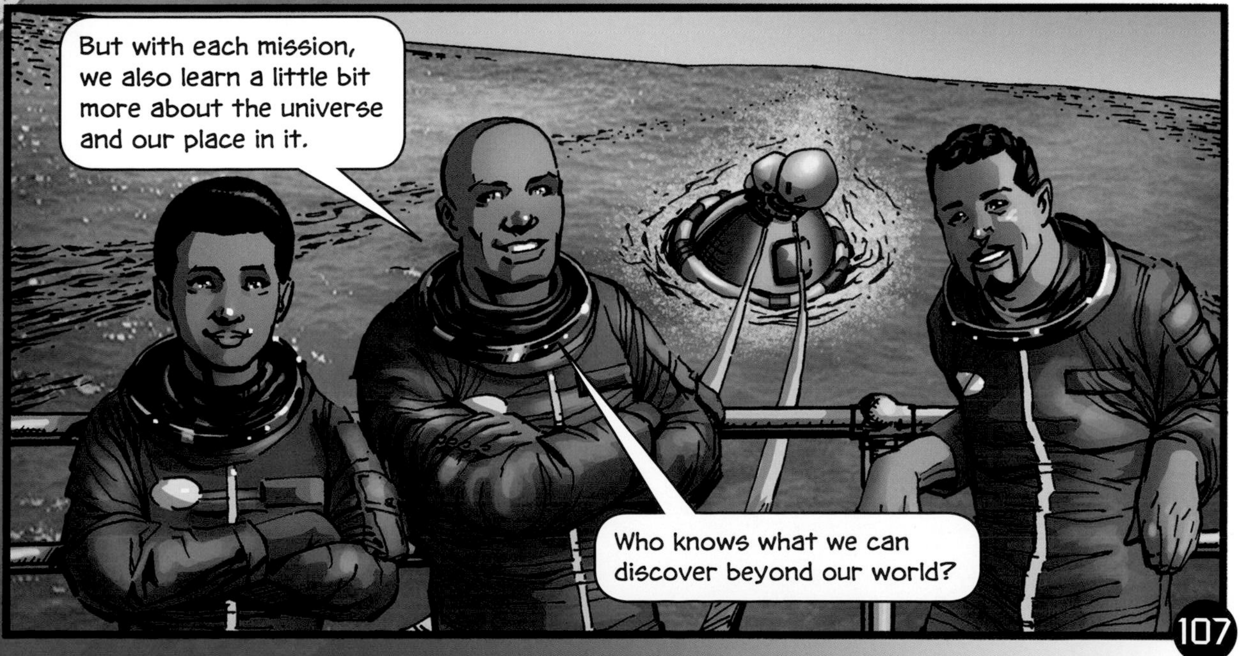
But with each mission, we also learn a little bit more about the universe and our place in it.
Who knows what we can discover beyond our world?

MORE ABOUT SPACE TRAVEL

- Rockets are different than jet engines. Jet engines require oxygen from the air to burn the fuel that they carry. Rocket engines need oxygen too. But they fly above the atmosphere where there's no air. Rockets have to carry their own oxidizer. This substance provides the oxygen needed to make fuel burn in the airlessness of space.

- Space is so huge that astronomers measure distances in light-years. One light-year is the distance that light travels in one year. But just how far can light go in that time? In one year, it travels 6 trillion miles (10 trillion km). For light to reach the closest star to the sun, Proxima Centauri, it travels for four years. In comparison, our fastest spacecraft would take 19,000 years to travel the same distance.

- Between 1969 and 1972, the United States sent 12 astronauts to the moon's surface in separate missions. Neil Armstrong and Buzz Aldrin became the first people to step on the moon in July 1969. About 18 months later astronaut Alan Shepard hit a few golf balls while he was there. In December 1972, astronauts Eugene Cernan and Harrison Schmitt became the last men to walk on the moon. No one has been there since.

- It takes many months of study and training to become an astronaut. Astronauts have to learn their craft's systems, flight safety and operations, and land and water survival techniques. They also have to learn how to perform their duties in space. Floating in water is similar to floating in space. Astronauts train in their space suits in huge tanks of water.

MORE ABOUT MAX AXIOM

SUPER SCIENTIST

Real name: Maxwell J. Axiom

Hometown: Seattle, Washington

Height: 6'1"   Weight: 192 lbs.

Eyes: Brown   Hair: None

Super capabilities: Super intelligence; able to shrink to the size of an atom; sunglasses give X-ray vision; lab coat allows for travel through time and space.

Origin: Since birth, Max Axiom seemed destined for greatness. His mother, a marine biologist, taught her son about the mysteries of the sea. His father, a nuclear physicist and volunteer park ranger, taught Max about the wonders of earth and sky.

One day on a wilderness hike, a megacharged lightning bolt struck Max with blinding fury. When he awoke, Max discovered a newfound energy and set out to learn as much about science as possible. He traveled the globe, earning degrees in every aspect of the field. Upon his return, he was ready to share his knowledge and new identity with the world. He had become Max Axiom, Super Scientist.

aerial (AYR-ee-uhl)—relating to something that happens in the skies

android (AN-droid)—a robot that looks, thinks, and acts very similar to a human being

antenna (an-TEN-uh)—a wire or dish that sends or receives radio waves

artificial (ar-tuh-FI-shuhl)—made by people

atmosphere (AT-muhss-fihr)—the mixture of gases that surrounds Earth

automate (AW-tah-mayt)—a mechanical process that is programmed to follow a set of instructions

autonomous (aw-TAH-nuh-muhss)—able to control oneself; autonomous robots are not operated remotely by a person

biomimetic (by-oh-mi-MET-ik)—imitating the design of a living thing

bipedal (bi-PE-duhl)—something that walks on two feet

dehydrated (dee-HY-dray-tuhd)—having the water removed

duplex (DOO-pleks)—having two parts

electromagnetic spectrum (i-lek-troh-mag-NET-ic SPEK-truhm)—the wide range of energy given off by the sun

engineer (en-juh-NEER)—someone trained to design and build machines, vehicles, bridges, roads, or other structures

exhaust (ig-ZAWST)—the waste gases produced by an engine

filter (FIL-tuhr)—a device that cleans liquids or gases as they pass through it

frequency (FREE-kwuhn-see)—the number of sound waves that pass a location in a certain amount of time

garment (GAR-muhnt)—a piece of clothing

Global Positioning System (GLOH-buhl puh-ZI-shuh-ning SISS-tuhm)—an electronic tool used to find the location of an object; this system is often called GPS

gravity (GRAV-uh-tee)—a force that pulls objects with mass together; gravity pulls objects down toward the center of Earth

grid (GRID)—a pattern of evenly spaced, or parallel, lines that cross

hertz (HURTS)—a unit for measuring the frequency of vibrations and waves; one hertz equals one wave per second

hydraulic (hye-DRAW-lik)—having to do with a system powered by fluid forced through pipes or chambers

infrared (in-fruh-RED)—light waves in the electromagnetic spectrum between visible light and microwaves

irrigate (IHR-uh-gate)—to supply water for crops

module (MOJ-ool)—a separate section that can be linked to other parts

orbit (OR-bit)—to travel around an object in space; an orbit is also the path an object follows while circling an object in space

oxidizer (OK-si-dahy-zer)—a substance that allows rocket fuel to burn in space

piston (PIS-tuhn)—a part inside a hydraulic machine that moves up and down to expand and compress fluid

pitch (PICH)—the angle of the blades on an aircraft; pitch determines whether an aircraft moves up or down

pivot (PIV-uht)—to turn or balance on a point

pneumatic (noo-MAT-ik)—operated by compressed air

radiation (ray-dee-AY-shuhn)—rays of energy given off by certain elements

radio wave (RAY-dee-oh WAYV)—a type of electromagnetic wave; electromagnetic waves are caused by electricity and magnetism

reconnaisance (ree-KAH-nuh-suhnss)—a mission to gather information about an enemy

region (REE-juhn)—a large area

rotor (ROH-tur)—the system of rotating blades on a helicopter; a rotor provides force to lift a helicopter or drone into the air

rural (RUR-uhl)—of the countryside; away from cities and towns

satellite (SAT-uh-lite)—a spacecraft that circles Earth; satellites gather and send information

sensor (SEN-sur)—an instrument that detects physical changes in the environment

simplex (SIM-pleks)—having one part

surveillance (suhr-VAY-luhnss)—the act of keeping very close watch on someone, someplace, or something

taxidermy (TAK-suh-dur-mee)—preparing, stuffing, and mounting skins of animals to make them look alive

terrain (tuh-RAYN)—the surface of the land

throttle (THROT-uhl)—a lever, pedal, or handle used to control the speed of an engine

tsunami (tsoo-NAH-mee)—a large, destructive wave caused by an underwater earthquake

weightlessness (WATE-liss-ness)—a state in which a person feels free of the pull of Earth's gravity

INDEX

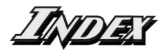